STAR-LORD AND KITTY PRYDE

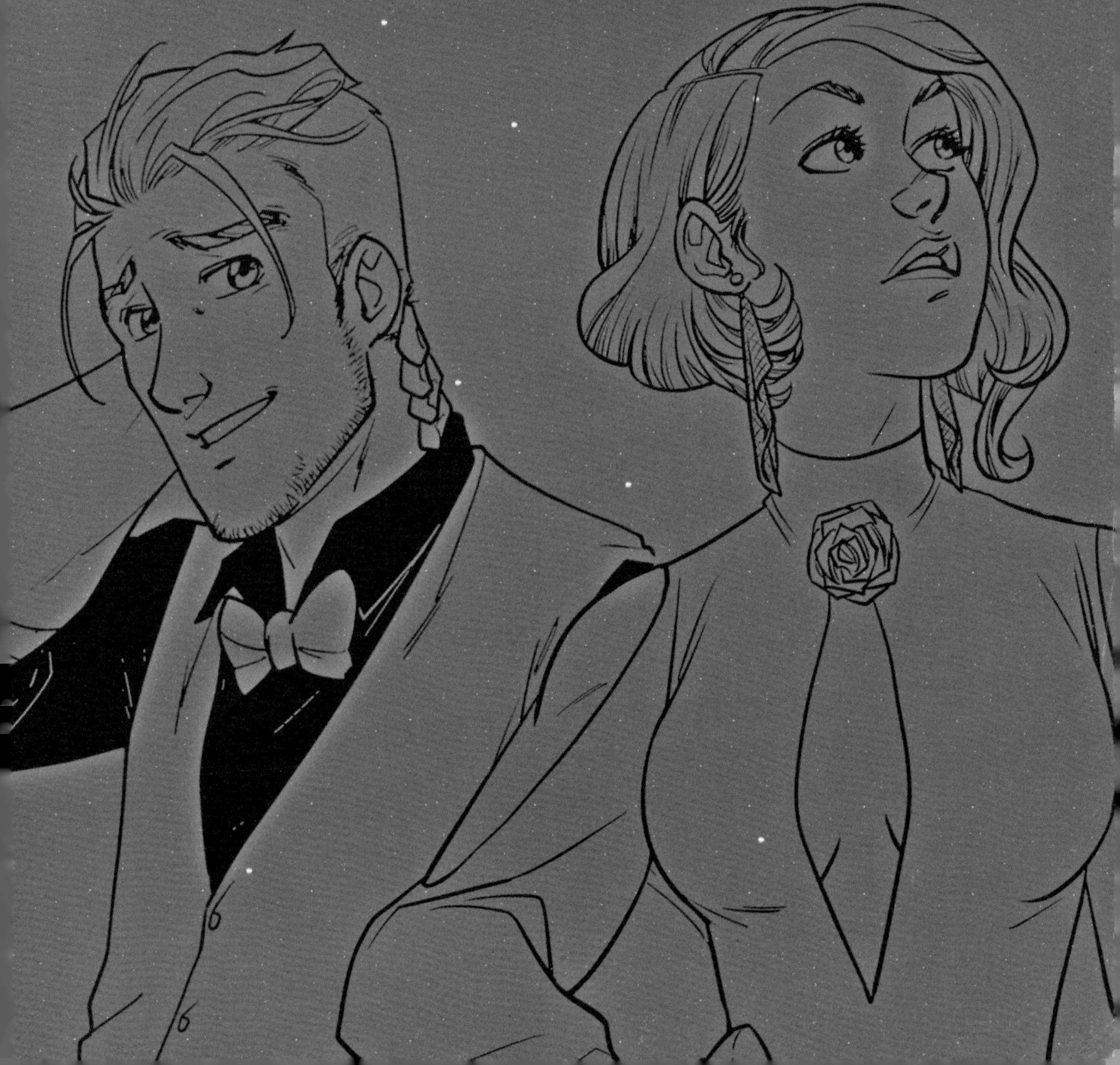

Collection Editor SARAH BRUNSTAD
Associate Managing Editor ALEX STARBUCK
Editors, Special Projects JENNIFER GRÜNWALD & MARK D. BEAZLEY
Senior Editor, Special Projects JEFF YOUNGQUIST
SVP Print, Sales & Marketing DAVID GABRIEL
Book Design: Adam Del Re

Editor in Chief AXEL ALONSO
Chief Creative Officer JOE QUESADA
Publisher DAN BUCKLEY
Executive Producer ALAN FINE

STAR-LORD & KITTY PRYDE. Contains material originally published in magazine form as STAR-LORD & KITTY PRYDE #1-3, GUARDIANS OF THE GALAXY & X-MEN: THE BLACK VORTEX OMEGA #1 and GENERATION NEXT #1. First printing 2015. ISBN# 978-0-7851-9843-7. Published by MARVEL WORLDWIDE, INC., a subsidiary of MARVEL ENTERTAINMENT, LLC. OFFICE OF PUBLICATION: 135 West 50th Street, New York, NY 10020. Copyright © 2015 MARVEL No similarity between any of the names, characters, persons, and/or institutions in this magazine with those of any living or dead person or institution is intended, and any such similarity which may exist is purely coincidental. **Printed in Canada.** ALAN FINE, President, Marvel Entertainment; DAN BUCKLEY, President, TV, Publishing and Brand Management; JOE QUESADA, Chief Creative Officer; TOM BREVOORT, SVP of Publishing; DAVID BOGART, SVP of Operations & Procurement, Publishing; C.B. CEBULSKI, VP of International Development & Brand Management; DAVID GABRIEL, SVP Print, Sales & Marketing; JIM O'KEEFE, VP of Operations & Logistics; DAN CARR, Executive Director of Publishing Technology; SUSAN CRESPI, Editorial Operations Manager; ALEX MORALES, Publishing Operations Manager; STAN LEE, Chairman Emeritus. For information regarding advertising in Marvel Comics or on Marvel.com, please contact Jonathan Rheingold, VP of Custom Solutions & Ad Sales, at jrheingold@marvel.com. For Marvel subscription inquiries, please call 800-217-9158. **Manufactured between 10/7/2015 and 11/11/2015 by SOLISCO PRINTERS, SCOTT, QC, CANADA.**

10 9 8 7 6 5 4 3 2 1

STAR·LORD AND KITTY PRYDE

Writer
SAM HUMPHRIES

Artist
ALTI FIRMANSYAH

Colorist
JESSICA KHOLINNE

Letterer
VC's JOE SABINO

Cover Art
YASMINE PUTRIHDRAWN

Assistant Editor
CHRISTINA HARRINGTON

Editor
JAKE THOMAS

Executive Editor
MIKE MARTS

SECRET WARS

THE MULTIVERSE WAS DESTROYED!

THE HEROES OF EARTH-616 AND EARTH-1610 WERE POWERLESS TO SAVE IT!

NOW, ALL THAT REMAINS...IS **BATTLEWORLD**!

A MASSIVE, PATCHWORK PLANET COMPOSED OF THE FRAGMENTS OF WORLDS THAT NO LONGER EXIST, MAINTAINED BY THE IRON WILL OF ITS GOD AND MASTER, **VICTOR VON DOOM**!

EACH REGION IS A DOMAIN UNTO ITSELF!

STAR-LORD AND KITTY PRYDE

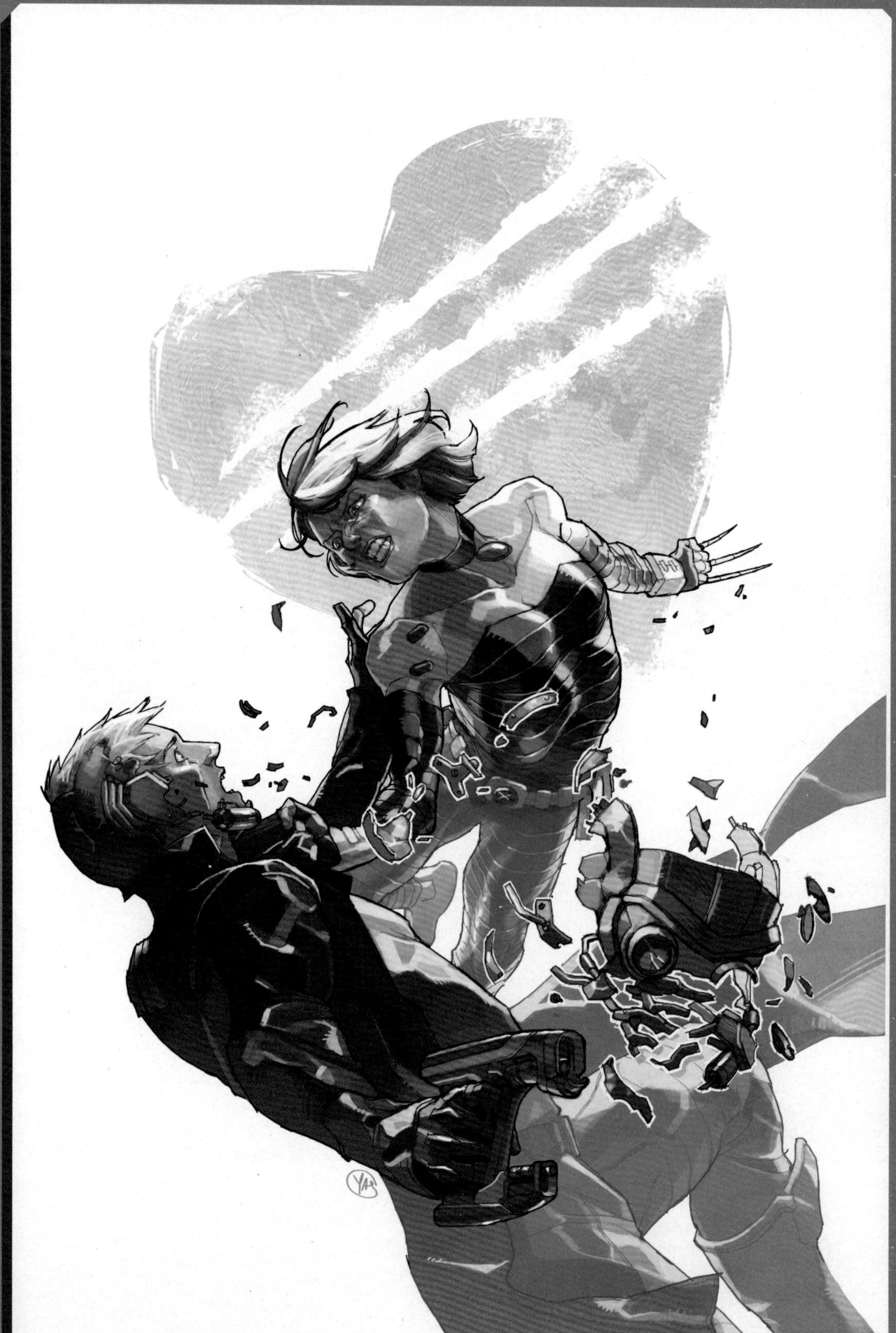

1

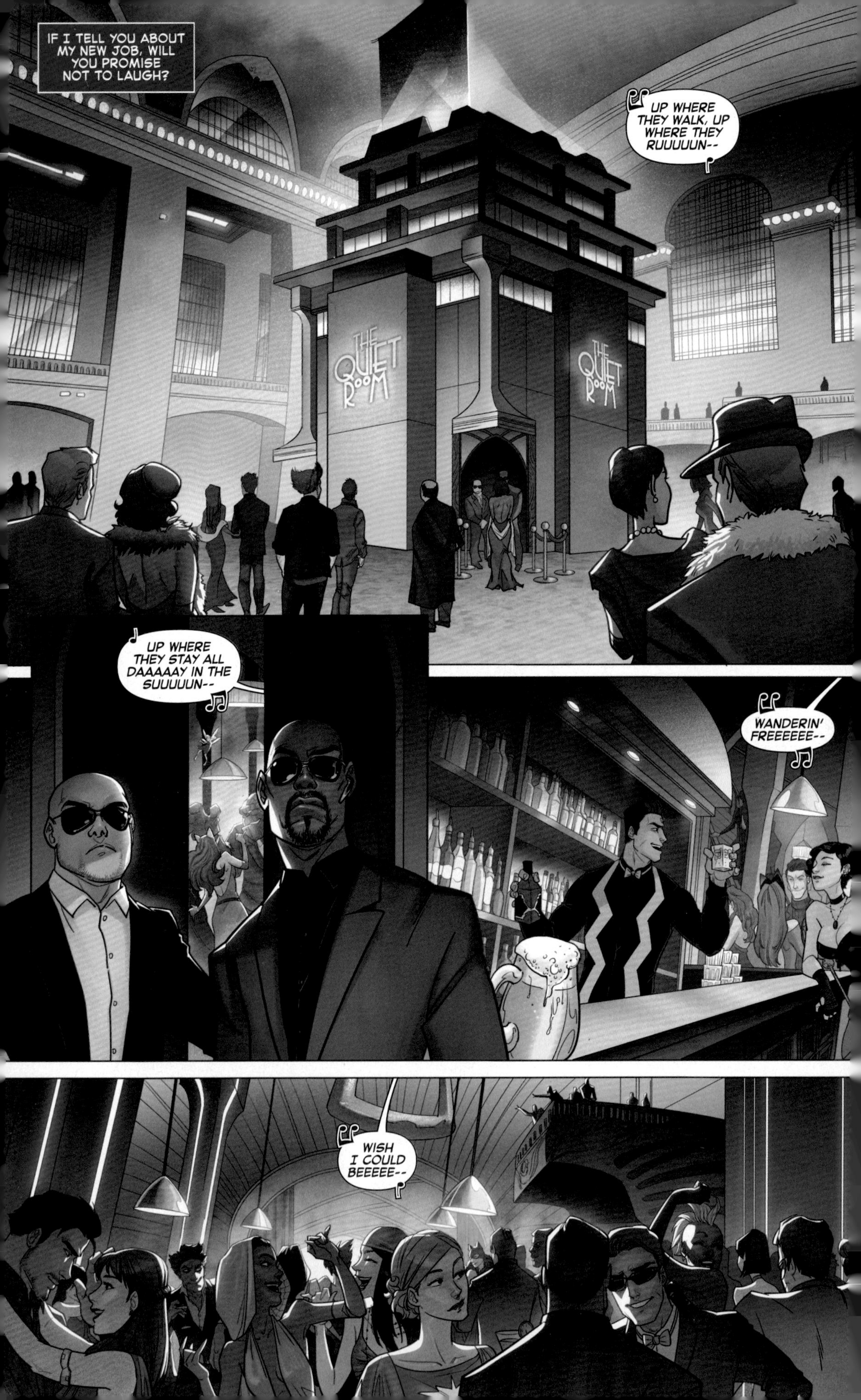
IF I TELL YOU ABOUT MY NEW JOB, WILL YOU PROMISE NOT TO LAUGH?
UP WHERE THEY WALK, UP WHERE THEY RUUUUUN--
THE QUIET ROOM
THE QUIET ROOM
UP WHERE THEY STAY ALL DAAAAAY IN THE SUUUUUN--
WANDERIN' FREEEEEE--
WISH I COULD BEEEEE--

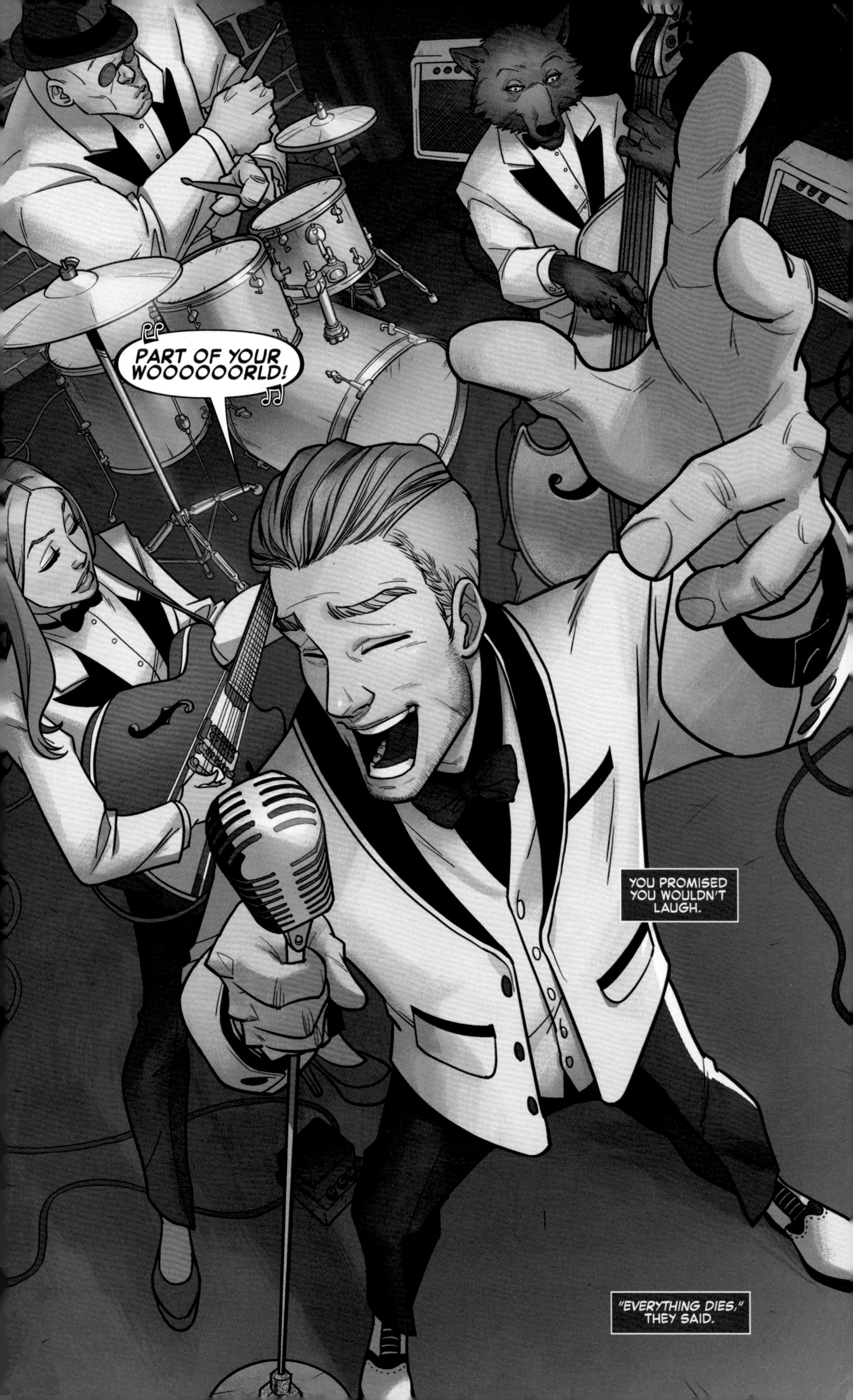
PART OF YOUR WOOOOOORLD!
YOU PROMISED YOU WOULDN'T LAUGH.
"EVERYTHING DIES," THEY SAID.

WELP, EVERYTHING *DIED.*

I SAW IT HAPPEN.

THE EARTH, THE SUN, THE MOON, THE STARS...

EVERY ICE CREAM SHOP, EVERY BLADE OF GRASS...EVERYONE WE EVER LOVED.

GONE.

EXCEPT FOR US.

REED RICHARDS, SMARTEST MAN EVER, BUILT US THIS COSMIC LIFE RAFT AND--

--DON'T ASK ME HOW, ASK REED, IF YOU WANNA GET BORED, BUT--

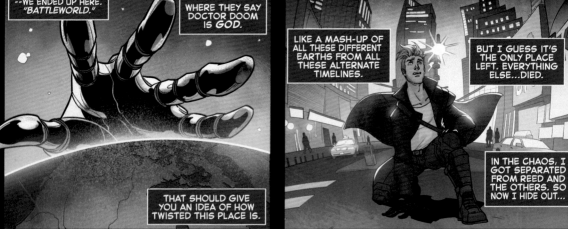

--WE ENDED UP HERE. "BATTLEWORLD."

WHERE THEY SAY DOCTOR DOOM IS *GOD.*

THAT SHOULD GIVE YOU AN IDEA OF HOW TWISTED THIS PLACE IS.

LIKE A MASH-UP OF ALL THESE DIFFERENT EARTHS FROM ALL THESE ALTERNATE TIMELINES.

BUT I GUESS IT'S THE ONLY PLACE LEFT. EVERYTHING ELSE...DIED.

IN THE CHAOS, I GOT SEPARATED FROM REED AND THE OTHERS. SO NOW I HIDE OUT...

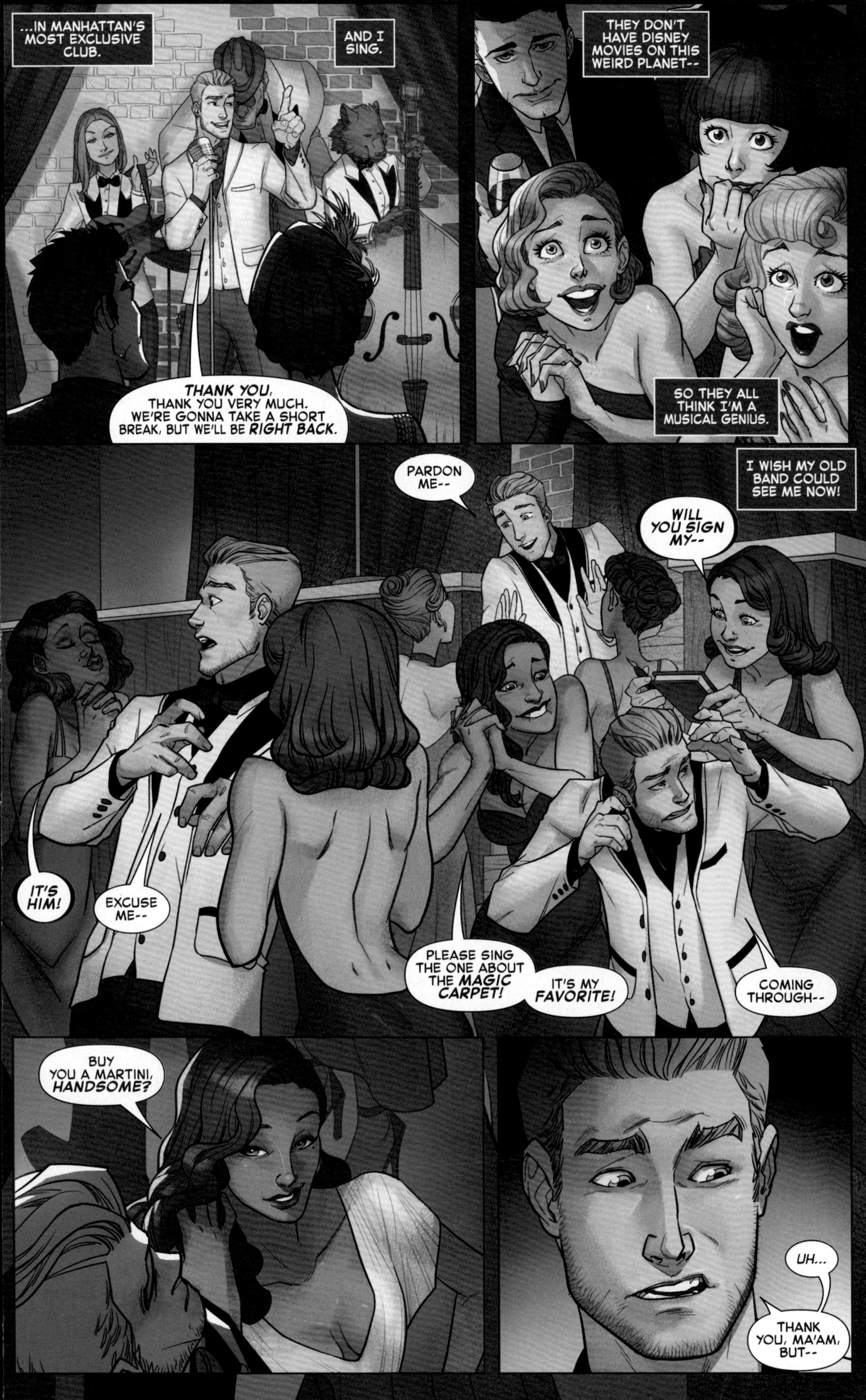

...IN MANHATTAN'S MOST EXCLUSIVE CLUB.
AND I SING.
THANK YOU, THANK YOU VERY MUCH. WE'RE GONNA TAKE A SHORT BREAK, BUT WE'LL BE RIGHT BACK.
THEY DON'T HAVE DISNEY MOVIES ON THIS WEIRD PLANET--
SO THEY ALL THINK I'M A MUSICAL GENIUS.
PARDON ME--
I WISH MY OLD BAND COULD SEE ME NOW!
WILL YOU SIGN MY--
IT'S HIM!
EXCUSE ME--
PLEASE SING THE ONE ABOUT THE MAGIC CARPET!
IT'S MY FAVORITE!
COMING THROUGH--
BUY YOU A MARTINI, HANDSOME?
UH...
THANK YOU, MA'AM, BUT--

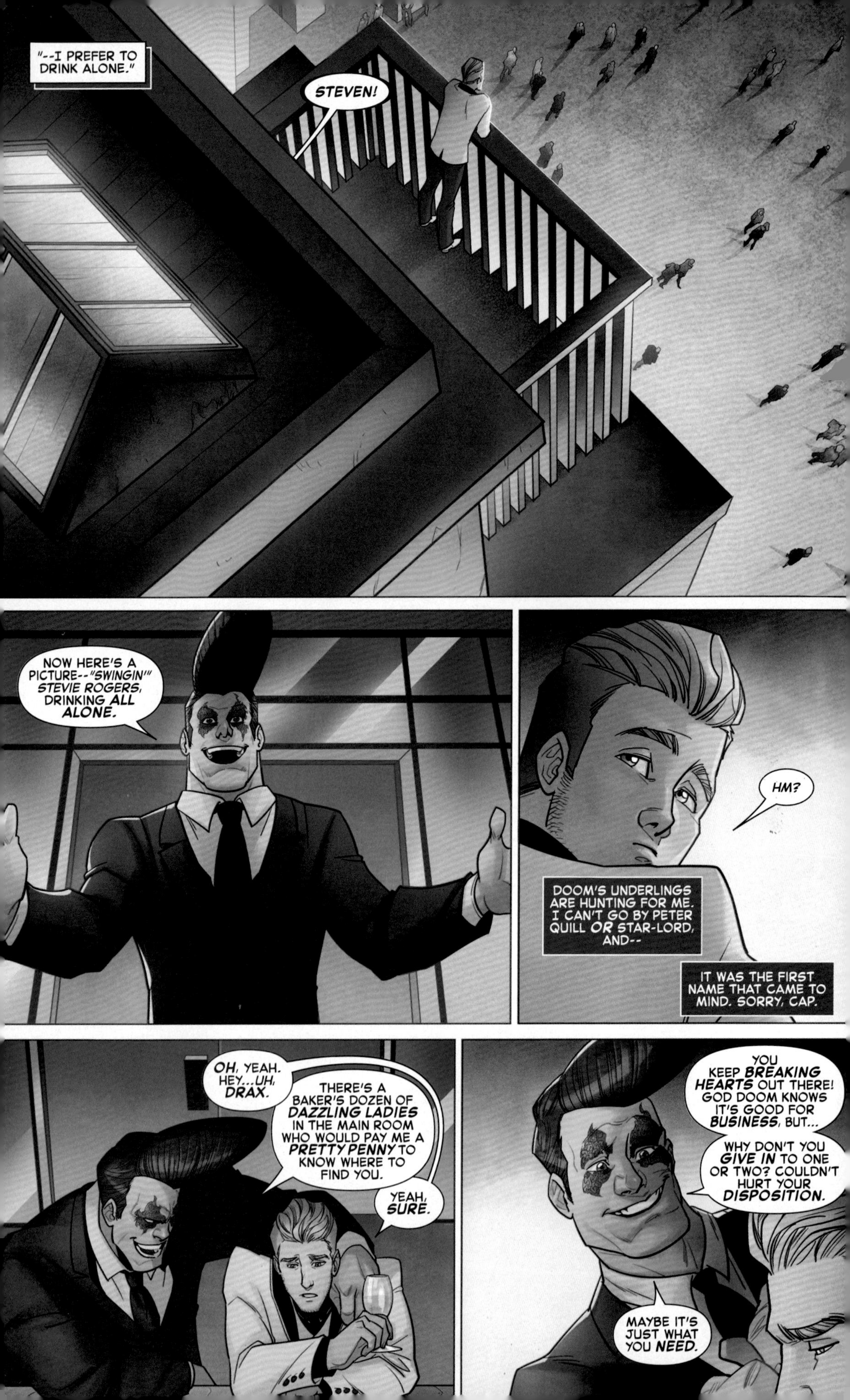
"--I PREFER TO DRINK ALONE."
STEVEN!
NOW HERE'S A PICTURE--"SWINGIN'" STEVIE ROGERS, DRINKING ALL ALONE.
HM?
DOOM'S UNDERLINGS ARE HUNTING FOR ME. I CAN'T GO BY PETER QUILL OR STAR-LORD, AND--
IT WAS THE FIRST NAME THAT CAME TO MIND. SORRY, CAP.
OH, YEAH. HEY...UH, DRAX.
THERE'S A BAKER'S DOZEN OF DAZZLING LADIES IN THE MAIN ROOM WHO WOULD PAY ME A PRETTY PENNY TO KNOW WHERE TO FIND YOU.
YEAH, SURE.
YOU KEEP BREAKING HEARTS OUT THERE! GOD DOOM KNOWS IT'S GOOD FOR BUSINESS, BUT...
WHY DON'T YOU GIVE IN TO ONE OR TWO? COULDN'T HURT YOUR DISPOSITION.
MAYBE IT'S JUST WHAT YOU NEED.

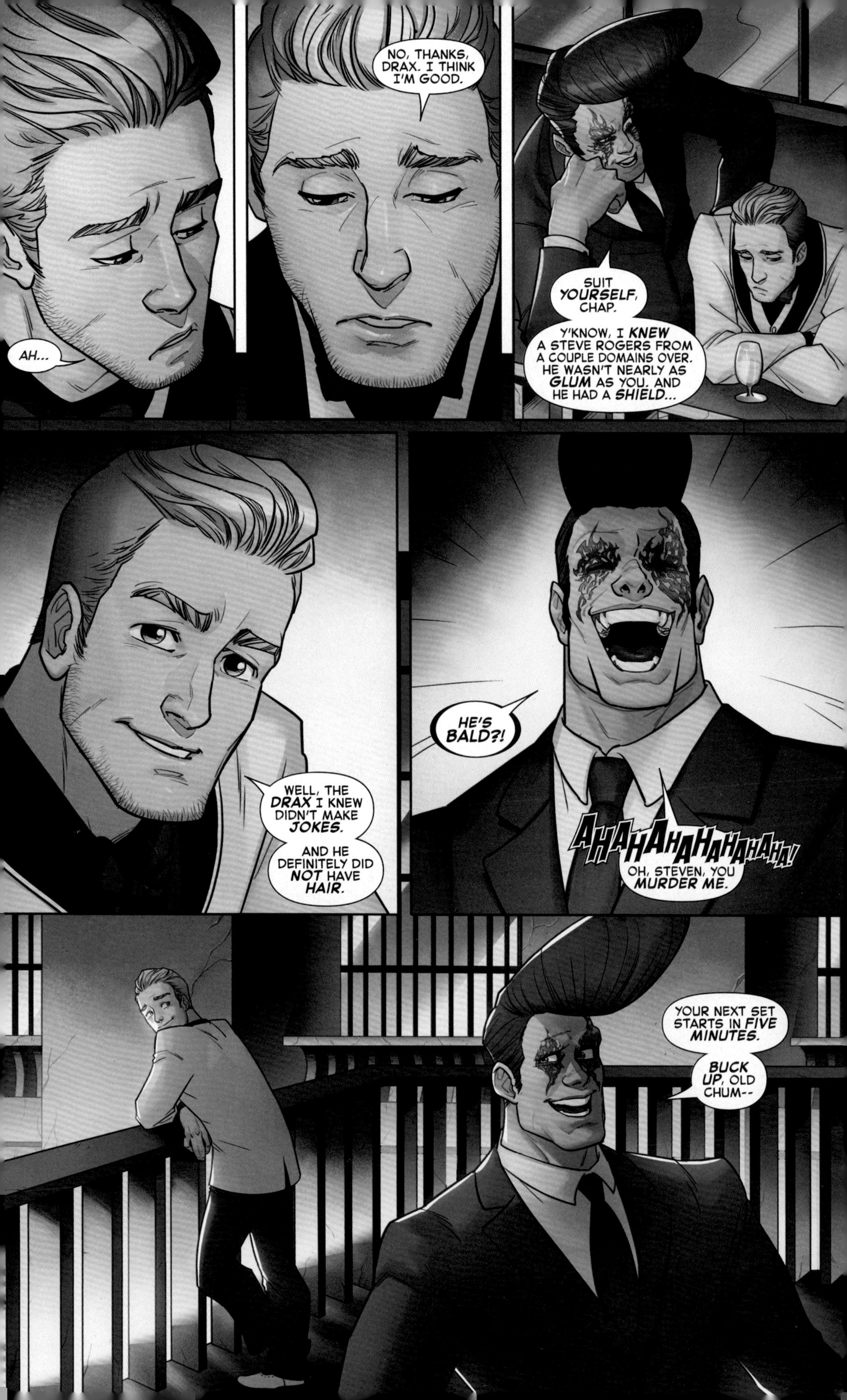
AH...
NO, THANKS, DRAX. I THINK I'M GOOD.
SUIT YOURSELF, CHAP.
Y'KNOW, I KNEW A STEVE ROGERS FROM A COUPLE DOMAINS OVER. HE WASN'T NEARLY AS GLUM AS YOU. AND HE HAD A SHIELD...
WELL, THE DRAX I KNEW DIDN'T MAKE JOKES.
AND HE DEFINITELY DID NOT HAVE HAIR.
HE'S BALD?!
AHAHAHAHAHAHAHAHA!
OH, STEVEN, YOU MURDER ME.
YOUR NEXT SET STARTS IN FIVE MINUTES.
BUCK UP, OLD CHUM--

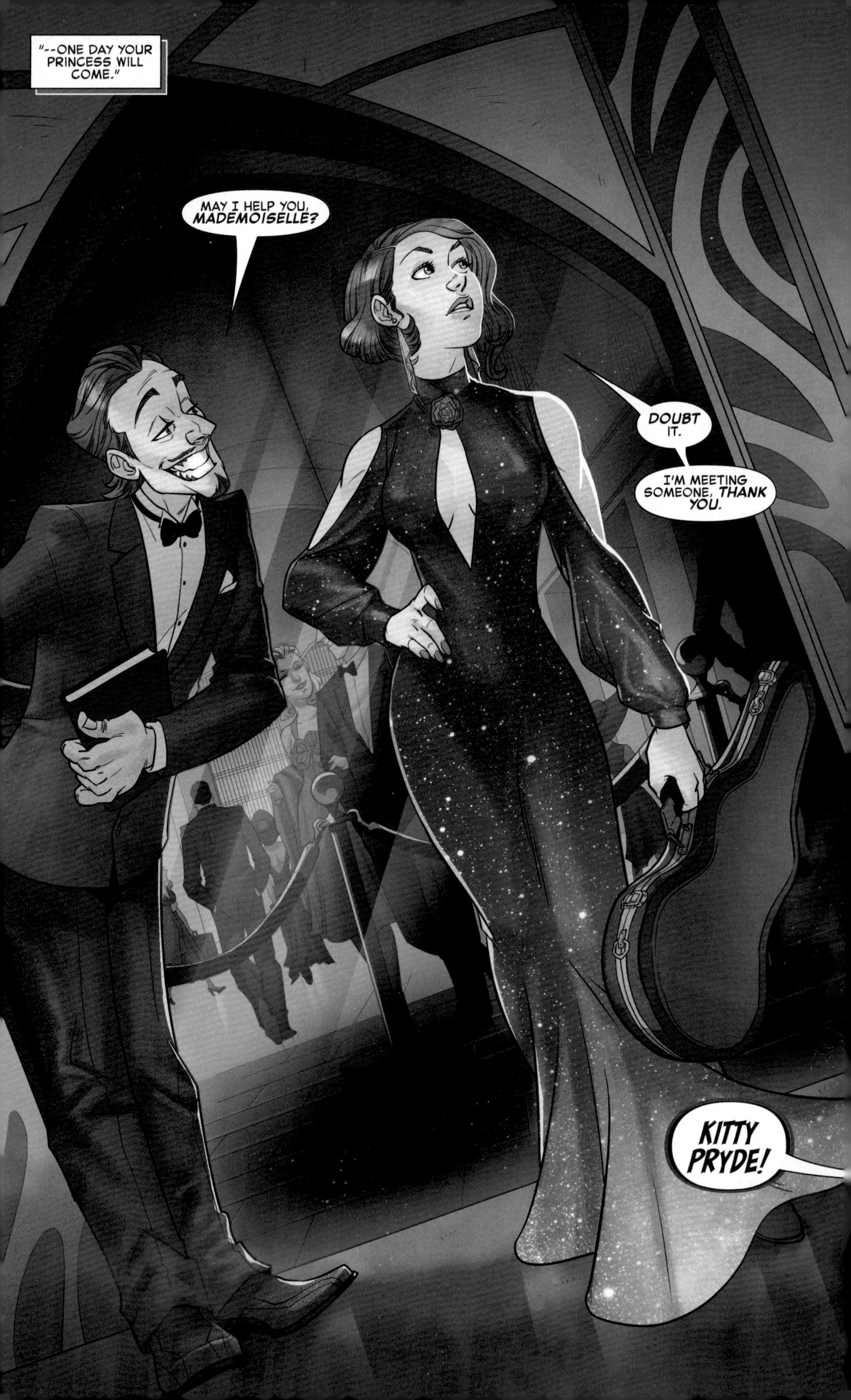
"--ONE DAY YOUR PRINCESS WILL COME."
MAY I HELP YOU, MADEMOISELLE?
DOUBT IT.
I'M MEETING SOMEONE, THANK YOU.
KITTY PRYDE!

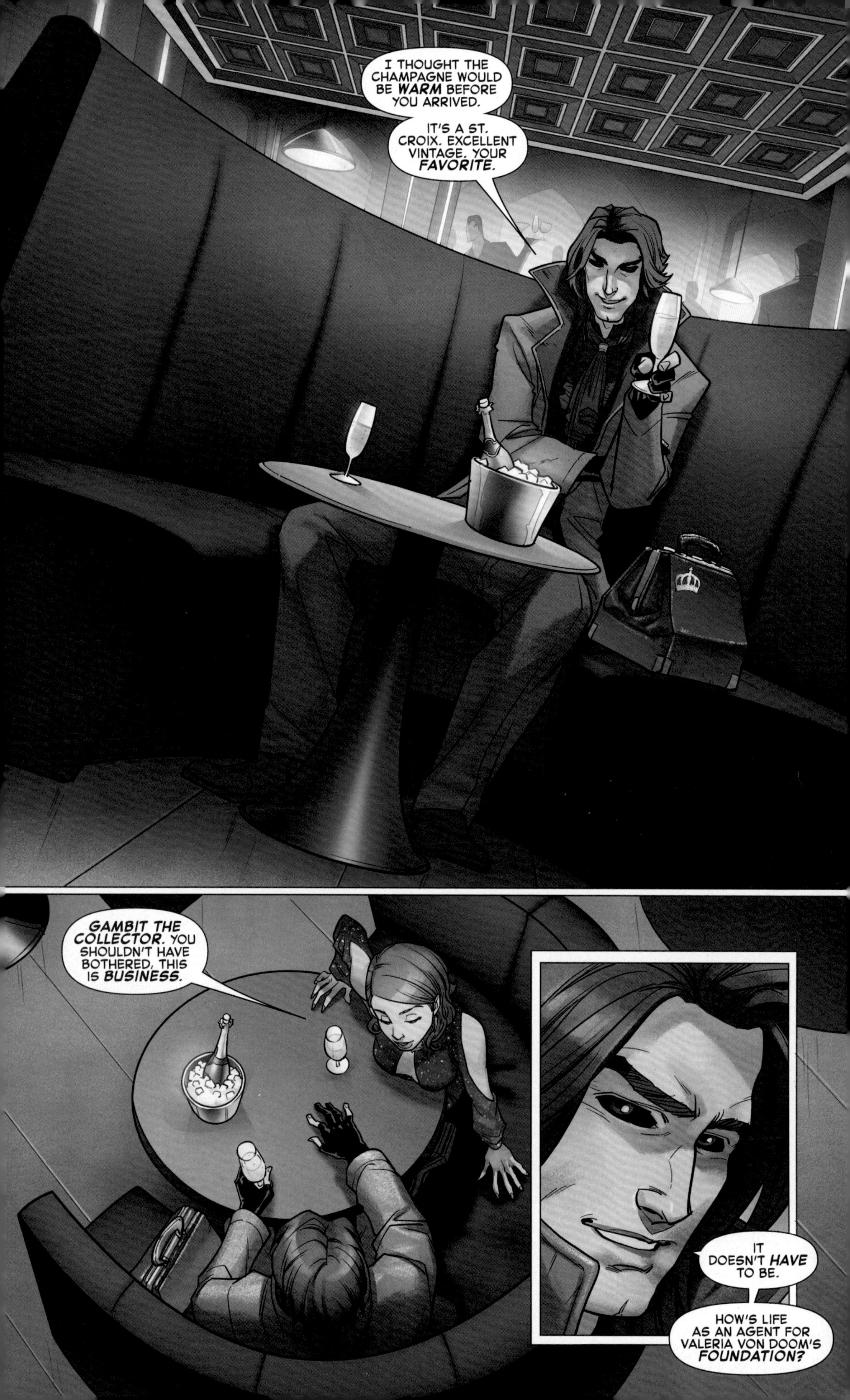
I THOUGHT THE CHAMPAGNE WOULD BE WARM BEFORE YOU ARRIVED.
IT'S A ST. CROIX. EXCELLENT VINTAGE. YOUR FAVORITE.
GAMBIT THE COLLECTOR. YOU SHOULDN'T HAVE BOTHERED, THIS IS BUSINESS.
IT DOESN'T HAVE TO BE.
HOW'S LIFE AS AN AGENT FOR VALERIA VON DOOM'S FOUNDATION?

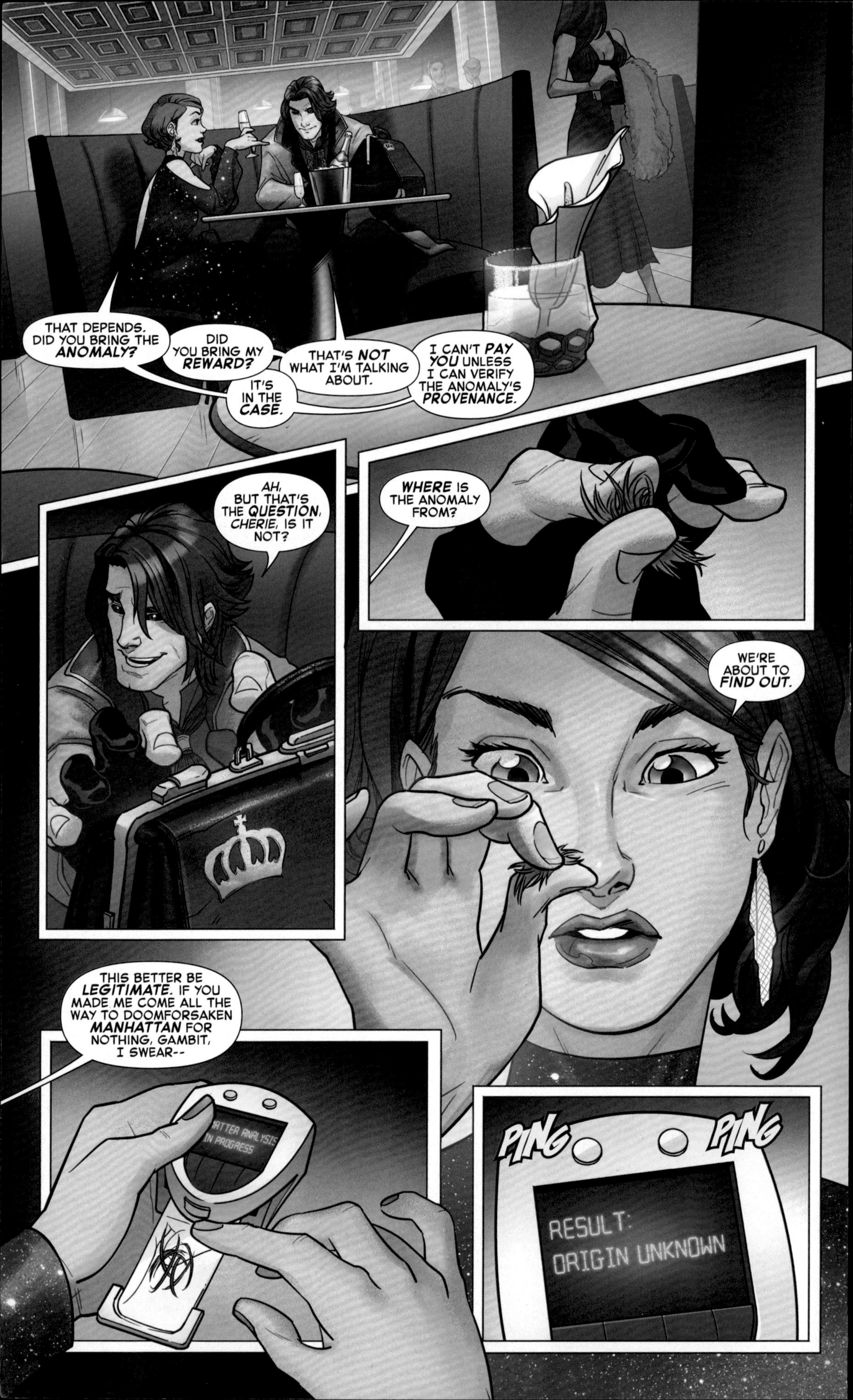
THAT DEPENDS. DID YOU BRING THE ANOMALY?
DID YOU BRING MY REWARD?
IT'S IN THE CASE.
THAT'S NOT WHAT I'M TALKING ABOUT.
I CAN'T PAY YOU UNLESS I CAN VERIFY THE ANOMALY'S PROVENANCE.
AH, BUT THAT'S THE QUESTION, CHERIE, IS IT NOT?
WHERE IS THE ANOMALY FROM?
WE'RE ABOUT TO FIND OUT.
THIS BETTER BE LEGITIMATE. IF YOU MADE ME COME ALL THE WAY TO DOOMFORSAKEN MANHATTAN FOR NOTHING, GAMBIT, I SWEAR--
IN PROGRESS
PING PING
RESULT:
ORIGIN UNKNOWN

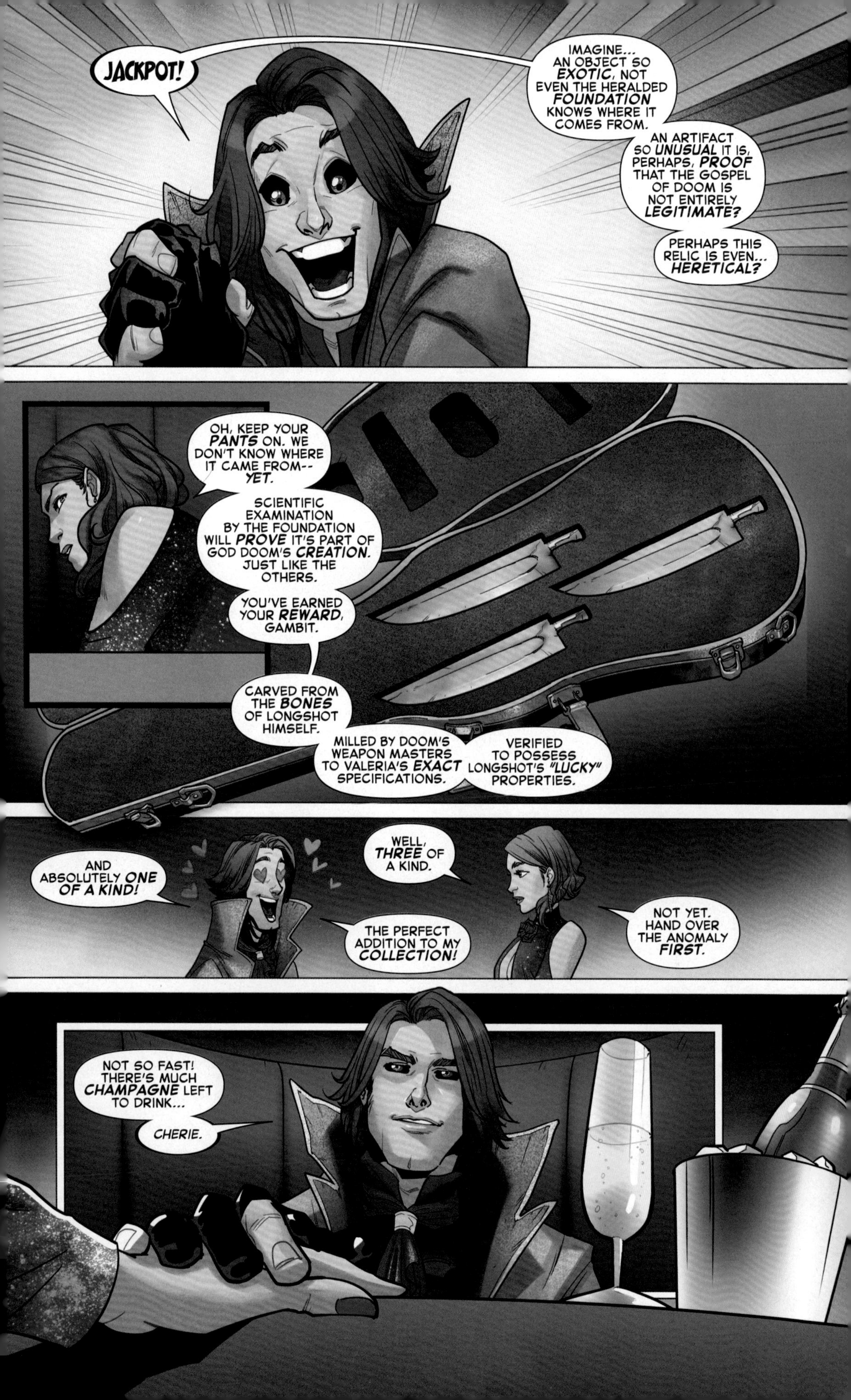

JACKPOT!
IMAGINE... AN OBJECT SO EXOTIC, NOT EVEN THE HERALDED FOUNDATION KNOWS WHERE IT COMES FROM.
AN ARTIFACT SO UNUSUAL IT IS, PERHAPS, PROOF THAT THE GOSPEL OF DOOM IS NOT ENTIRELY LEGITIMATE?
PERHAPS THIS RELIC IS EVEN... HERETICAL?
OH, KEEP YOUR PANTS ON. WE DON'T KNOW WHERE IT CAME FROM-- YET.
SCIENTIFIC EXAMINATION BY THE FOUNDATION WILL PROVE IT'S PART OF GOD DOOM'S CREATION. JUST LIKE THE OTHERS.
YOU'VE EARNED YOUR REWARD, GAMBIT.
CARVED FROM THE BONES OF LONGSHOT HIMSELF.
MILLED BY DOOM'S WEAPON MASTERS TO VALERIA'S EXACT SPECIFICATIONS.
VERIFIED TO POSSESS LONGSHOT'S "LUCKY" PROPERTIES.
AND ABSOLUTELY ONE OF A KIND!
WELL, THREE OF A KIND.
THE PERFECT ADDITION TO MY COLLECTION!
NOT YET. HAND OVER THE ANOMALY FIRST.
NOT SO FAST! THERE'S MUCH CHAMPAGNE LEFT TO DRINK...
CHERIE.

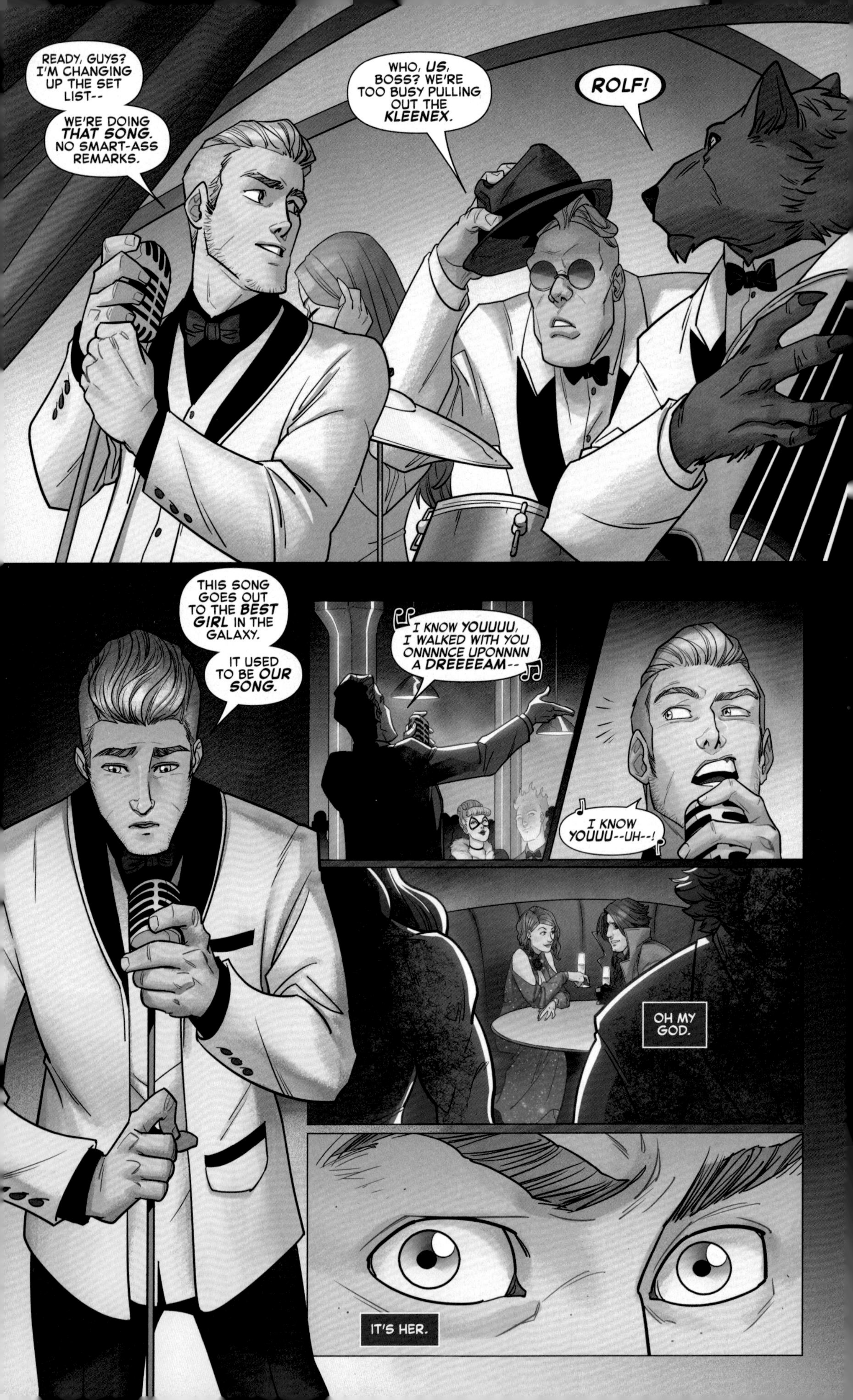
READY, GUYS? I'M CHANGING UP THE SET LIST--
WE'RE DOING THAT SONG. NO SMART-ASS REMARKS.
WHO, US, BOSS? WE'RE TOO BUSY PULLING OUT THE KLEENEX.
ROLF!
THIS SONG GOES OUT TO THE BEST GIRL IN THE GALAXY.
IT USED TO BE OUR SONG.
I KNOW YOUUUU, I WALKED WITH YOU ONNNNCE UPONNNN A DREEEEAM--
I KNOW YOUUU--UH--!
OH MY GOD.
IT'S HER.

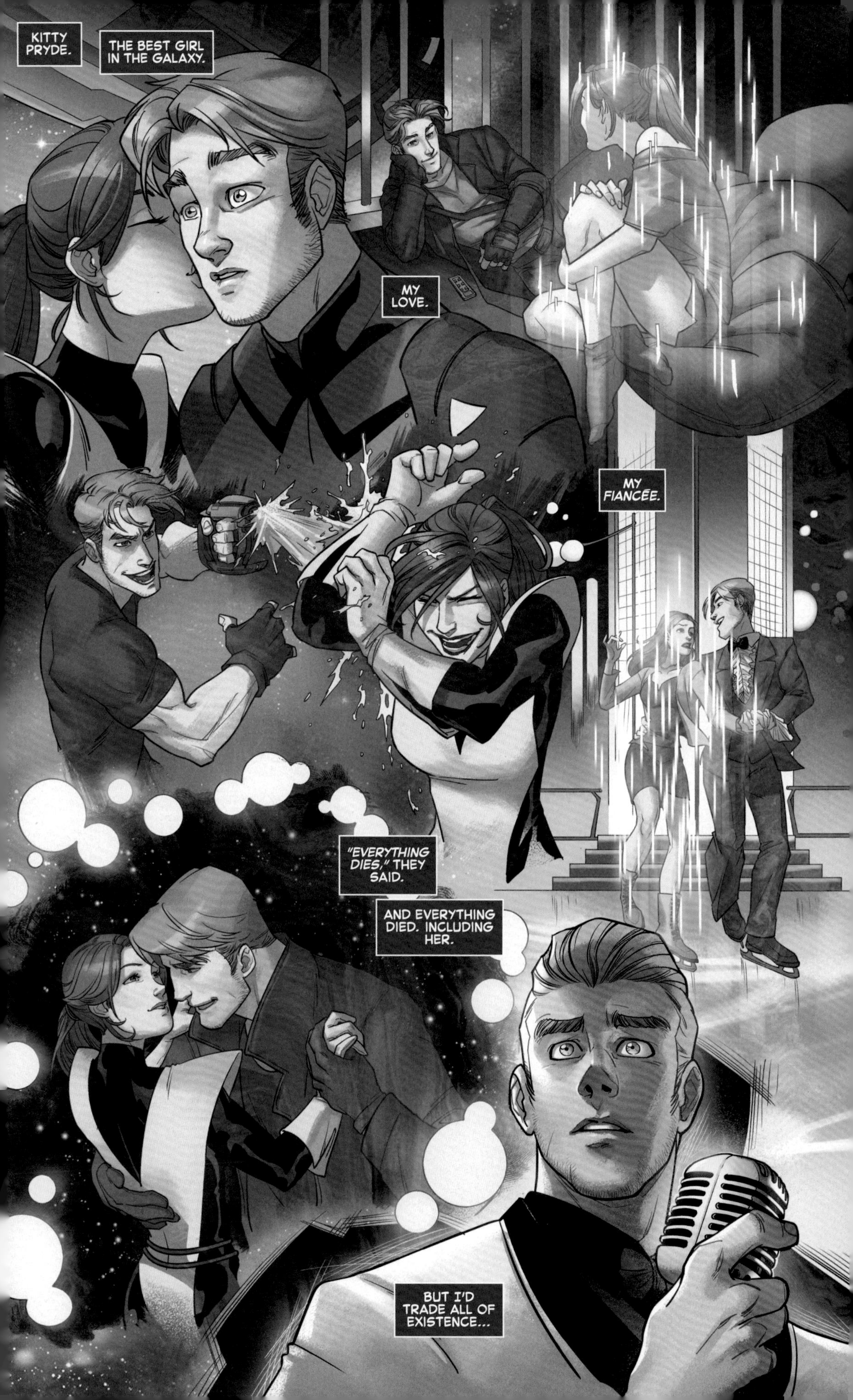
KITTY PRYDE.
THE BEST GIRL IN THE GALAXY.
MY LOVE.
MY FIANCÉE.
"EVERYTHING DIES," THEY SAID.
AND EVERYTHING DIED. INCLUDING HER.
BUT I'D TRADE ALL OF EXISTENCE...

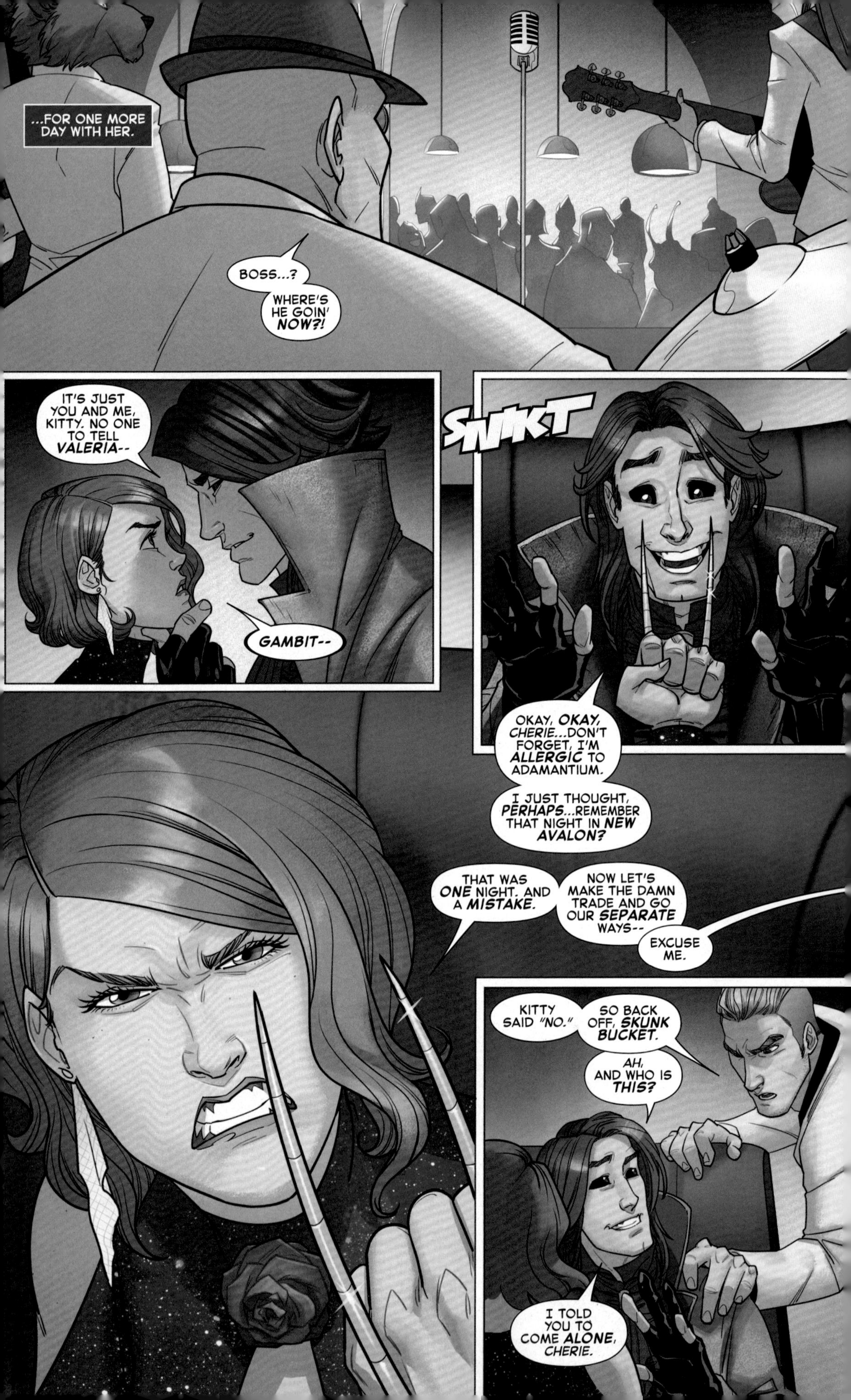

...FOR ONE MORE DAY WITH HER.
BOSS...?
WHERE'S HE GOIN' NOW?!
IT'S JUST YOU AND ME, KITTY. NO ONE TO TELL VALERIA--
GAMBIT--
SNIKT
OKAY, OKAY, CHERIE...DON'T FORGET, I'M ALLERGIC TO ADAMANTIUM.
I JUST THOUGHT, PERHAPS...REMEMBER THAT NIGHT IN NEW AVALON?
THAT WAS ONE NIGHT. AND A MISTAKE.
NOW LET'S MAKE THE DAMN TRADE AND GO OUR SEPARATE WAYS--
EXCUSE ME.
KITTY SAID "NO."
SO BACK OFF, SKUNK BUCKET.
AH, AND WHO IS THIS?
I TOLD YOU TO COME ALONE, CHERIE.

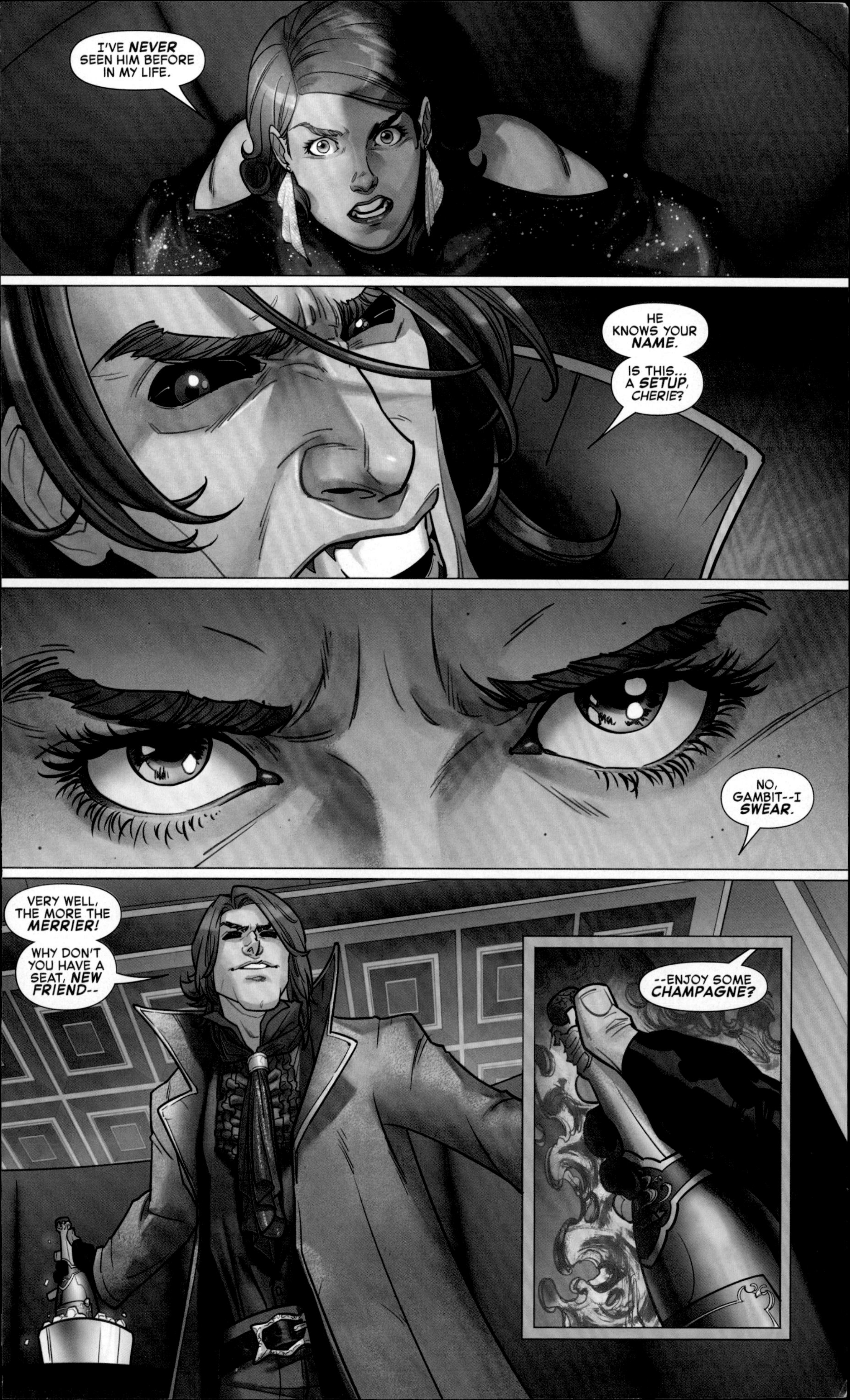
I'VE NEVER SEEN HIM BEFORE IN MY LIFE.
HE KNOWS YOUR NAME.
IS THIS... A SETUP, CHERIE?
NO, GAMBIT--I SWEAR.
VERY WELL, THE MORE THE MERRIER!
WHY DON'T YOU HAVE A SEAT, NEW FRIEND--
--ENJOY SOME CHAMPAGNE?

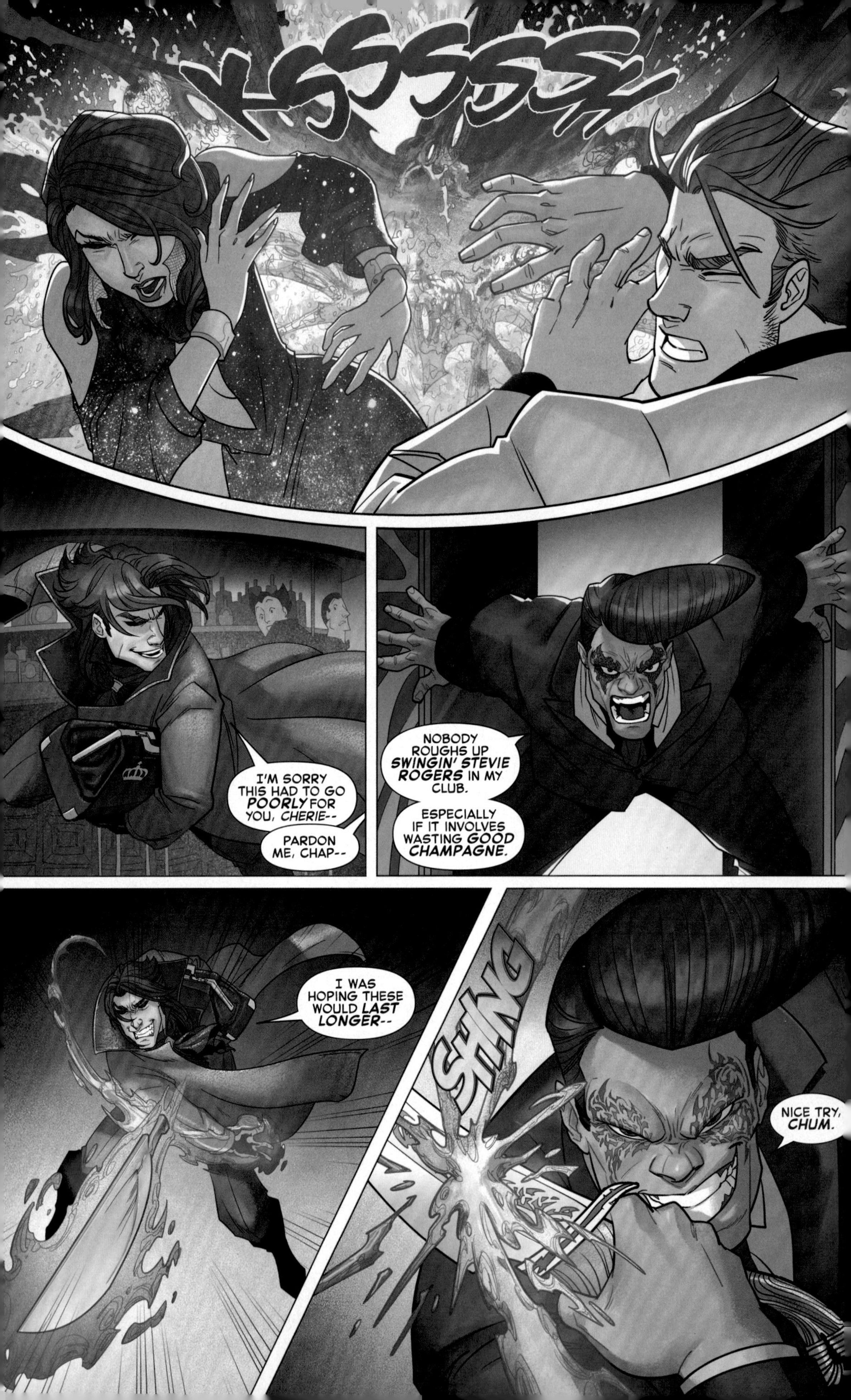

XSSSSH
I'M SORRY THIS HAD TO GO POORLY FOR YOU, CHERIE--
PARDON ME, CHAP--
NOBODY ROUGHS UP SWINGIN' STEVIE ROGERS IN MY CLUB.
ESPECIALLY IF IT INVOLVES WASTING GOOD CHAMPAGNE.
I WAS HOPING THESE WOULD LAST LONGER--
SHING
NICE TRY, CHUM.

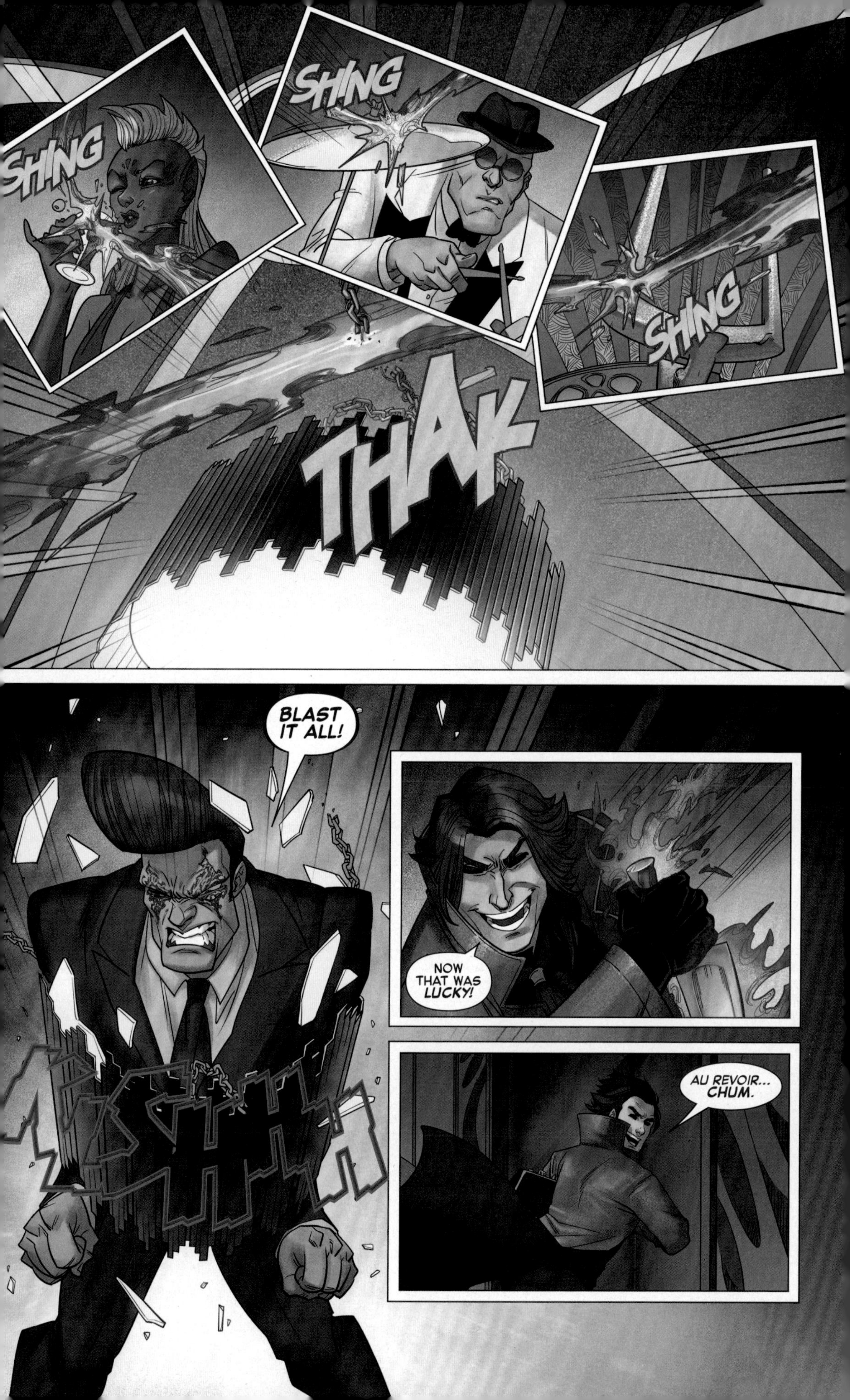
SHING
SHING
SHING
THAK
BLAST IT ALL!
NOW THAT WAS LUCKY!
AU REVOIR... CHUM.

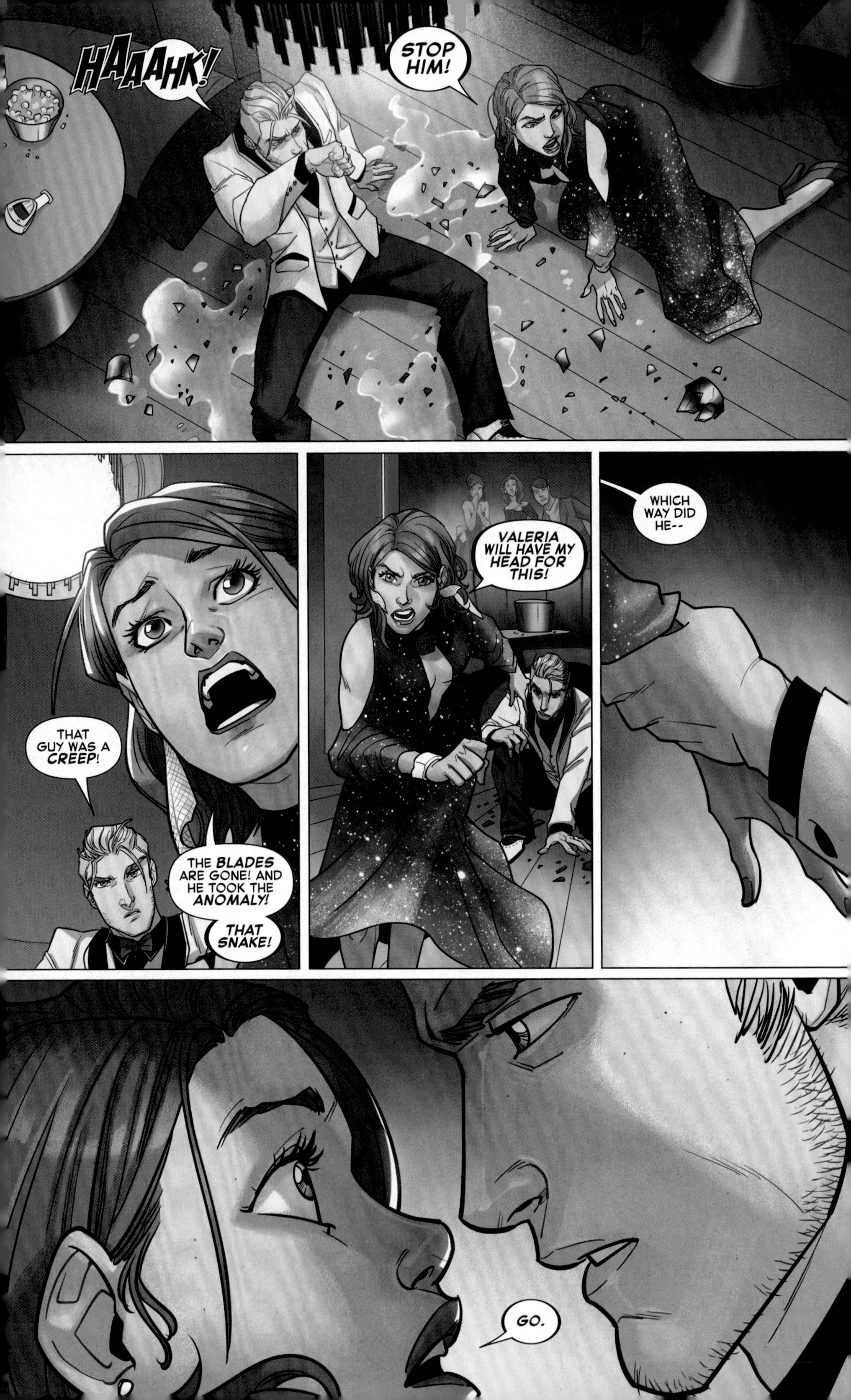
HAAAHK!
STOP HIM!
THAT GUY WAS A CREEP!
THE BLADES ARE GONE! AND HE TOOK THE ANOMALY!
THAT SNAKE!
VALERIA WILL HAVE MY HEAD FOR THIS!
WHICH WAY DID HE--
GO.

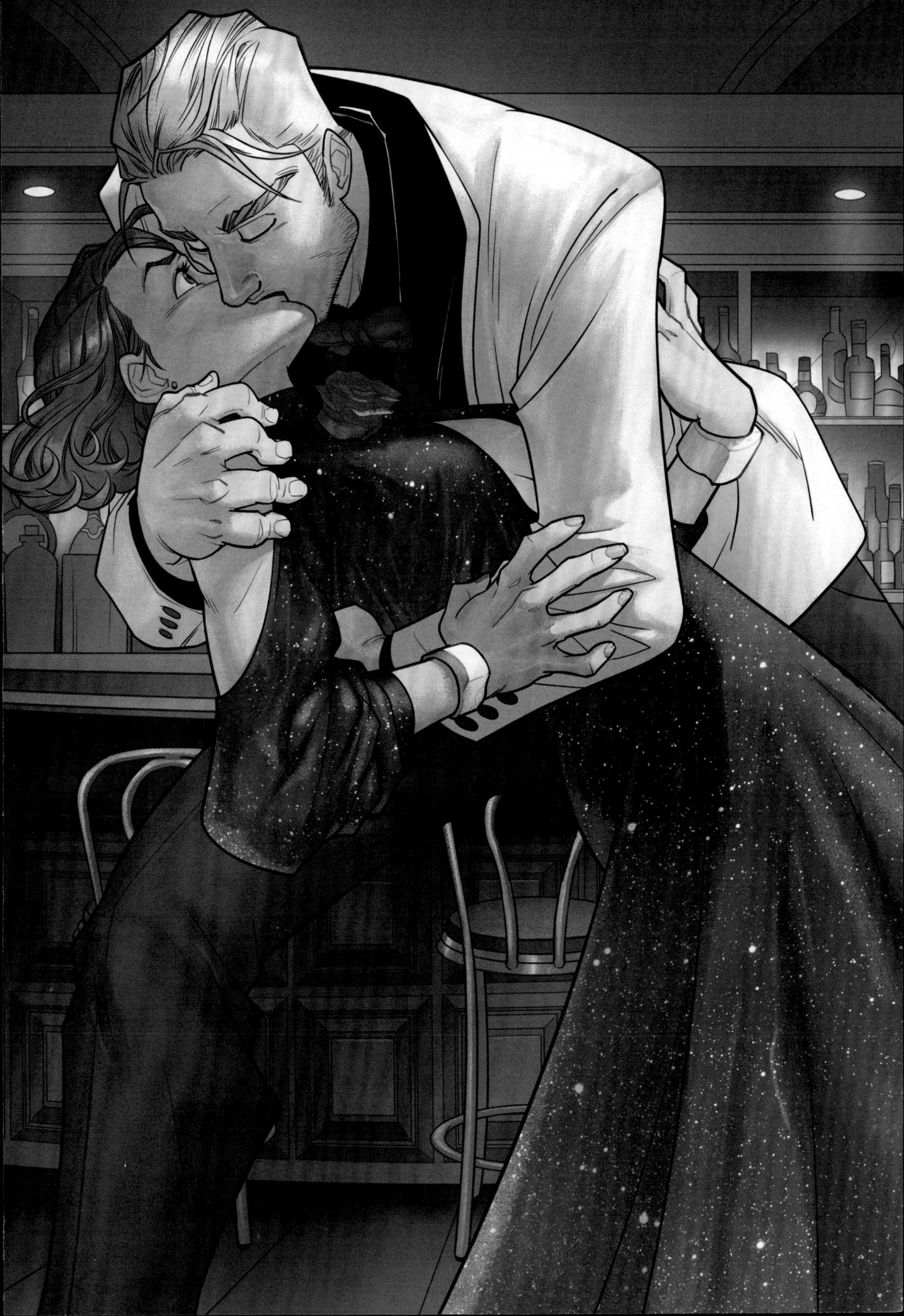

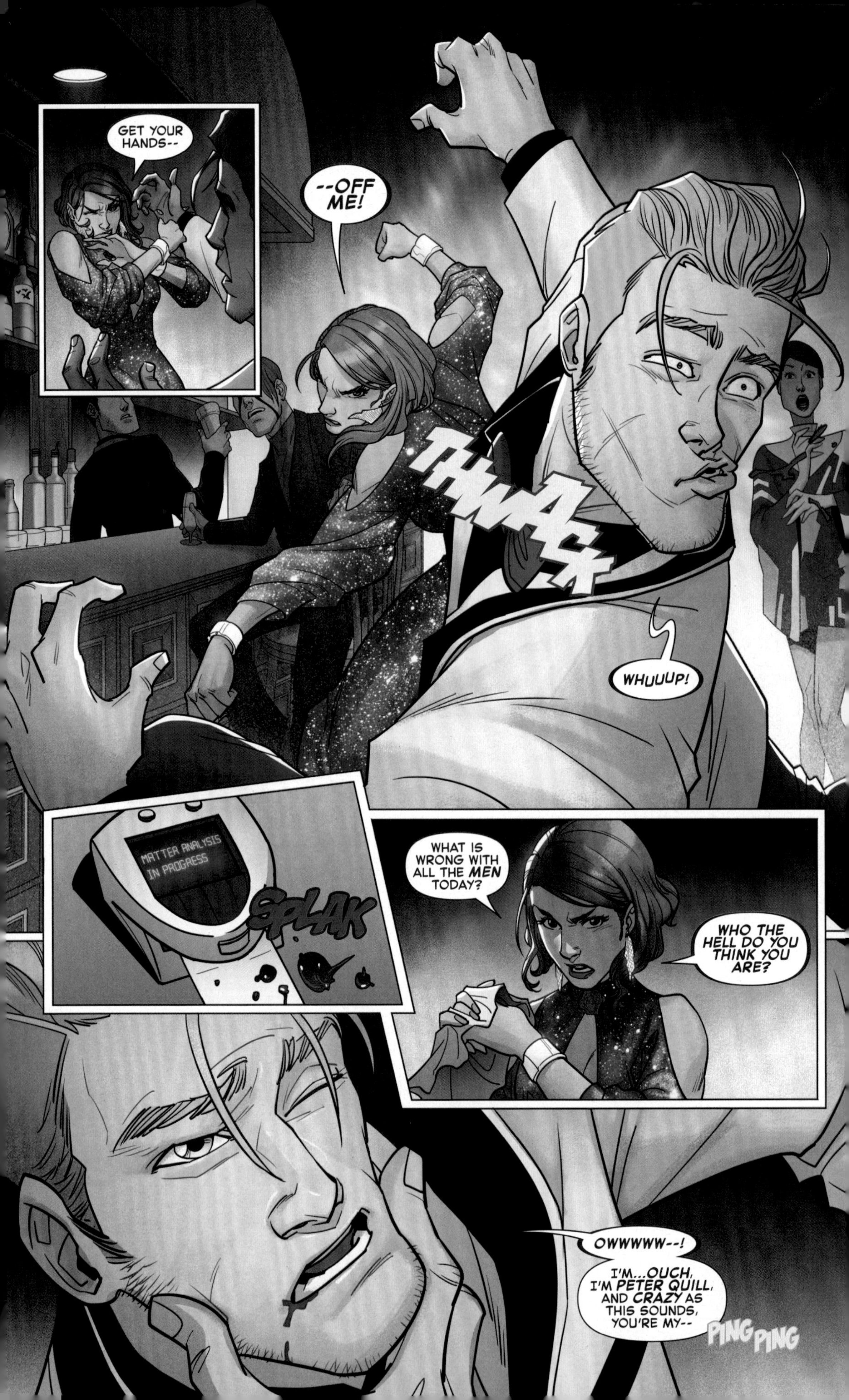
GET YOUR HANDS--
--OFF ME!
THWACK
WHUUUP!
MATTER ANALYSIS IN PROGRESS
SPLAK
WHAT IS WRONG WITH ALL THE MEN TODAY?
WHO THE HELL DO YOU THINK YOU ARE?
OWWWWW--!
I'M...OUCH, I'M PETER QUILL, AND CRAZY AS THIS SOUNDS, YOU'RE MY--
PING PING

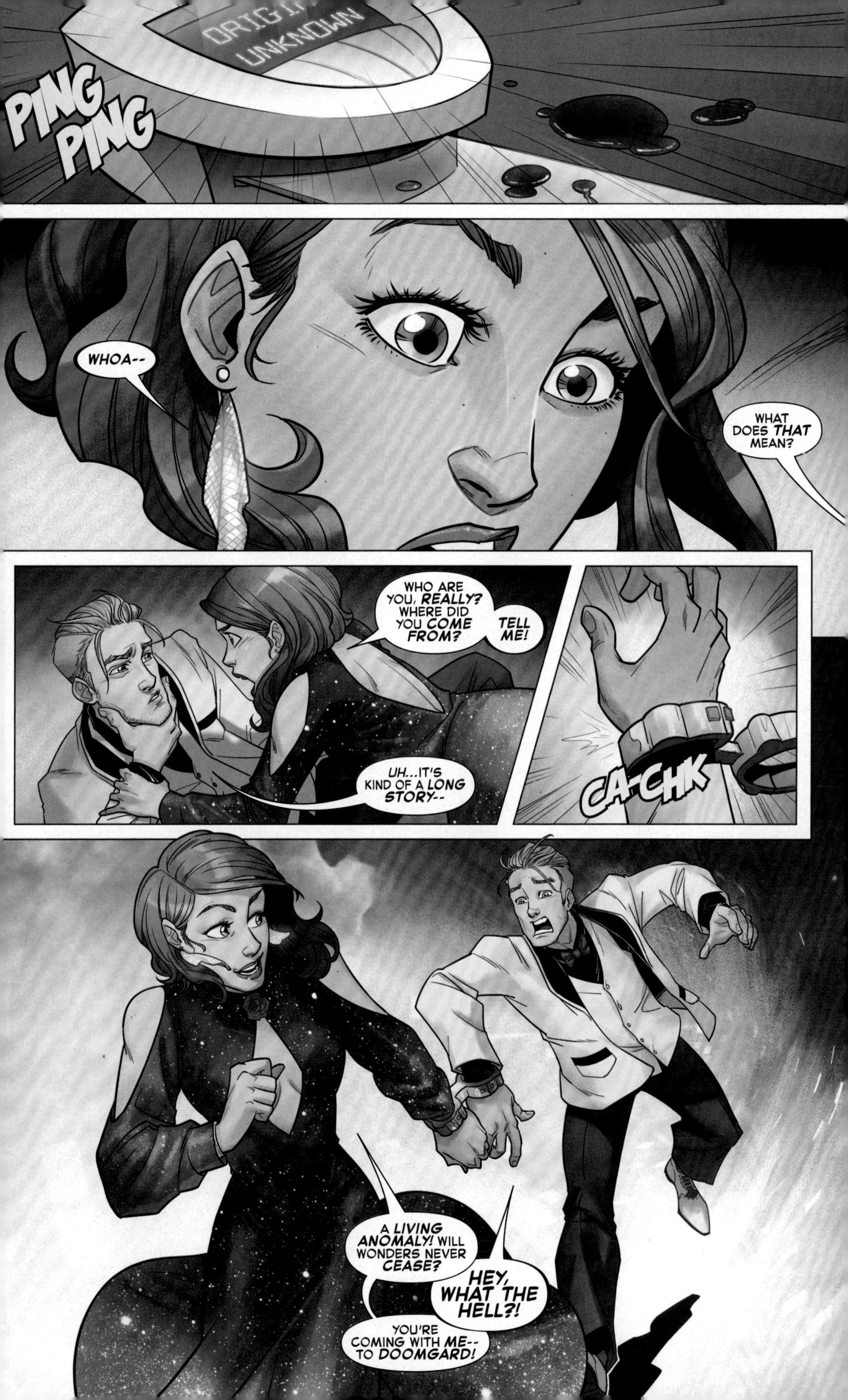
ORIGIN UNKNOWN
PING PING
WHOA--
WHAT DOES THAT MEAN?
WHO ARE YOU, REALLY? WHERE DID YOU COME FROM?
TELL ME!
UH...IT'S KIND OF A LONG STORY--
CA-CHK
A LIVING ANOMALY! WILL WONDERS NEVER CEASE?
HEY, WHAT THE HELL?!
YOU'RE COMING WITH ME-- TO DOOMGARD!

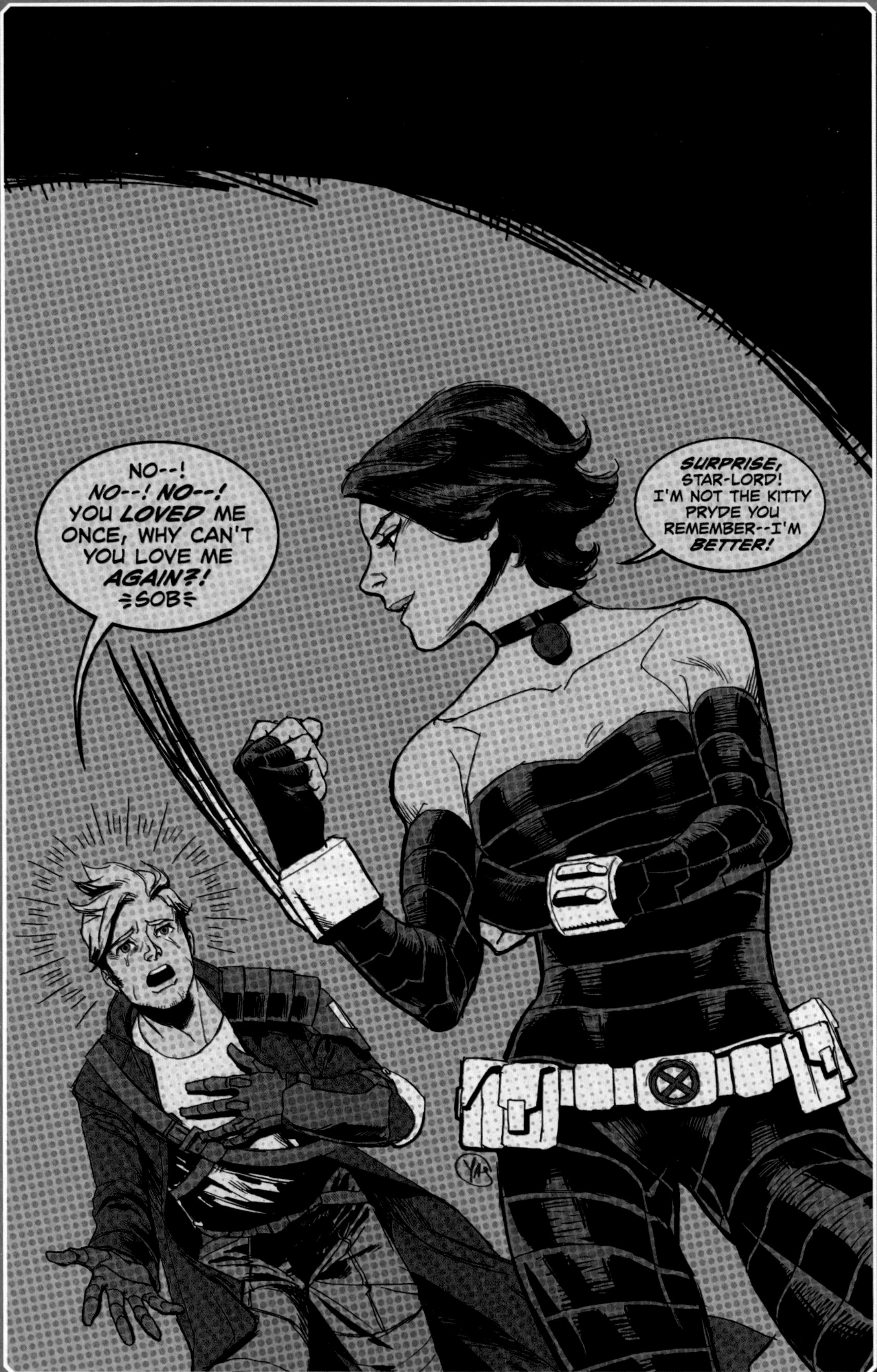

SURPRISE, STAR-LORD! I'M NOT THE KITTY PRYDE YOU REMEMBER--I'M BETTER!
NO--! NO--! NO--! YOU LOVED ME ONCE, WHY CAN'T YOU LOVE ME AGAIN?! ≡SOB≡

2

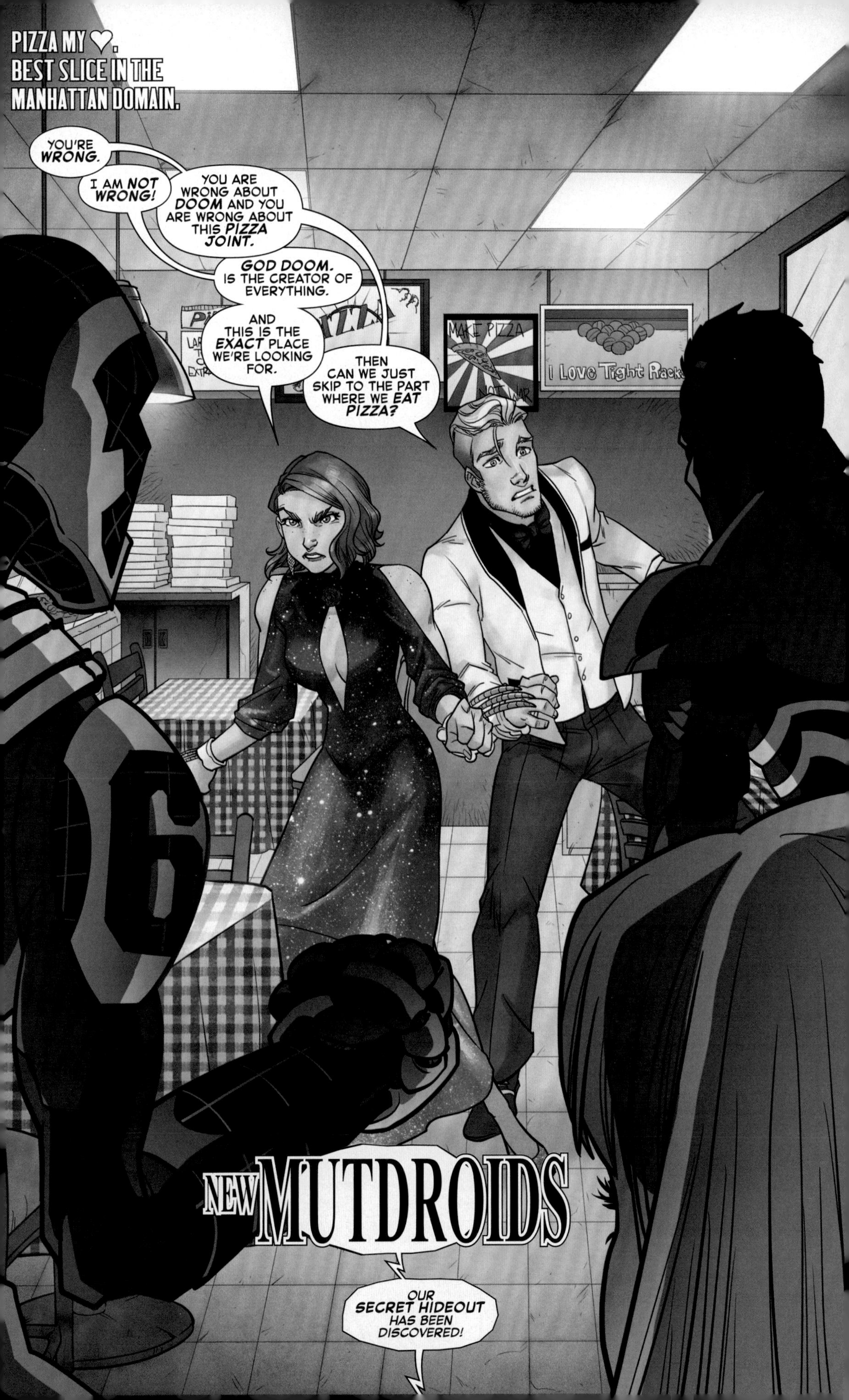

PIZZA MY ♥. BEST SLICE IN THE MANHATTAN DOMAIN.
YOU'RE WRONG.
I AM NOT WRONG!
YOU ARE WRONG ABOUT DOOM AND YOU ARE WRONG ABOUT THIS PIZZA JOINT.
GOD DOOM. IS THE CREATOR OF EVERYTHING.
AND THIS IS THE EXACT PLACE WE'RE LOOKING FOR.
THEN CAN WE JUST SKIP TO THE PART WHERE WE EAT PIZZA?
MAKE PIZZA
NEW MUTDROIDS
OUR SECRET HIDEOUT HAS BEEN DISCOVERED!

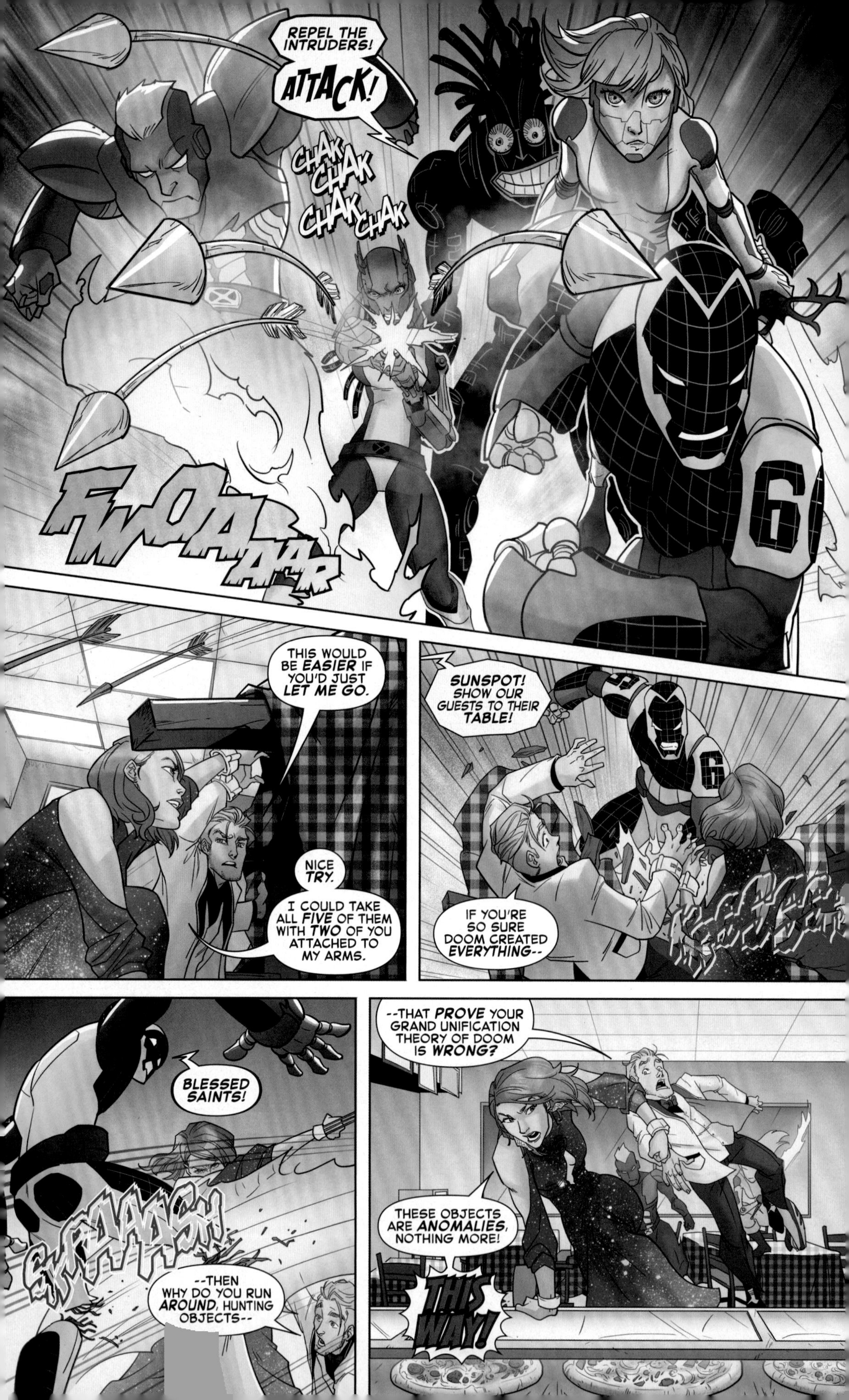
REPEL THE INTRUDERS!
ATTACK!
CHAK CHAK CHAK CHAK
FWOAAAR
THIS WOULD BE EASIER IF YOU'D JUST LET ME GO.
NICE TRY.
I COULD TAKE ALL FIVE OF THEM WITH TWO OF YOU ATTACHED TO MY ARMS.
SUNSPOT! SHOW OUR GUESTS TO THEIR TABLE!
IF YOU'RE SO SURE DOOM CREATED EVERYTHING--
BLESSED SAINTS!
SKRAASH
--THEN WHY DO YOU RUN AROUND, HUNTING OBJECTS--
--THAT PROVE YOUR GRAND UNIFICATION THEORY OF DOOM IS WRONG?
THESE OBJECTS ARE ANOMALIES, NOTHING MORE!
THIS WAY!

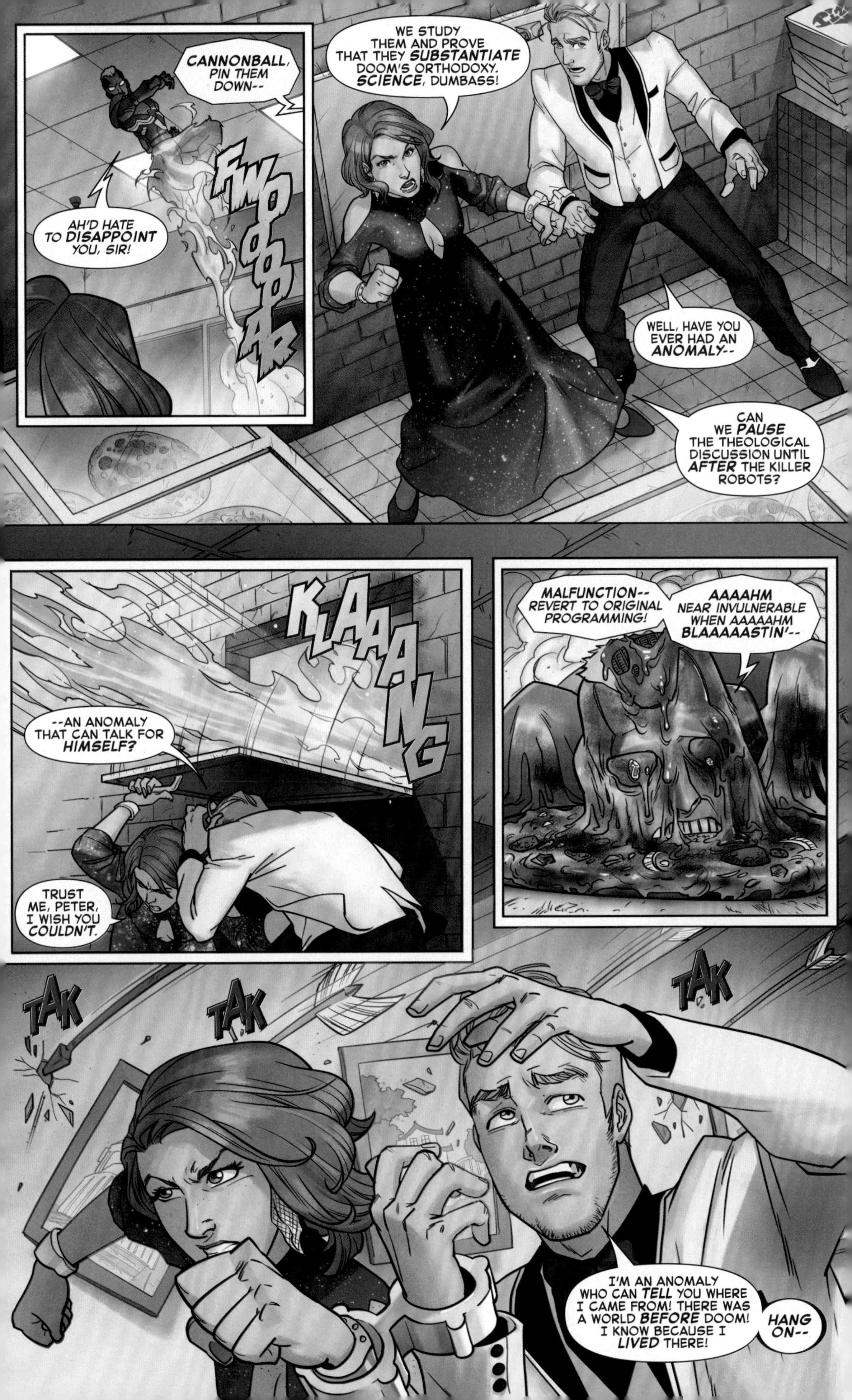
CANNONBALL, PIN THEM DOWN--
AH'D HATE TO DISAPPOINT YOU, SIR!
FWOOOOOOAR
WE STUDY THEM AND PROVE THAT THEY SUBSTANTIATE DOOM'S ORTHODOXY. SCIENCE, DUMBASS!
WELL, HAVE YOU EVER HAD AN ANOMALY--
CAN WE PAUSE THE THEOLOGICAL DISCUSSION UNTIL AFTER THE KILLER ROBOTS?
KLAAAANG
--AN ANOMALY THAT CAN TALK FOR HIMSELF?
TRUST ME, PETER, I WISH YOU COULDN'T.
MALFUNCTION-- REVERT TO ORIGINAL PROGRAMMING!
AAAAHM NEAR INVULNERABLE WHEN AAAAAHM BLAAAAASTIN'--
TAK
TAK
TAK
I'M AN ANOMALY WHO CAN TELL YOU WHERE I CAME FROM! THERE WAS A WORLD BEFORE DOOM! I KNOW BECAUSE I LIVED THERE!
HANG ON--

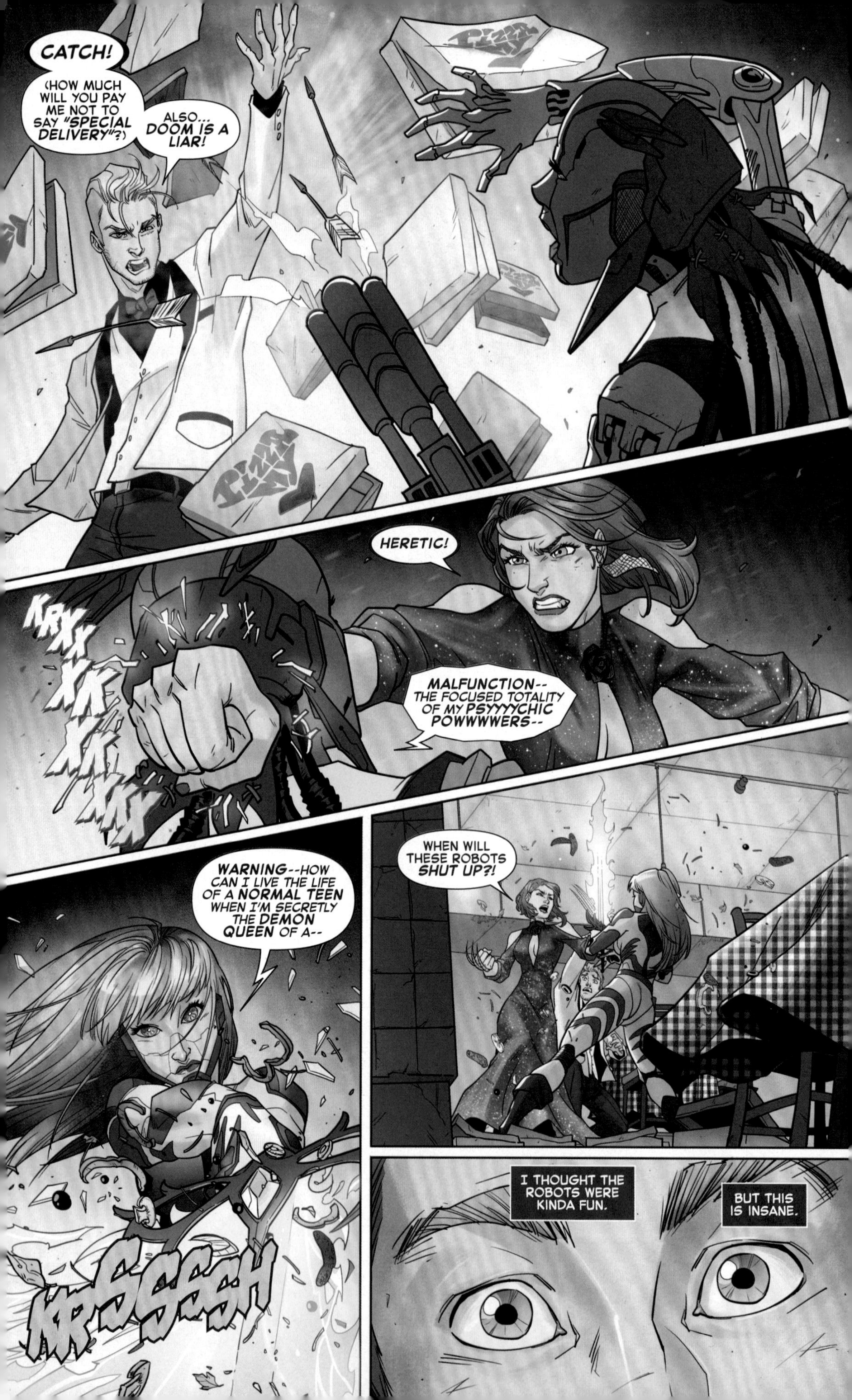

CATCH!
(HOW MUCH WILL YOU PAY ME NOT TO SAY "SPECIAL DELIVERY"?)
ALSO... DOOM IS A LIAR!
HERETIC!
KRXXXXXXXK
MALFUNCTION-- THE FOCUSED TOTALITY OF MY PSYYYYCHIC POWWWWERS--
WARNING--HOW CAN I LIVE THE LIFE OF A NORMAL TEEN WHEN I'M SECRETLY THE DEMON QUEEN OF A--
KRSSSSH
WHEN WILL THESE ROBOTS SHUT UP?!
I THOUGHT THE ROBOTS WERE KINDA FUN.
BUT THIS IS INSANE.

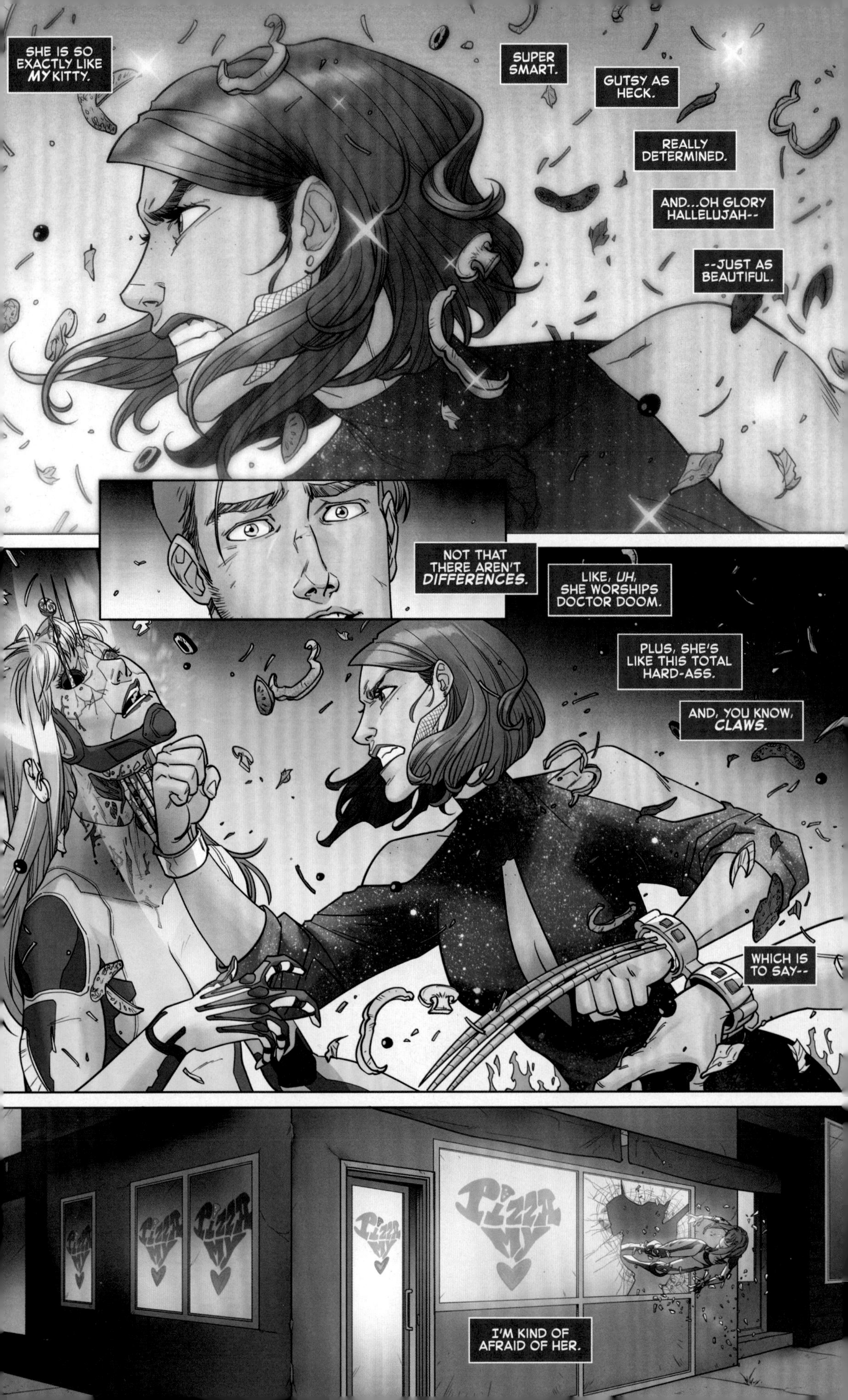
SHE IS SO EXACTLY LIKE *MY* KITTY.
SUPER SMART.
GUTSY AS HECK.
REALLY DETERMINED.
AND...OH GLORY HALLELUJAH--
--JUST AS BEAUTIFUL.
NOT THAT THERE AREN'T *DIFFERENCES*.
LIKE, *UH*, SHE WORSHIPS DOCTOR DOOM.
PLUS, SHE'S LIKE THIS TOTAL HARD-ASS.
AND, YOU KNOW, *CLAWS*.
WHICH IS TO SAY--
PIZZA MY
PIZZA MY
PIZZA MY
PIZZA MY
I'M KIND OF AFRAID OF HER.

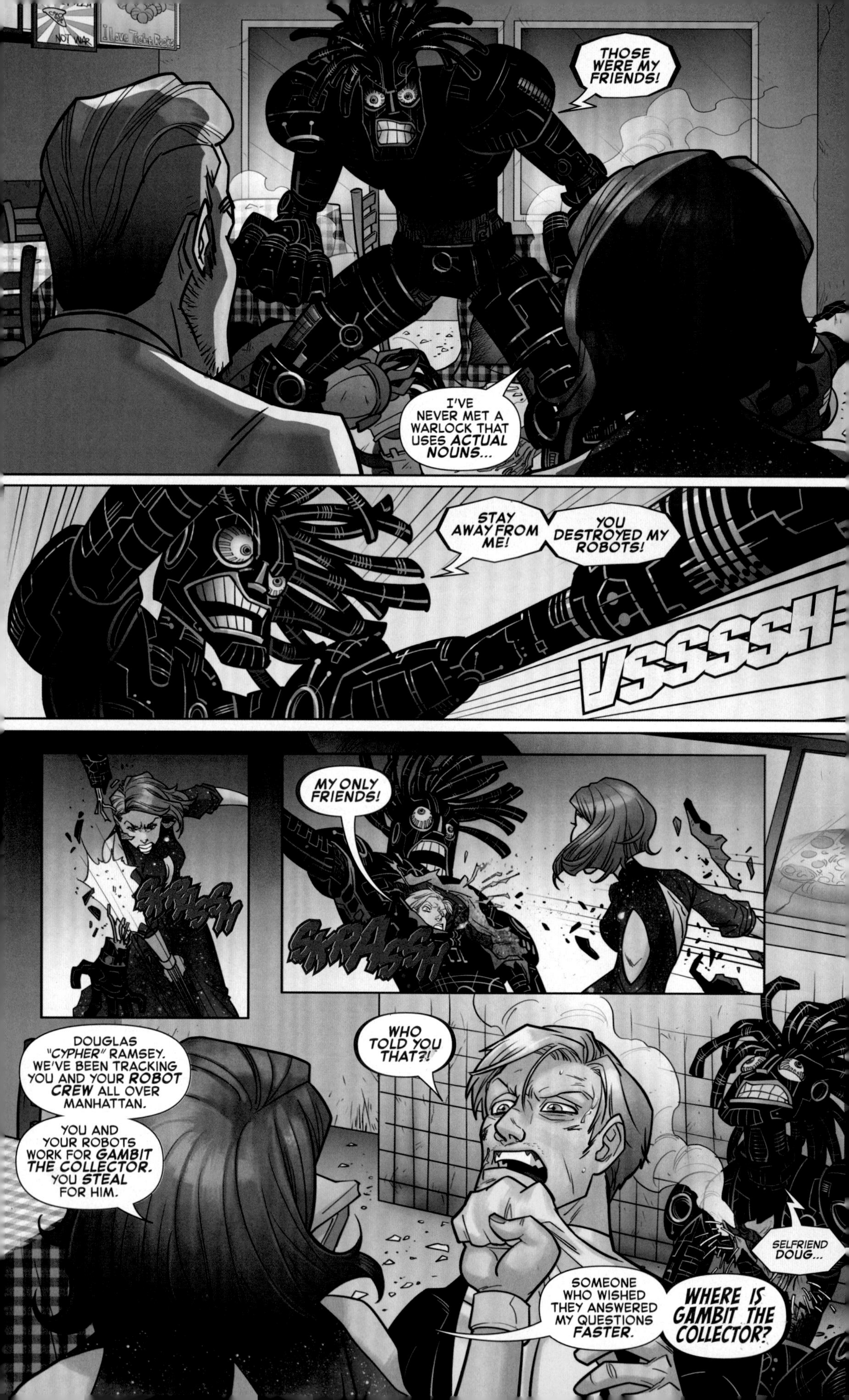
THOSE WERE MY FRIENDS!
I'VE NEVER MET A WARLOCK THAT USES ACTUAL NOUNS...
STAY AWAY FROM ME!
YOU DESTROYED MY ROBOTS!
VSSSSSH
SKRASSH
MY ONLY FRIENDS!
SKRASSH
DOUGLAS "CYPHER" RAMSEY. WE'VE BEEN TRACKING YOU AND YOUR ROBOT CREW ALL OVER MANHATTAN.
YOU AND YOUR ROBOTS WORK FOR GAMBIT THE COLLECTOR. YOU STEAL FOR HIM.
WHO TOLD YOU THAT?!
SOMEONE WHO WISHED THEY ANSWERED MY QUESTIONS FASTER.
WHERE IS GAMBIT THE COLLECTOR?
SELFRIEND DOUG...

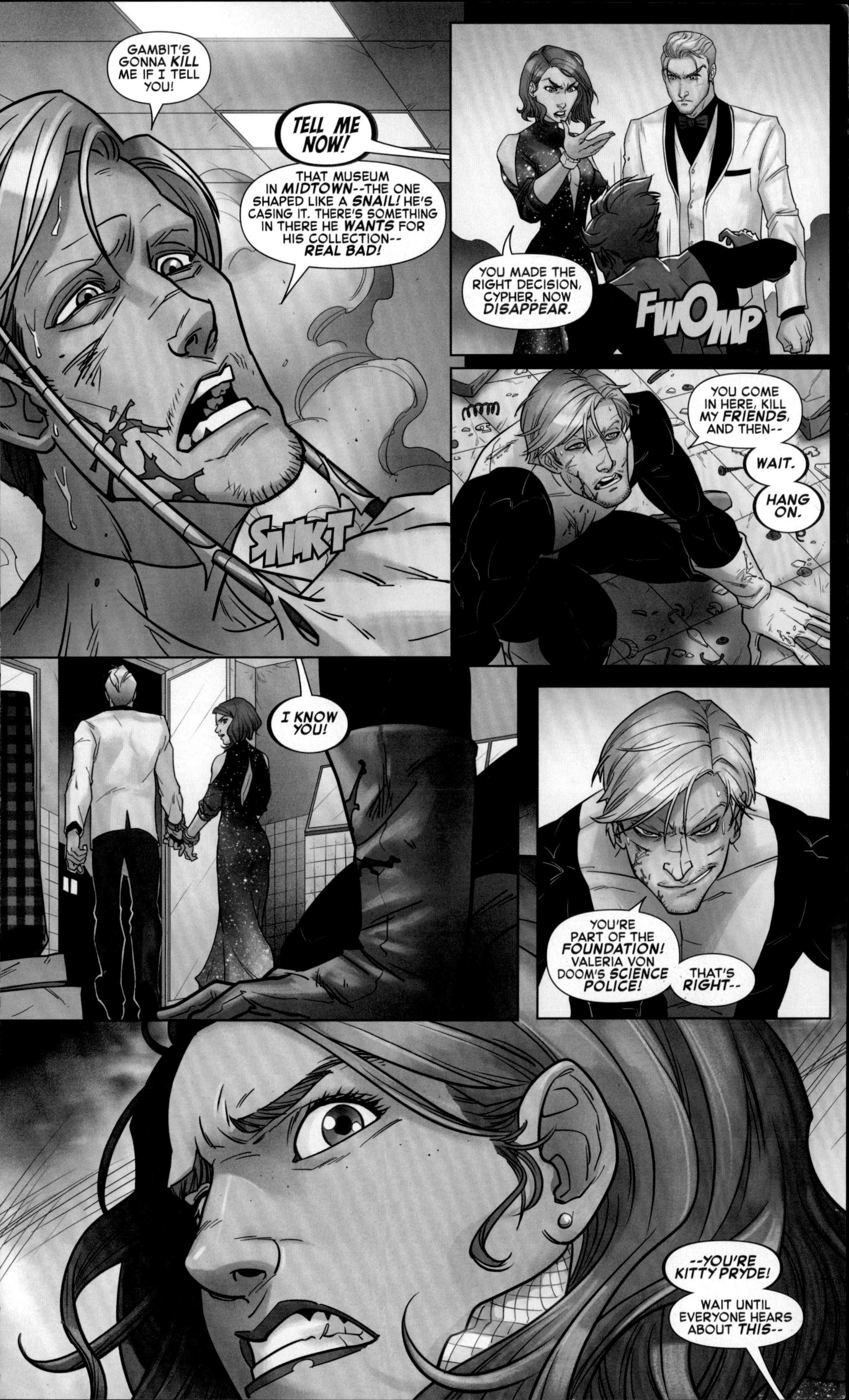
GAMBIT'S GONNA KILL ME IF I TELL YOU!
TELL ME NOW!
THAT MUSEUM IN MIDTOWN--THE ONE SHAPED LIKE A SNAIL! HE'S CASING IT. THERE'S SOMETHING IN THERE HE WANTS FOR HIS COLLECTION-- REAL BAD!
SNIKT
YOU MADE THE RIGHT DECISION, CYPHER. NOW DISAPPEAR.
FWOMP
YOU COME IN HERE, KILL MY FRIENDS, AND THEN--
WAIT.
HANG ON.
I KNOW YOU!
YOU'RE PART OF THE FOUNDATION! VALERIA VON DOOM'S SCIENCE POLICE!
THAT'S RIGHT--
--YOU'RE KITTY PRYDE!
WAIT UNTIL EVERYONE HEARS ABOUT THIS--

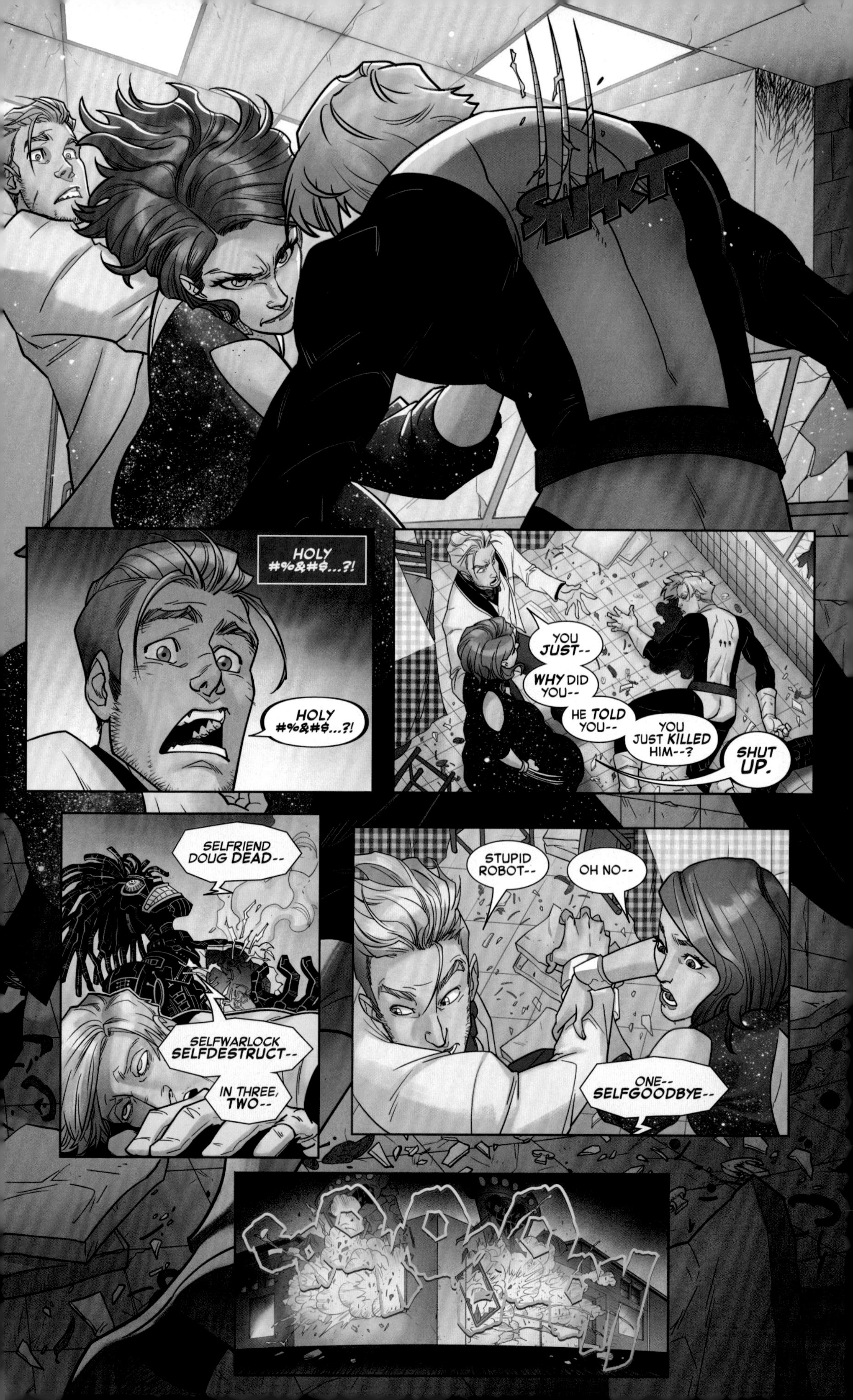
SNIKT
HOLY #%&#$...?!
HOLY #%&#$...?!
YOU JUST--
WHY DID YOU--
HE TOLD YOU--
YOU JUST KILLED HIM--?
SHUT UP.
SELFRIEND DOUG DEAD--
SELFWARLOCK SELFDESTRUCT--
IN THREE, TWO--
STUPID ROBOT--
OH NO--
ONE-- SELFGOODBYE--

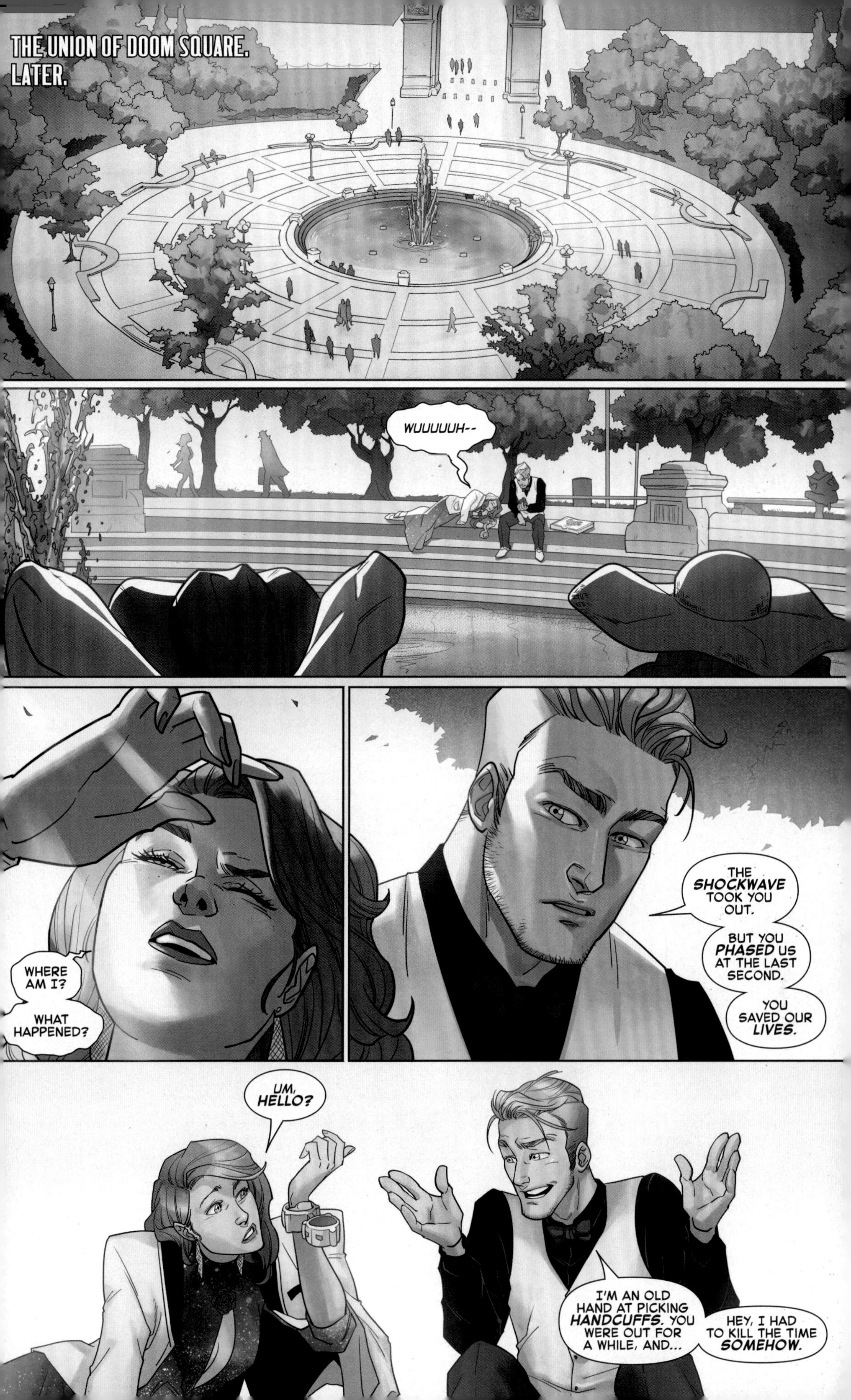
THE UNION OF DOOM SQUARE. LATER.
WUUUUUH--
WHERE AM I?
WHAT HAPPENED?
THE SHOCKWAVE TOOK YOU OUT.
BUT YOU PHASED US AT THE LAST SECOND.
YOU SAVED OUR LIVES.
UM, HELLO?
I'M AN OLD HAND AT PICKING HANDCUFFS. YOU WERE OUT FOR A WHILE, AND...
HEY, I HAD TO KILL THE TIME SOMEHOW.

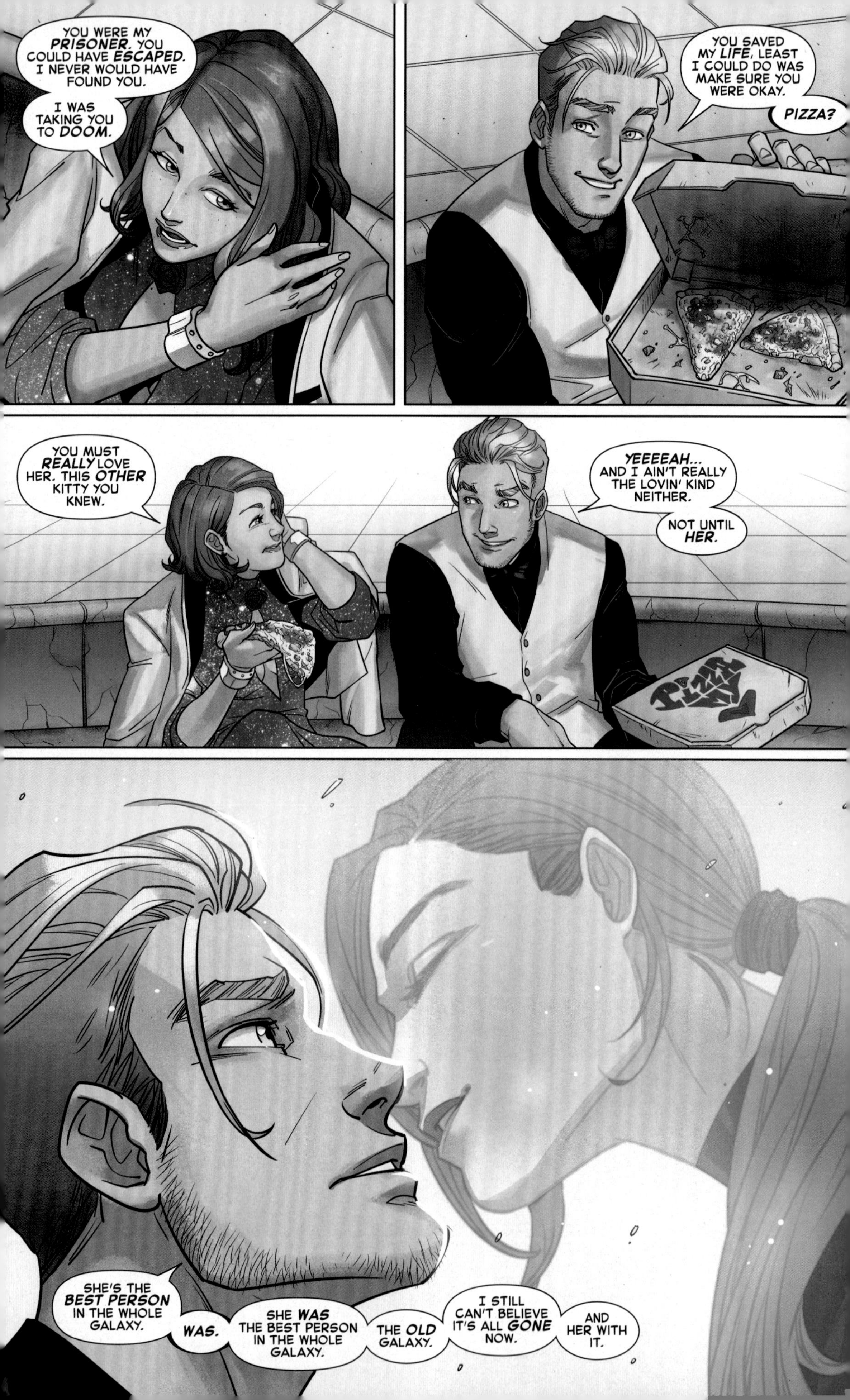
YOU WERE MY PRISONER. YOU COULD HAVE ESCAPED. I NEVER WOULD HAVE FOUND YOU.
I WAS TAKING YOU TO DOOM.
YOU SAVED MY LIFE, LEAST I COULD DO WAS MAKE SURE YOU WERE OKAY.
PIZZA?
YOU MUST REALLY LOVE HER. THIS OTHER KITTY YOU KNEW.
YEEEEAH... AND I AIN'T REALLY THE LOVIN' KIND NEITHER.
NOT UNTIL HER.
SHE'S THE BEST PERSON IN THE WHOLE GALAXY.
WAS.
SHE WAS THE BEST PERSON IN THE WHOLE GALAXY.
THE OLD GALAXY.
I STILL CAN'T BELIEVE IT'S ALL GONE NOW.
AND HER WITH IT.

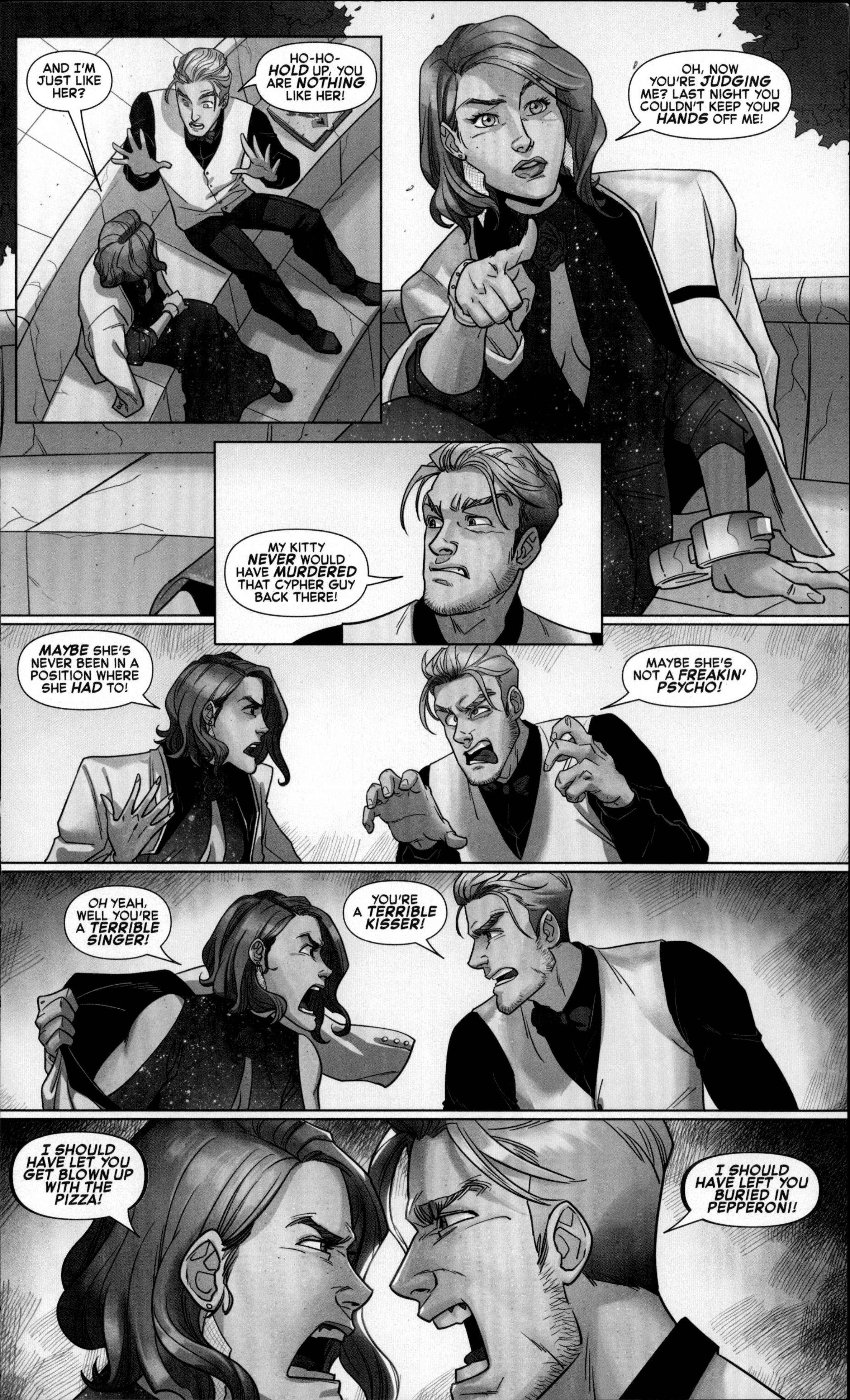
AND I'M JUST LIKE HER?
HO-HO-HOLD UP, YOU ARE NOTHING LIKE HER!
OH, NOW YOU'RE JUDGING ME? LAST NIGHT YOU COULDN'T KEEP YOUR HANDS OFF ME!
MY KITTY NEVER WOULD HAVE MURDERED THAT CYPHER GUY BACK THERE!
MAYBE SHE'S NEVER BEEN IN A POSITION WHERE SHE HAD TO!
MAYBE SHE'S NOT A FREAKIN' PSYCHO!
OH YEAH, WELL YOU'RE A TERRIBLE SINGER!
YOU'RE A TERRIBLE KISSER!
I SHOULD HAVE LET YOU GET BLOWN UP WITH THE PIZZA!
I SHOULD HAVE LEFT YOU BURIED IN PEPPERONI!

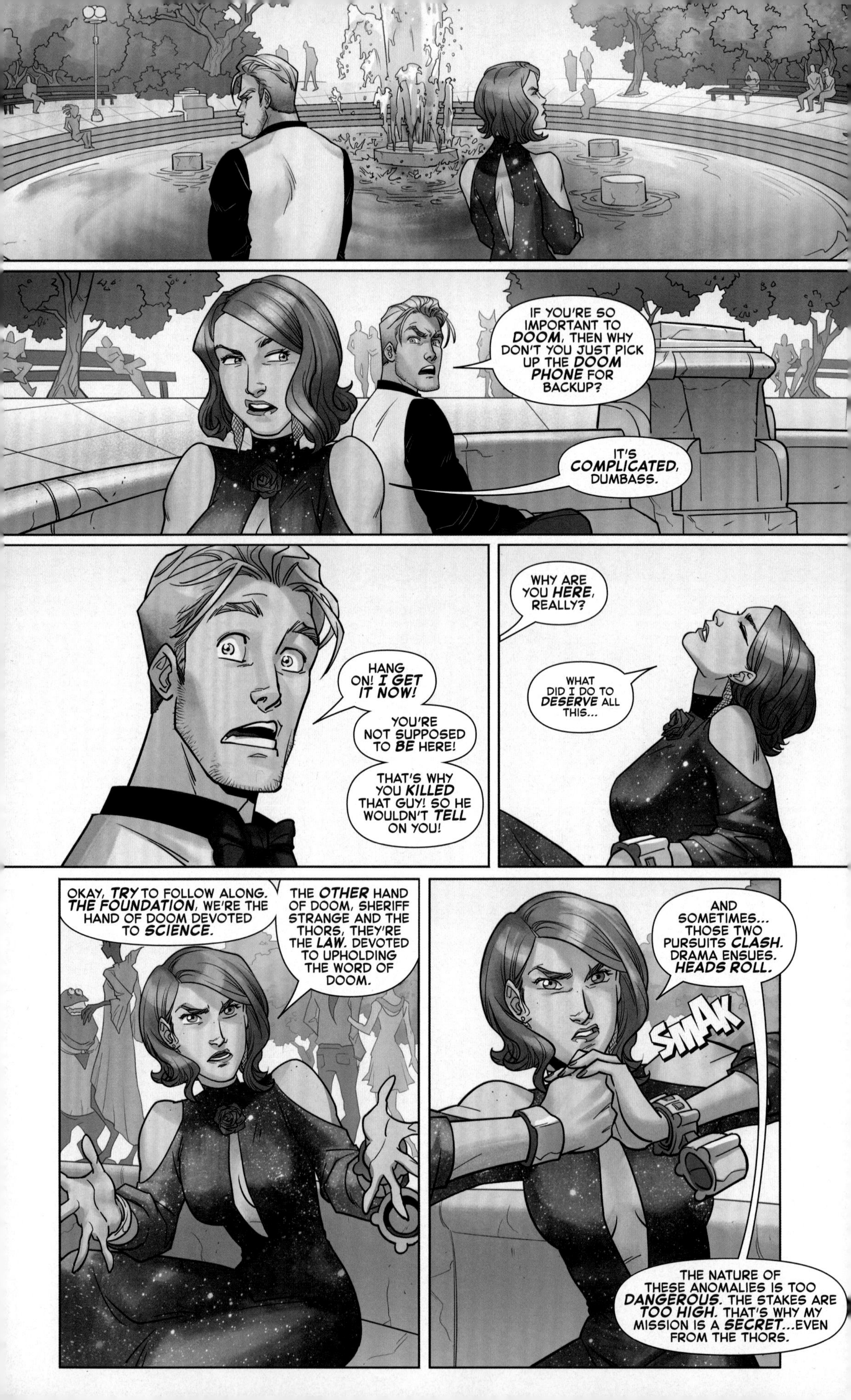
IF YOU'RE SO IMPORTANT TO DOOM, THEN WHY DON'T YOU JUST PICK UP THE DOOM PHONE FOR BACKUP?
IT'S COMPLICATED, DUMBASS.
HANG ON! I GET IT NOW!
YOU'RE NOT SUPPOSED TO BE HERE!
THAT'S WHY YOU KILLED THAT GUY! SO HE WOULDN'T TELL ON YOU!
WHY ARE YOU HERE, REALLY?
WHAT DID I DO TO DESERVE ALL THIS...
OKAY, TRY TO FOLLOW ALONG. THE FOUNDATION, WE'RE THE HAND OF DOOM DEVOTED TO SCIENCE.
THE OTHER HAND OF DOOM, SHERIFF STRANGE AND THE THORS, THEY'RE THE LAW. DEVOTED TO UPHOLDING THE WORD OF DOOM.
AND SOMETIMES... THOSE TWO PURSUITS CLASH. DRAMA ENSUES. HEADS ROLL.
SMAK
THE NATURE OF THESE ANOMALIES IS TOO DANGEROUS. THE STAKES ARE TOO HIGH. THAT'S WHY MY MISSION IS A SECRET...EVEN FROM THE THORS.

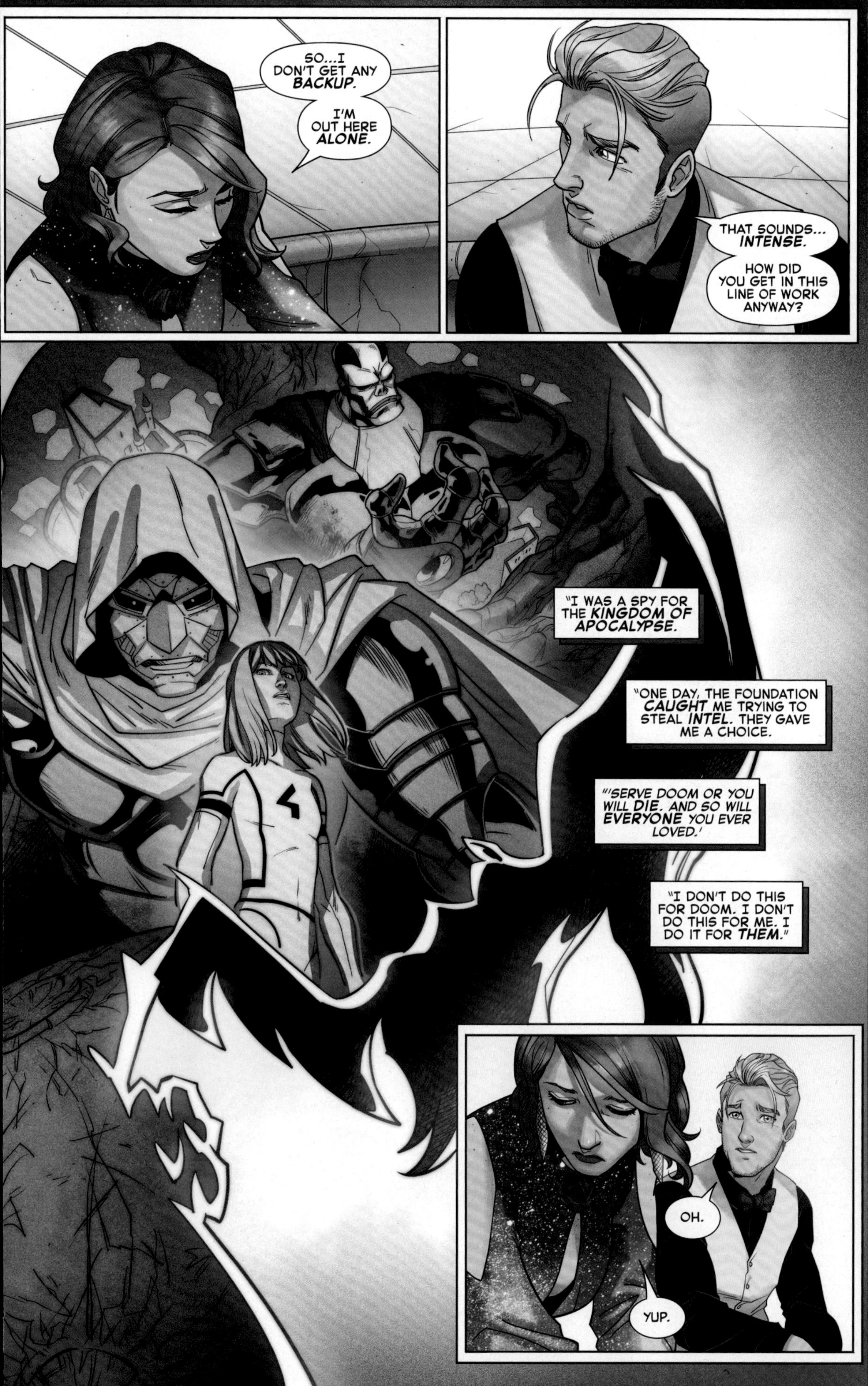
SO...I DON'T GET ANY BACKUP.
I'M OUT HERE ALONE.
THAT SOUNDS... INTENSE.
HOW DID YOU GET IN THIS LINE OF WORK ANYWAY?
"I WAS A SPY FOR THE KINGDOM OF APOCALYPSE.
"ONE DAY, THE FOUNDATION CAUGHT ME TRYING TO STEAL INTEL. THEY GAVE ME A CHOICE.
"'SERVE DOOM OR YOU WILL DIE. AND SO WILL EVERYONE YOU EVER LOVED.'
"I DON'T DO THIS FOR DOOM. I DON'T DO THIS FOR ME. I DO IT FOR THEM."
OH.
YUP.

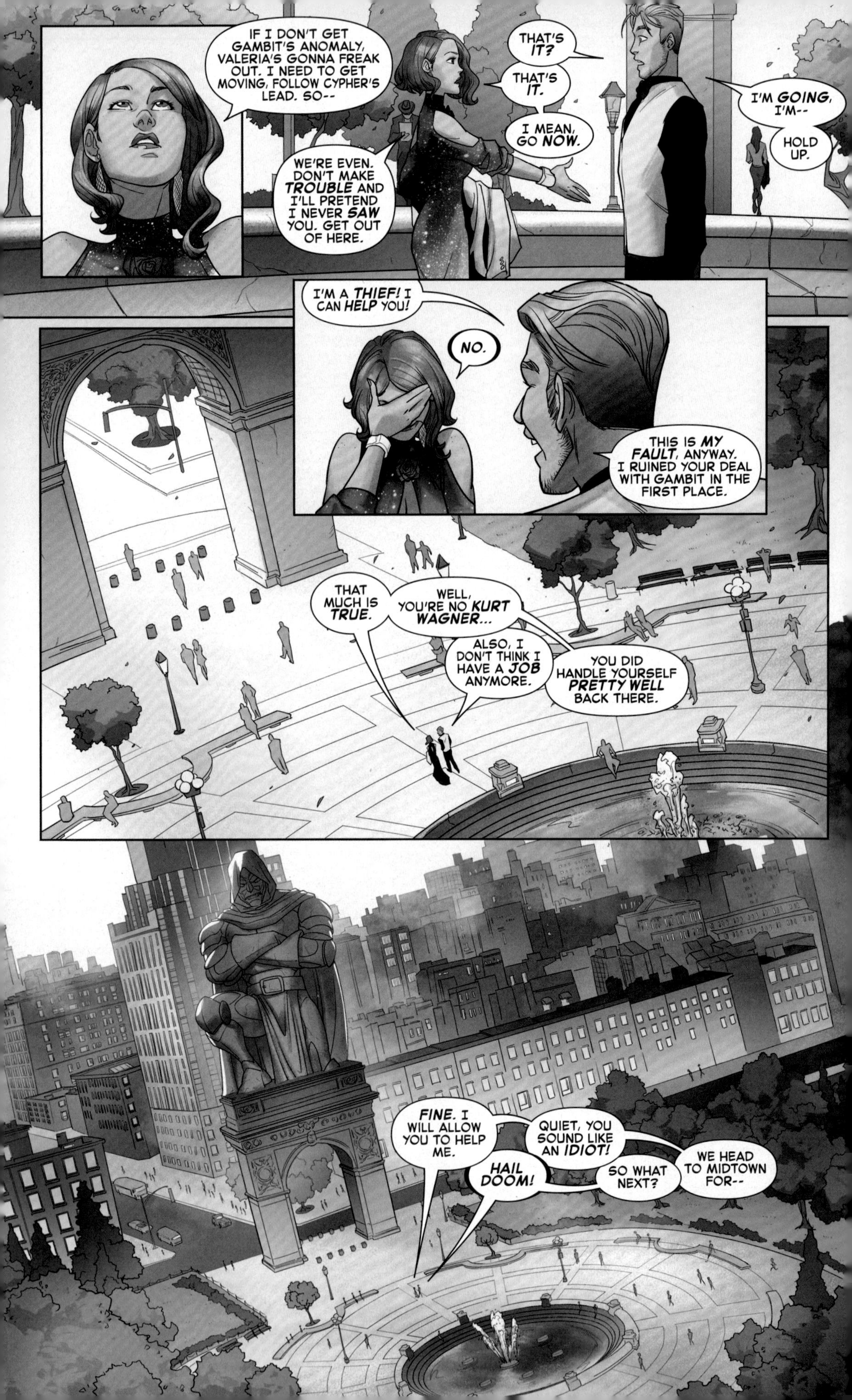
IF I DON'T GET GAMBIT'S ANOMALY, VALERIA'S GONNA FREAK OUT. I NEED TO GET MOVING, FOLLOW CYPHER'S LEAD. SO--
WE'RE EVEN. DON'T MAKE TROUBLE AND I'LL PRETEND I NEVER SAW YOU. GET OUT OF HERE.
THAT'S IT?
THAT'S IT.
I MEAN, GO NOW.
I'M GOING, I'M--
HOLD UP.
I'M A THIEF! I CAN HELP YOU!
NO.
THIS IS MY FAULT, ANYWAY. I RUINED YOUR DEAL WITH GAMBIT IN THE FIRST PLACE.
THAT MUCH IS TRUE.
WELL, YOU'RE NO KURT WAGNER...
YOU DID HANDLE YOURSELF PRETTY WELL BACK THERE.
ALSO, I DON'T THINK I HAVE A JOB ANYMORE.
FINE. I WILL ALLOW YOU TO HELP ME.
QUIET, YOU SOUND LIKE AN IDIOT!
WE HEAD TO MIDTOWN FOR--
HAIL DOOM!
SO WHAT NEXT?

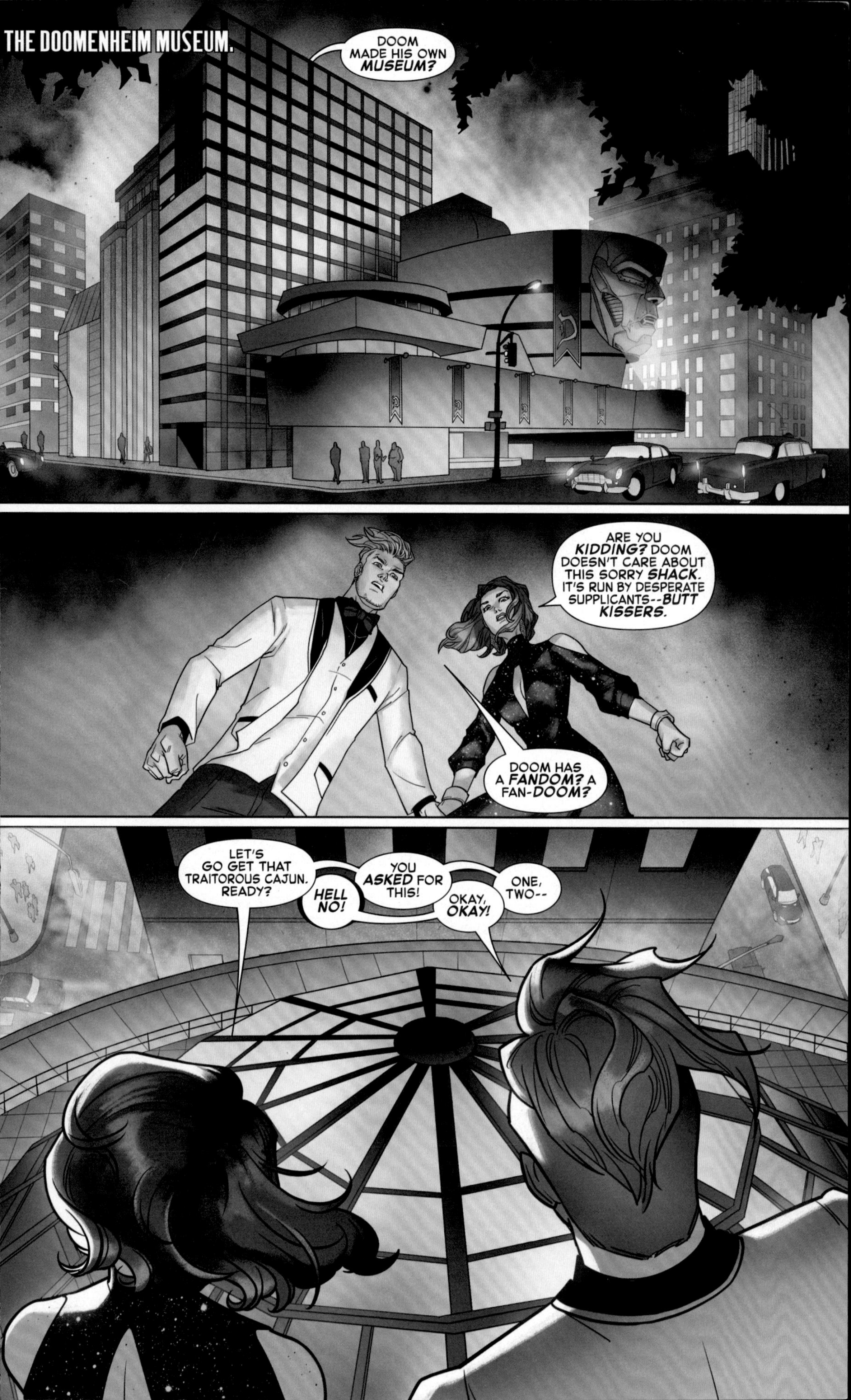
THE DOOMENHEIM MUSEUM.
DOOM MADE HIS OWN MUSEUM?
ARE YOU KIDDING? DOOM DOESN'T CARE ABOUT THIS SORRY SHACK. IT'S RUN BY DESPERATE SUPPLICANTS--BUTT KISSERS.
DOOM HAS A FANDOM? A FAN-DOOM?
LET'S GO GET THAT TRAITOROUS CAJUN. READY?
HELL NO!
YOU ASKED FOR THIS!
OKAY, OKAY!
ONE, TWO--

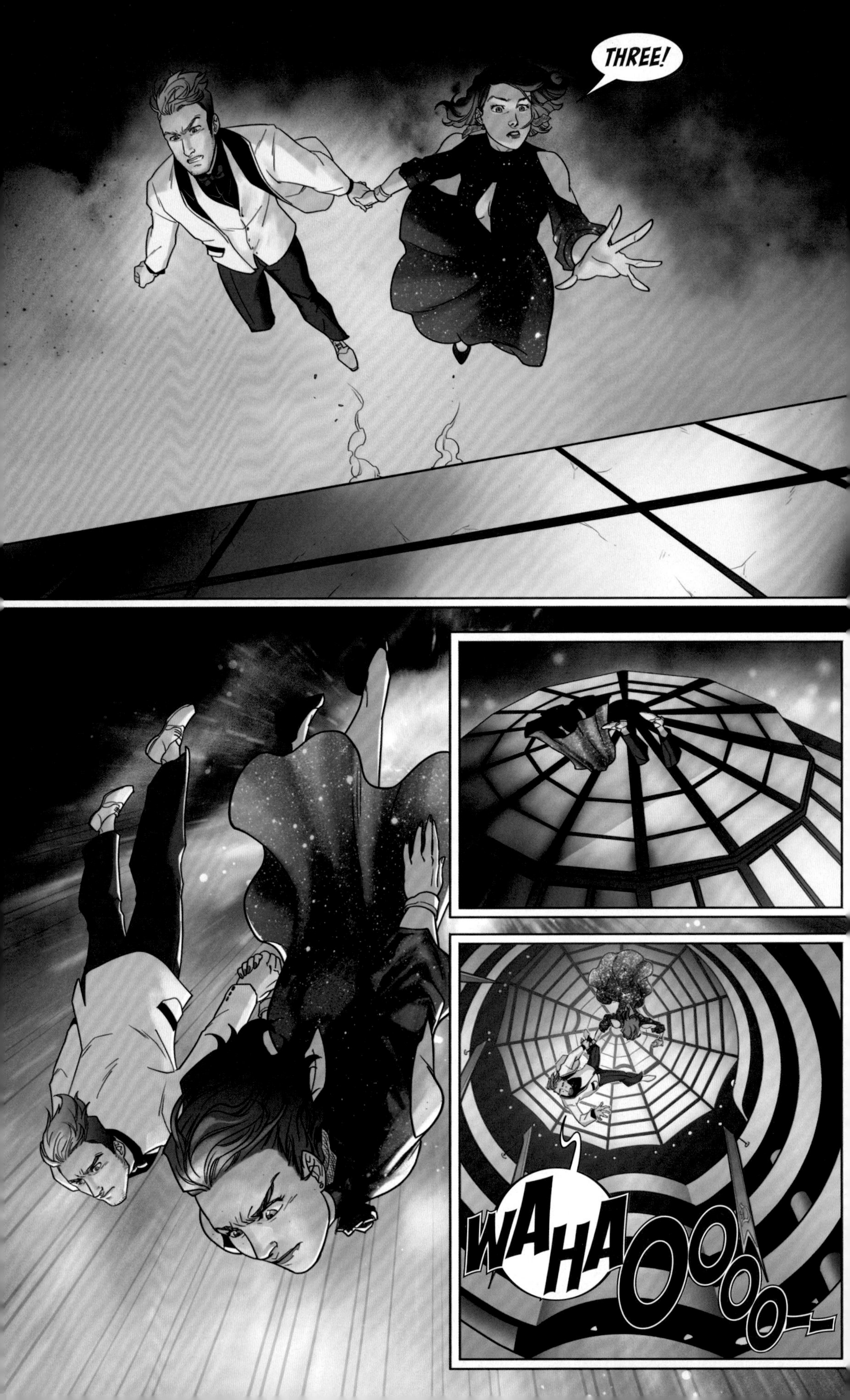
THREE!
WAHAOOOO–!

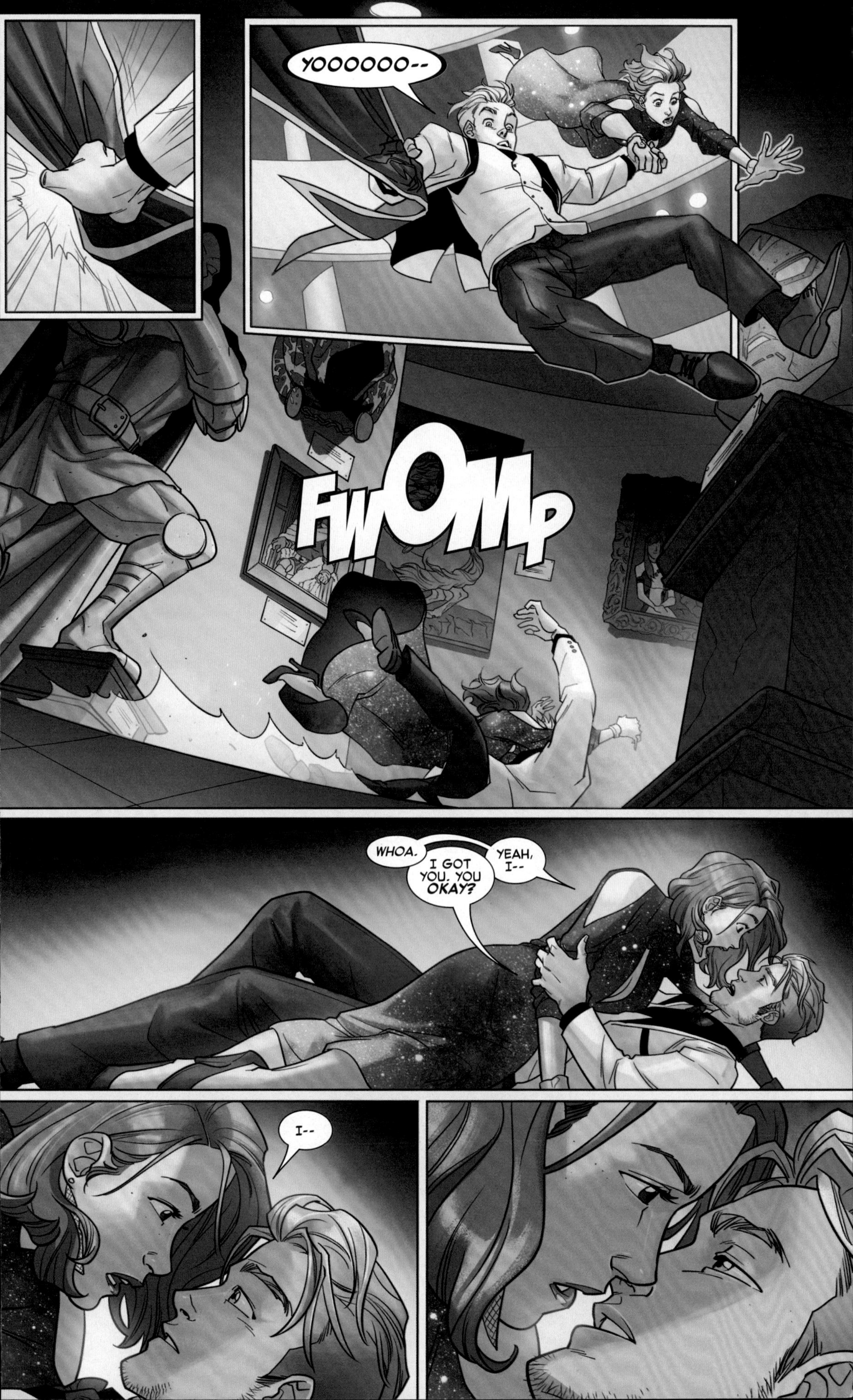
YOOOOOO--
FWOMP
WHOA.
I GOT YOU. YOU OKAY?
YEAH, I--
I--

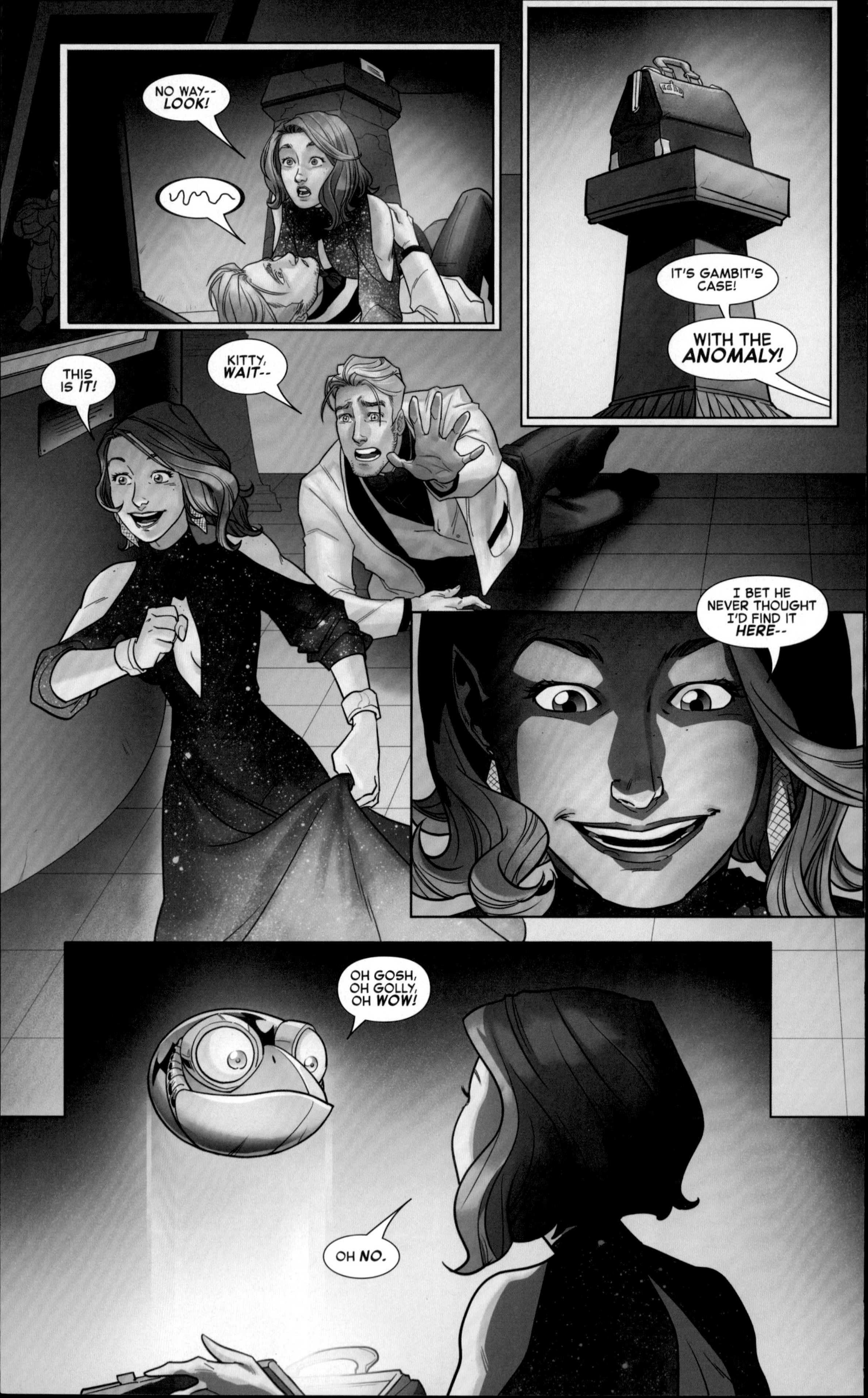
NO WAY-- LOOK!
IT'S GAMBIT'S CASE!
WITH THE ANOMALY!
THIS IS IT!
KITTY, WAIT--
I BET HE NEVER THOUGHT I'D FIND IT HERE--
OH GOSH, OH GOLLY, OH WOW!
OH NO.

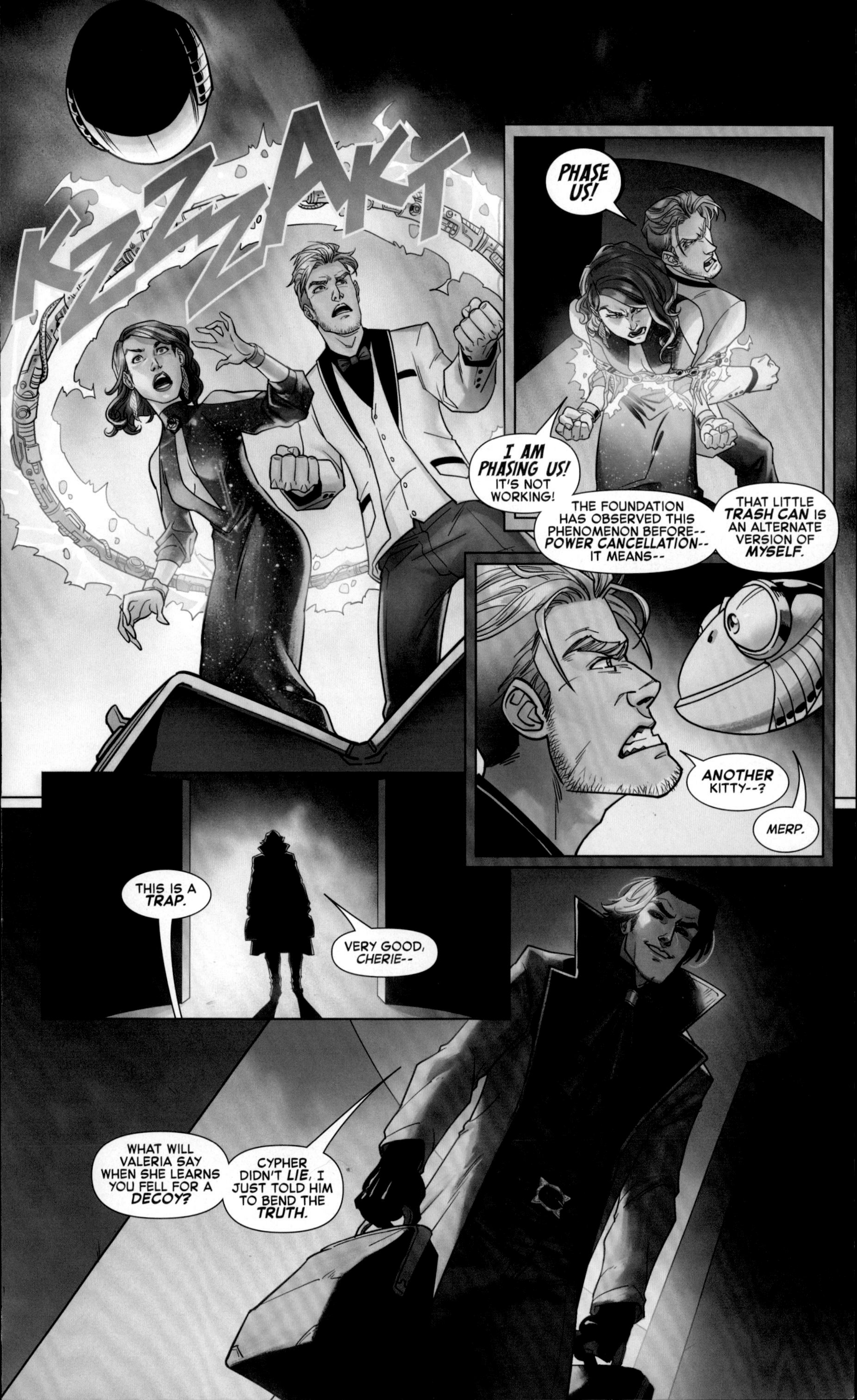
KZZZAKT
PHASE US!
I AM PHASING US! IT'S NOT WORKING!
THE FOUNDATION HAS OBSERVED THIS PHENOMENON BEFORE-- POWER CANCELLATION-- IT MEANS--
THAT LITTLE TRASH CAN IS AN ALTERNATE VERSION OF MYSELF.
ANOTHER KITTY--?
MERP.
THIS IS A TRAP.
VERY GOOD, CHERIE--
WHAT WILL VALERIA SAY WHEN SHE LEARNS YOU FELL FOR A DECOY?
CYPHER DIDN'T LIE, I JUST TOLD HIM TO BEND THE TRUTH.

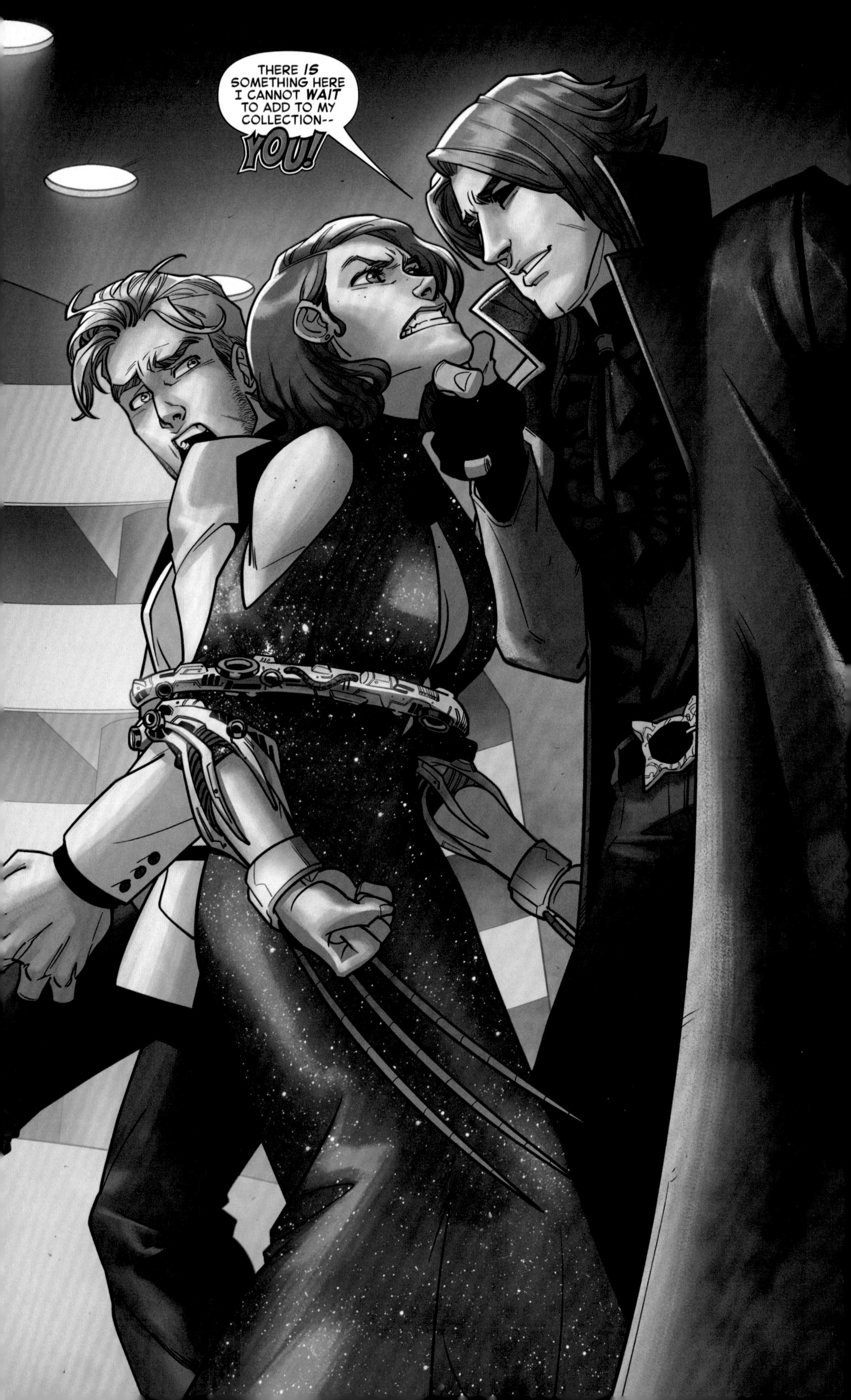
THERE IS SOMETHING HERE I CANNOT WAIT TO ADD TO MY COLLECTION--
YOU!

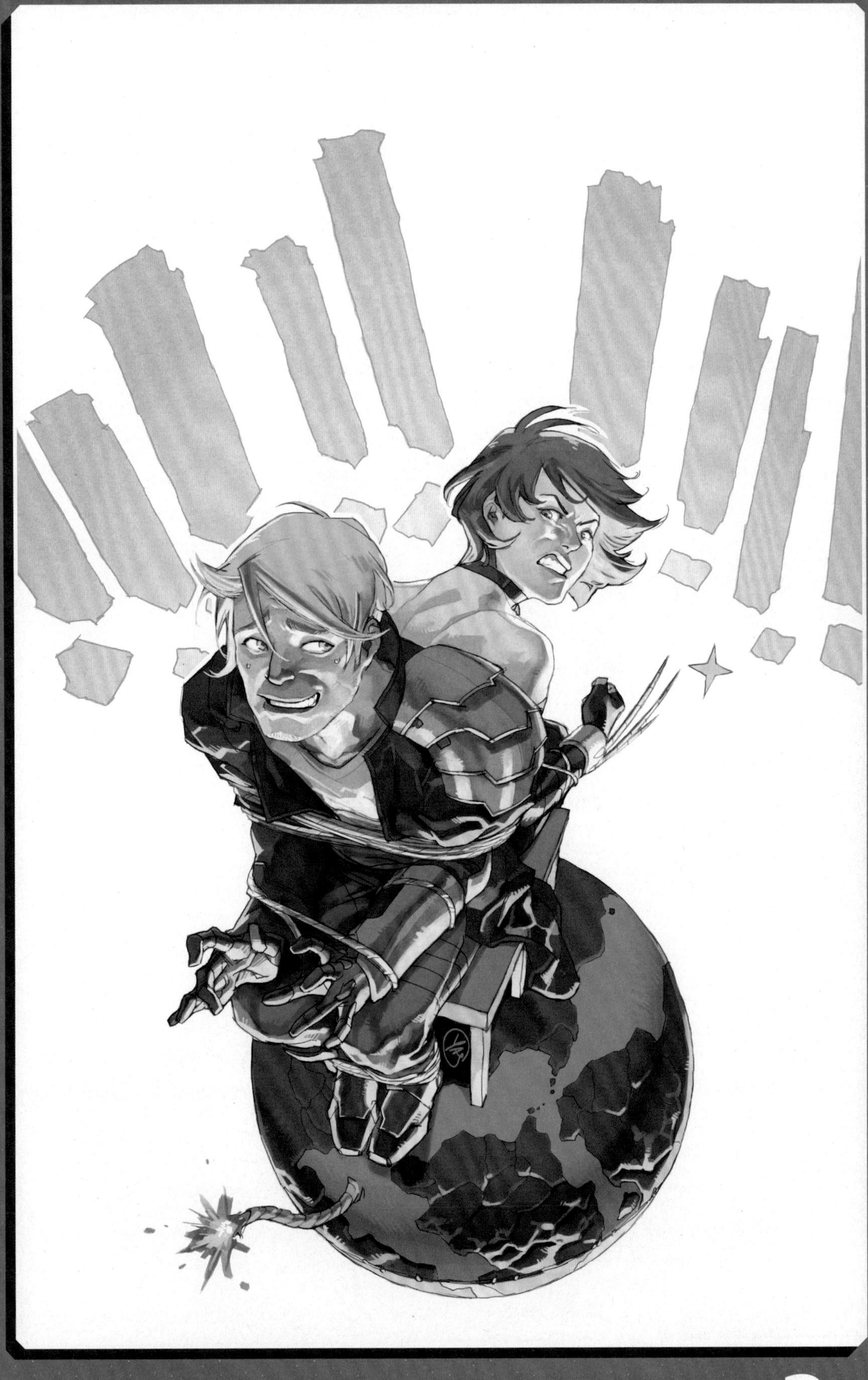

3

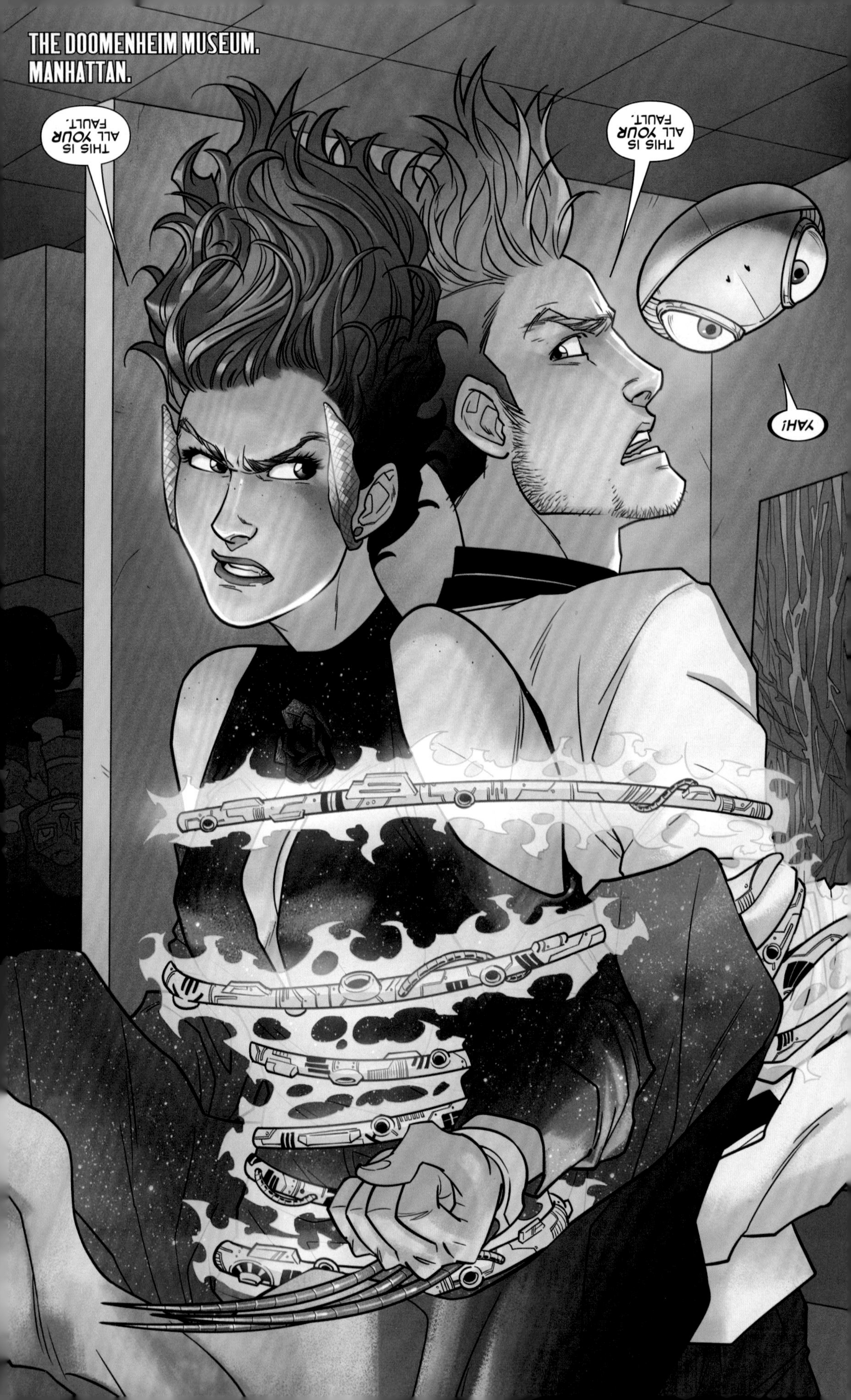
THE DOOMENHEIM MUSEUM.
MANHATTAN.
THIS IS ALL YOUR FAULT.
THIS IS ALL YOUR FAULT.
YAH!

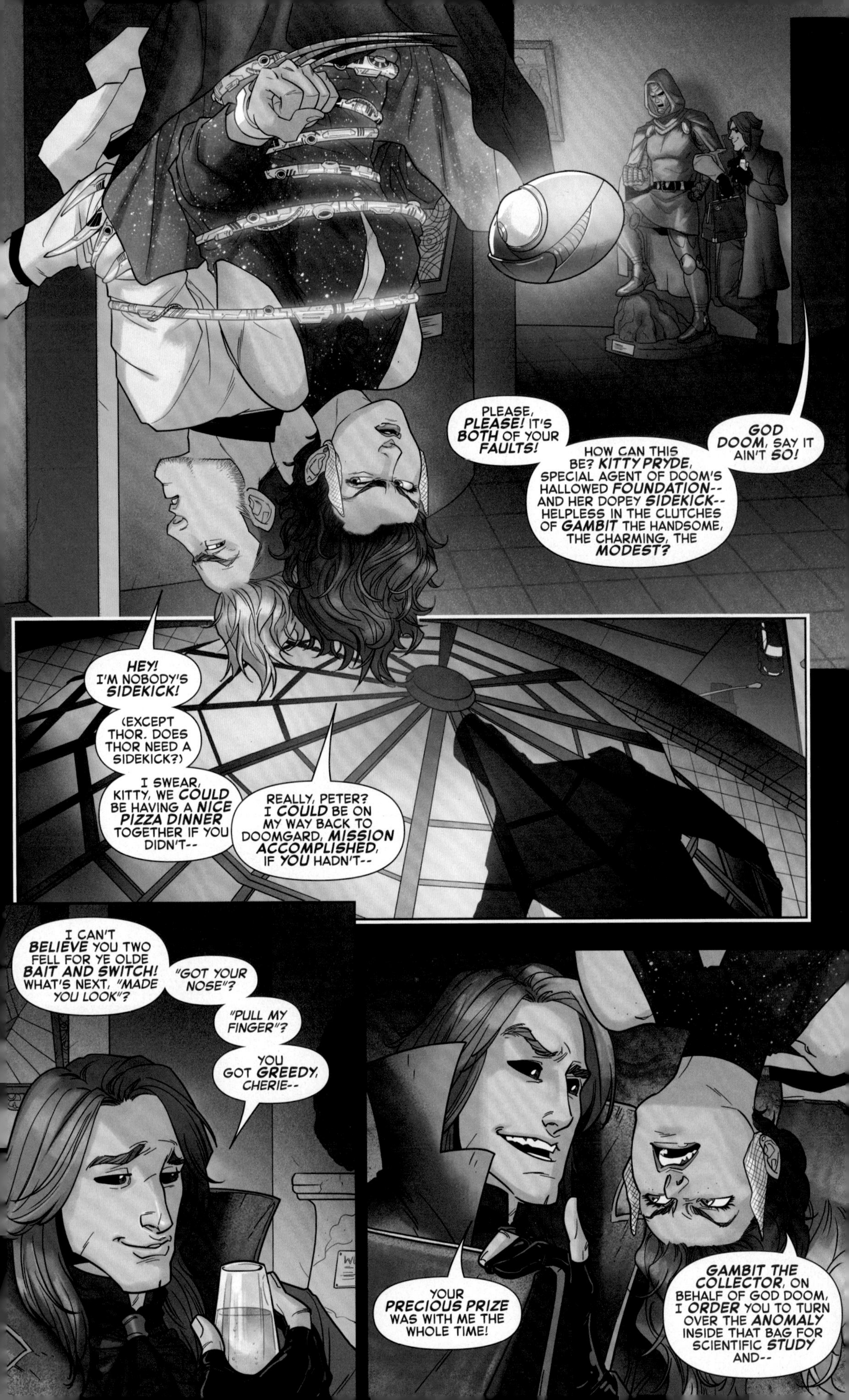
GOD DOOM, SAY IT AIN'T SO!
HOW CAN THIS BE? KITTY PRYDE, SPECIAL AGENT OF DOOM'S HALLOWED FOUNDATION-- AND HER DOPEY SIDEKICK-- HELPLESS IN THE CLUTCHES OF GAMBIT THE HANDSOME, THE CHARMING, THE MODEST?
PLEASE, PLEASE! IT'S BOTH OF YOUR FAULTS!
HEY! I'M NOBODY'S SIDEKICK!
(EXCEPT THOR. DOES THOR NEED A SIDEKICK?)
I SWEAR, KITTY, WE COULD BE HAVING A NICE PIZZA DINNER TOGETHER IF YOU DIDN'T--
REALLY, PETER? I COULD BE ON MY WAY BACK TO DOOMGARD, MISSION ACCOMPLISHED, IF YOU HADN'T--
I CAN'T BELIEVE YOU TWO FELL FOR YE OLDE BAIT AND SWITCH! WHAT'S NEXT, "MADE YOU LOOK"?
"GOT YOUR NOSE"?
"PULL MY FINGER"?
YOU GOT GREEDY, CHERIE--
YOUR PRECIOUS PRIZE WAS WITH ME THE WHOLE TIME!
GAMBIT THE COLLECTOR, ON BEHALF OF GOD DOOM, I ORDER YOU TO TURN OVER THE ANOMALY INSIDE THAT BAG FOR SCIENTIFIC STUDY AND--

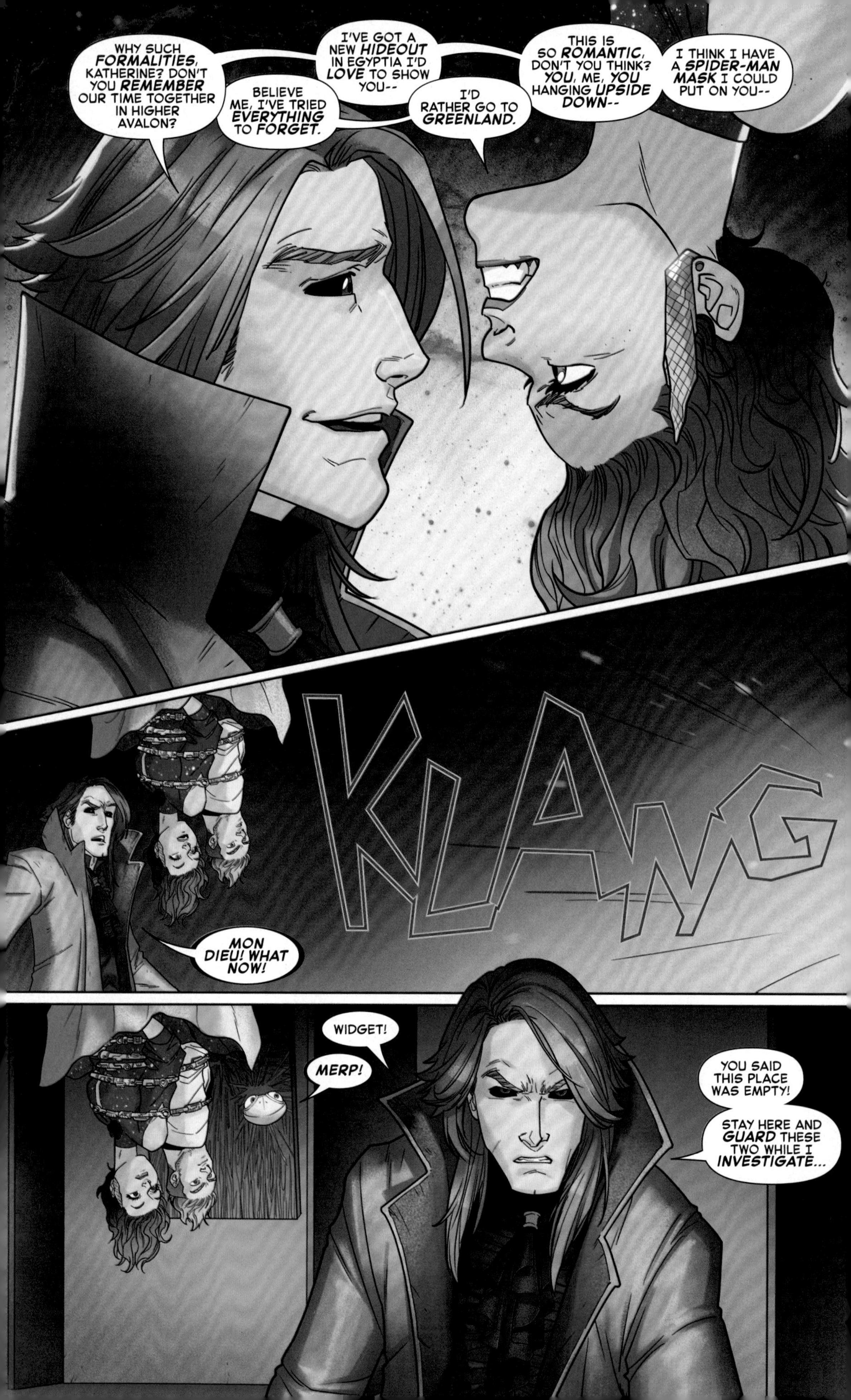

WHY SUCH FORMALITIES, KATHERINE? DON'T YOU REMEMBER OUR TIME TOGETHER IN HIGHER AVALON?
BELIEVE ME, I'VE TRIED EVERYTHING TO FORGET.
I'VE GOT A NEW HIDEOUT IN EGYPTIA I'D LOVE TO SHOW YOU--
I'D RATHER GO TO GREENLAND.
THIS IS SO ROMANTIC, DON'T YOU THINK? YOU, ME, YOU HANGING UPSIDE DOWN--
I THINK I HAVE A SPIDER-MAN MASK I COULD PUT ON YOU--
KLANG
MON DIEU! WHAT NOW!
WIDGET!
MERP!
YOU SAID THIS PLACE WAS EMPTY!
STAY HERE AND GUARD THESE TWO WHILE I INVESTIGATE...

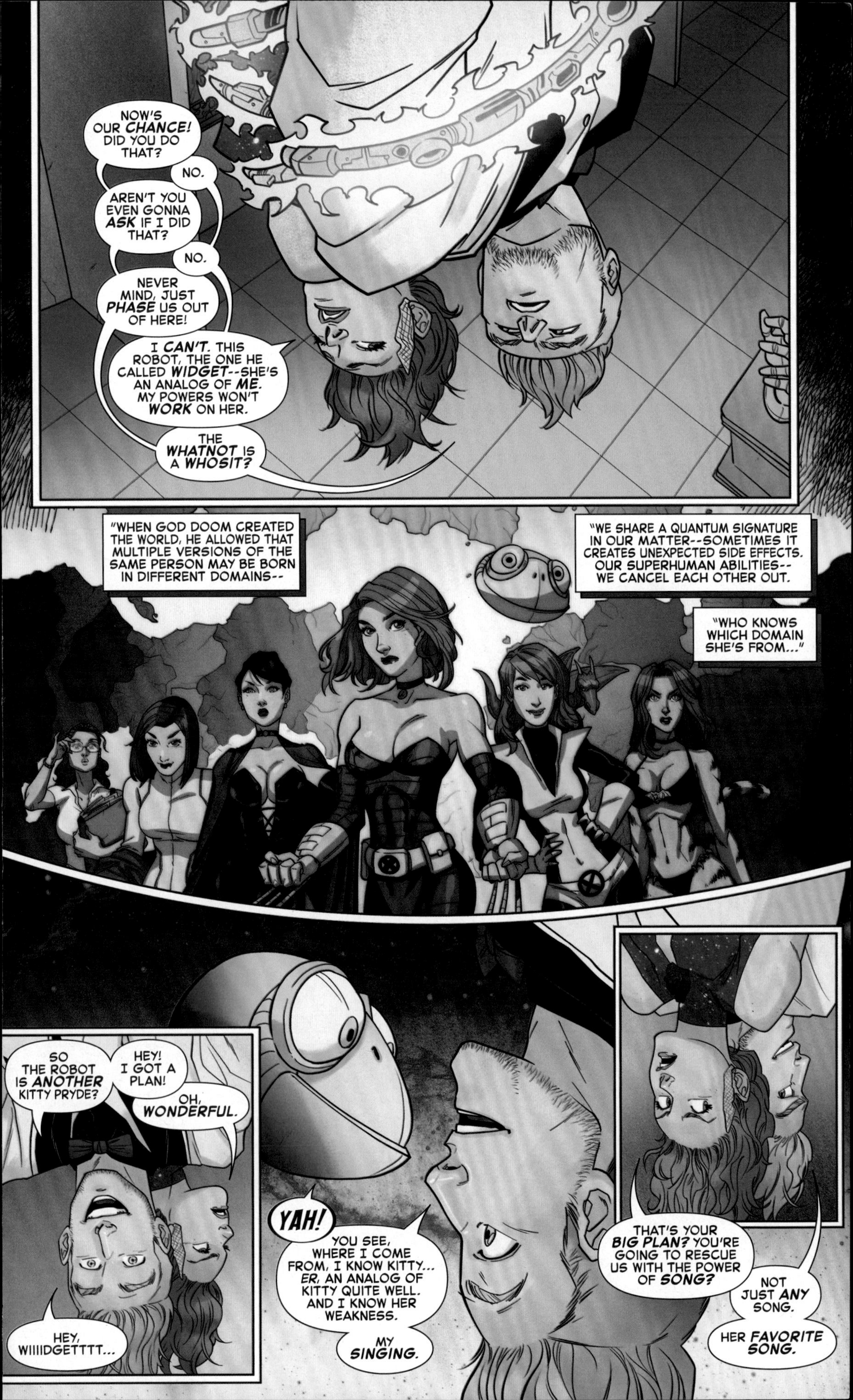
NOW'S OUR CHANCE! DID YOU DO THAT?
NO.
AREN'T YOU EVEN GONNA ASK IF I DID THAT?
NO.
NEVER MIND, JUST PHASE US OUT OF HERE!
I CAN'T. THIS ROBOT, THE ONE HE CALLED WIDGET--SHE'S AN ANALOG OF ME. MY POWERS WON'T WORK ON HER.
THE WHATNOT IS A WHOSIT?
"WHEN GOD DOOM CREATED THE WORLD, HE ALLOWED THAT MULTIPLE VERSIONS OF THE SAME PERSON MAY BE BORN IN DIFFERENT DOMAINS--
"WE SHARE A QUANTUM SIGNATURE IN OUR MATTER--SOMETIMES IT CREATES UNEXPECTED SIDE EFFECTS. OUR SUPERHUMAN ABILITIES--WE CANCEL EACH OTHER OUT.
"WHO KNOWS WHICH DOMAIN SHE'S FROM..."
SO THE ROBOT IS ANOTHER KITTY PRYDE?
HEY! I GOT A PLAN!
OH, WONDERFUL.
HEY, WIIIIDGETTTT...
YAH!
YOU SEE, WHERE I COME FROM, I KNOW KITTY... ER, AN ANALOG OF KITTY QUITE WELL. AND I KNOW HER WEAKNESS.
MY SINGING.
THAT'S YOUR BIG PLAN? YOU'RE GOING TO RESCUE US WITH THE POWER OF SONG?
NOT JUST ANY SONG.
HER FAVORITE SONG.

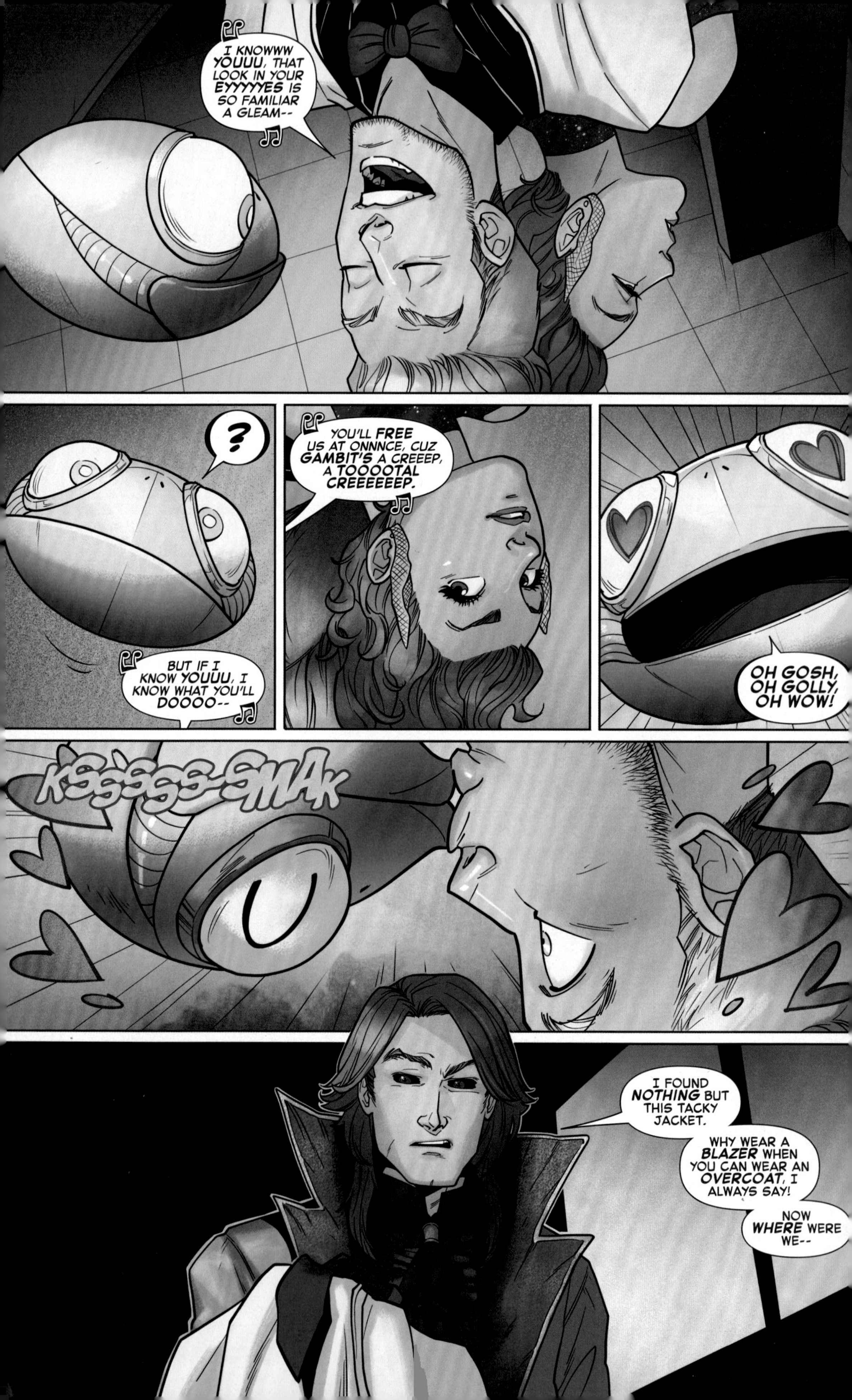
I KNOWWW YOUUU, THAT LOOK IN YOUR EYYYYYES IS SO FAMILIAR A GLEAM--
?
BUT IF I KNOW YOUUU, I KNOW WHAT YOU'LL DOOOO--
YOU'LL FREE US AT ONNNCE, CUZ GAMBIT'S A CREEEP, A TOOOOTAL CREEEEEEP.
OH GOSH, OH GOLLY, OH WOW!
KSSSSSS-SMAK
I FOUND NOTHING BUT THIS TACKY JACKET.
WHY WEAR A BLAZER WHEN YOU CAN WEAR AN OVERCOAT, I ALWAYS SAY!
NOW WHERE WERE WE--

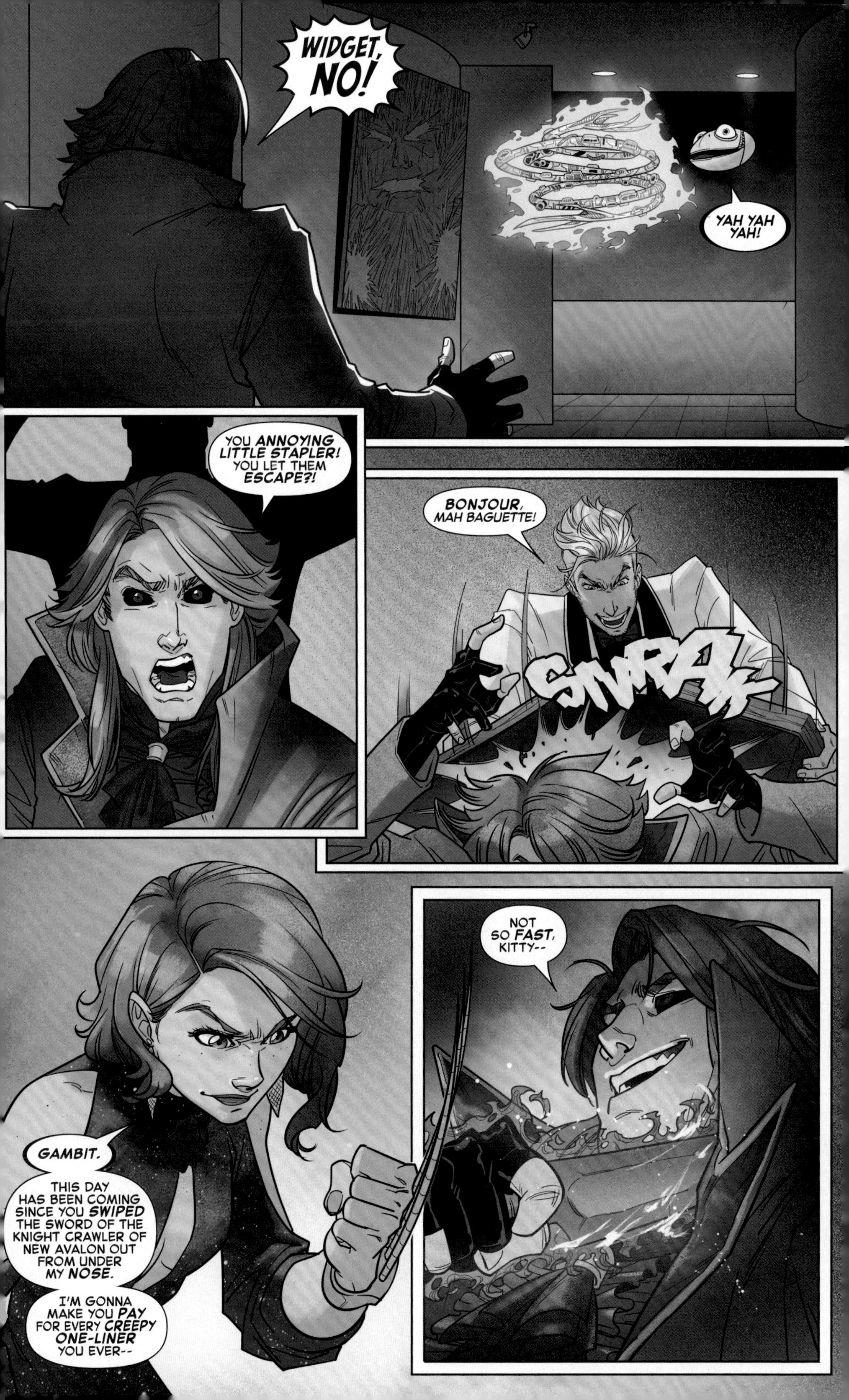
WIDGET, NO!
YAH YAH YAH!
YOU ANNOYING LITTLE STAPLER! YOU LET THEM ESCAPE?!
BONJOUR, MAH BAGUETTE!
SNRAK
GAMBIT.
THIS DAY HAS BEEN COMING SINCE YOU SWIPED THE SWORD OF THE KNIGHT CRAWLER OF NEW AVALON OUT FROM UNDER MY NOSE.
I'M GONNA MAKE YOU PAY FOR EVERY CREEPY ONE-LINER YOU EVER--
NOT SO FAST, KITTY--

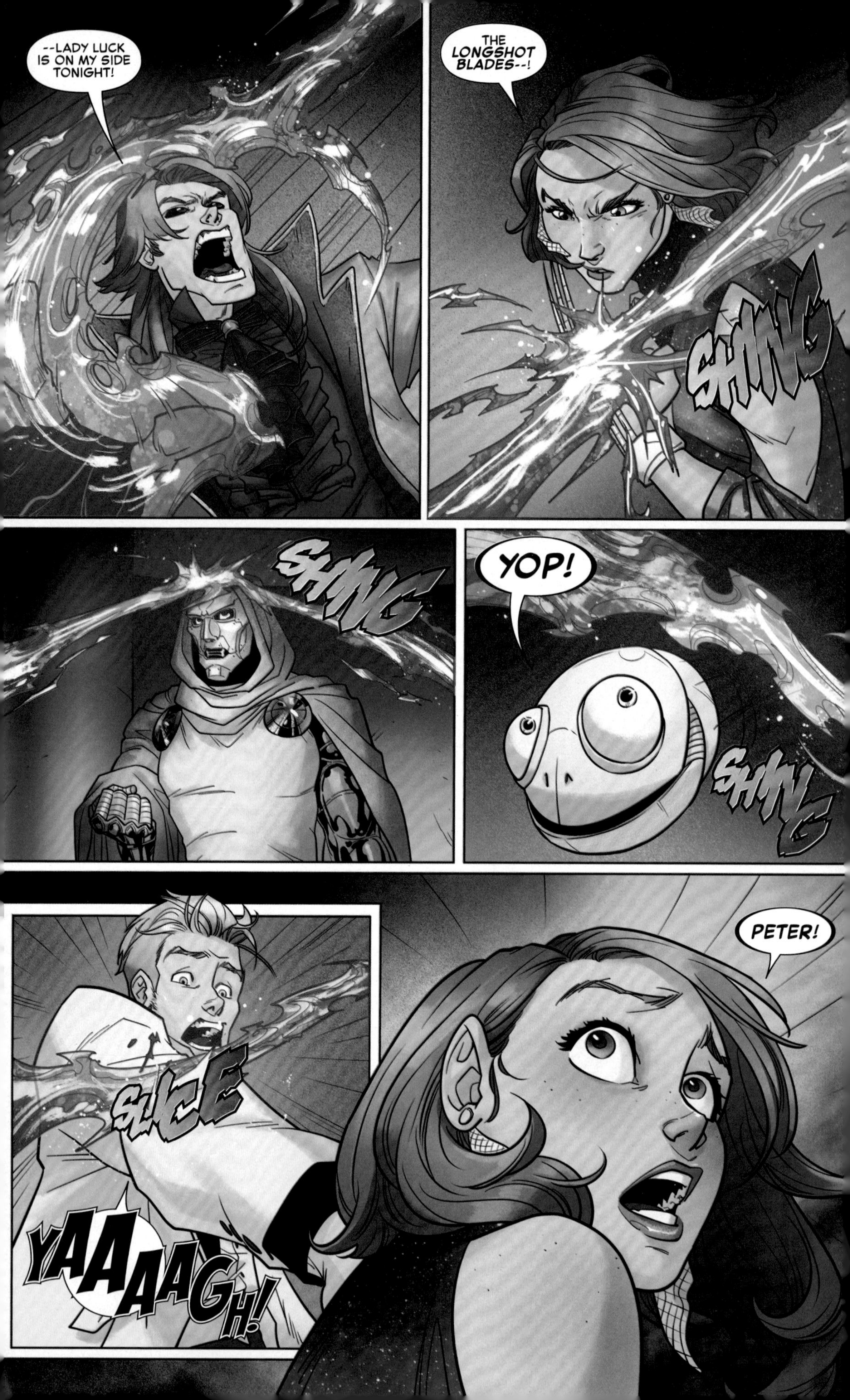
--LADY LUCK IS ON MY SIDE TONIGHT!
THE LONGSHOT BLADES--!
SHING
SHING
YOP!
SHING
SLICE
YAAAAAGH!
PETER!

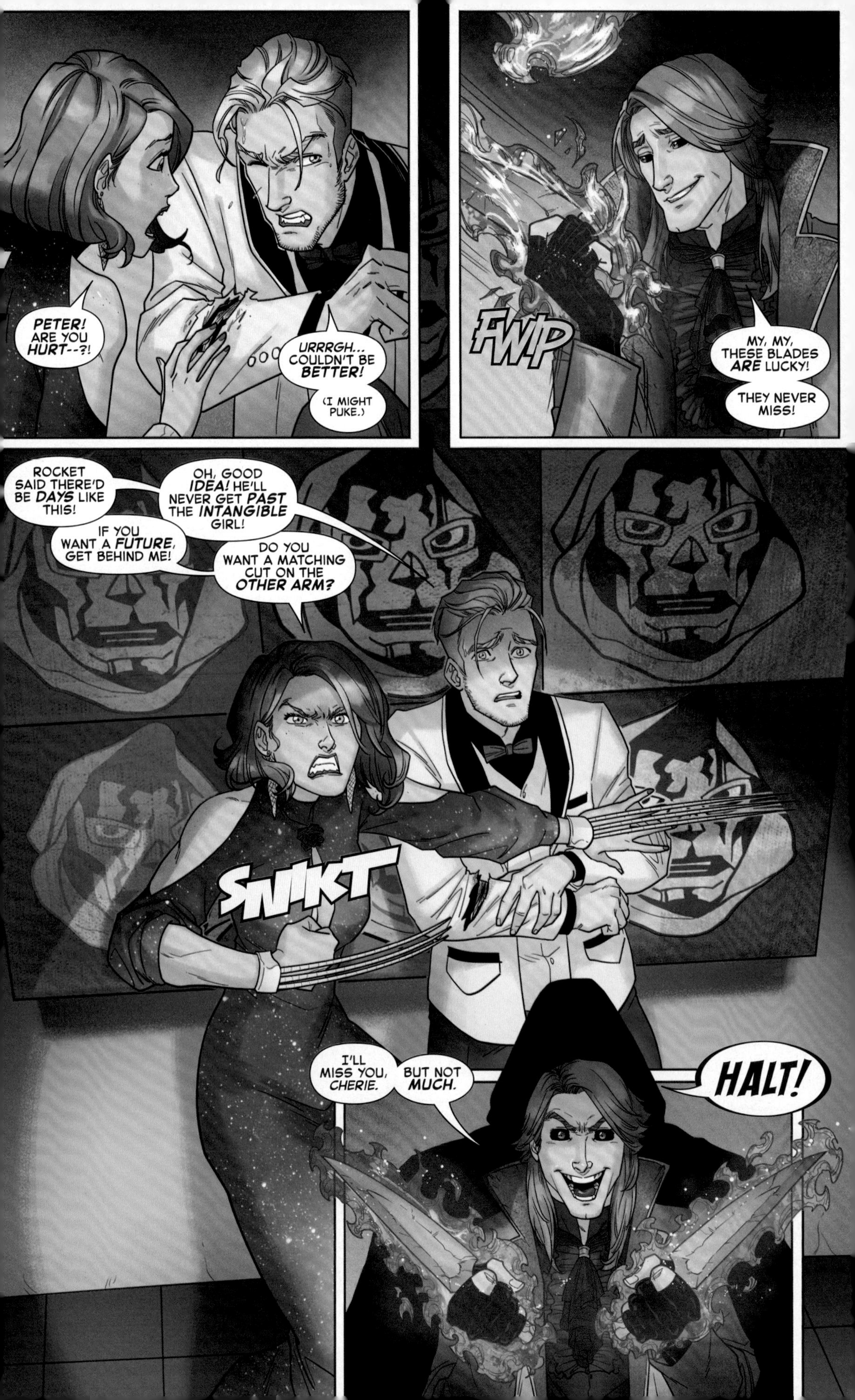

PETER! ARE YOU HURT--?!
URRRGH... COULDN'T BE BETTER!
(I MIGHT PUKE.)
FWIP
MY, MY, THESE BLADES ARE LUCKY!
THEY NEVER MISS!
ROCKET SAID THERE'D BE DAYS LIKE THIS!
OH, GOOD IDEA! HE'LL NEVER GET PAST THE INTANGIBLE GIRL!
IF YOU WANT A FUTURE, GET BEHIND ME!
DO YOU WANT A MATCHING CUT ON THE OTHER ARM?
SNIKT
I'LL MISS YOU, CHERIE.
BUT NOT MUCH.
HALT!

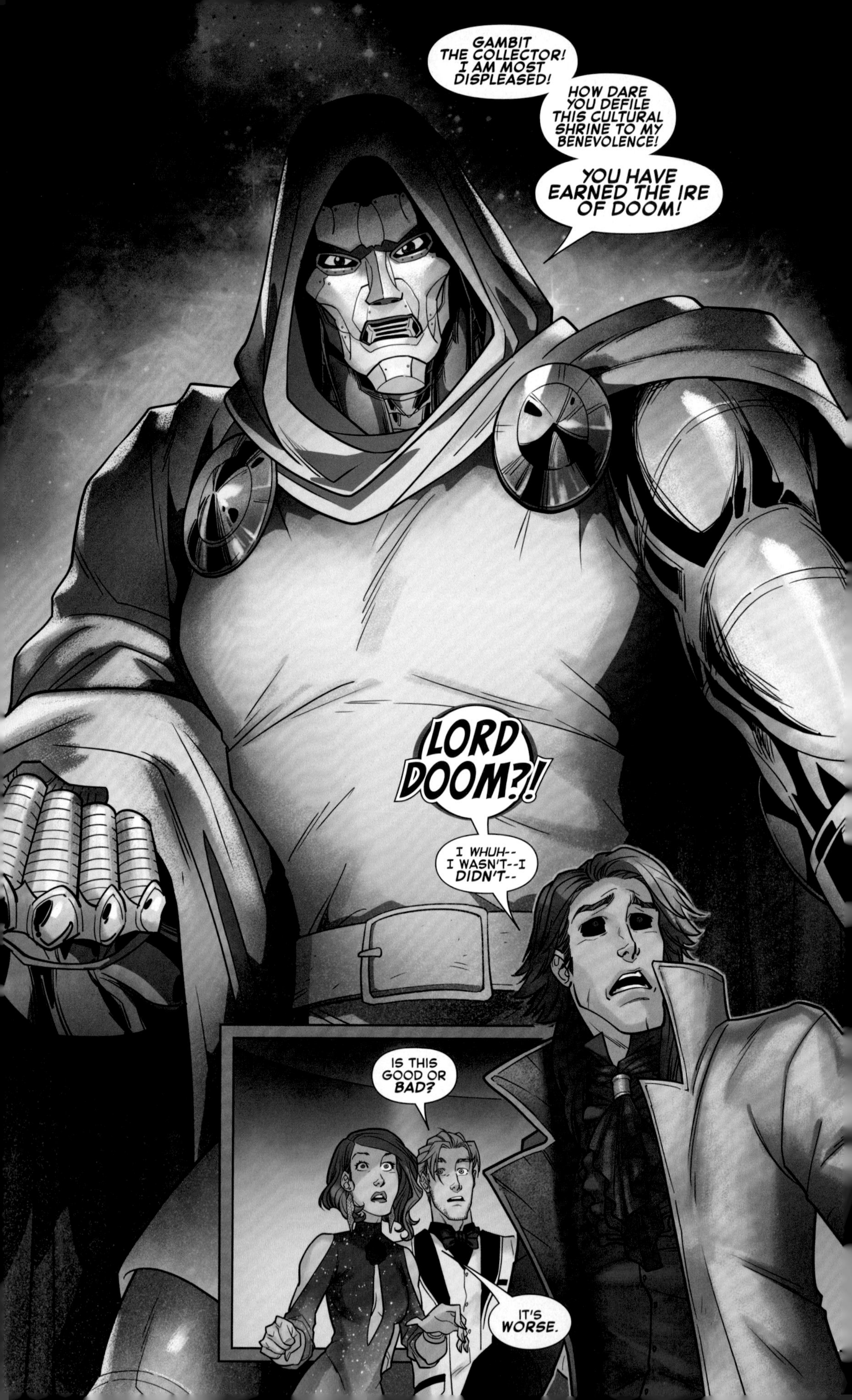
GAMBIT THE COLLECTOR! I AM MOST DISPLEASED!
HOW DARE YOU DEFILE THIS CULTURAL SHRINE TO MY BENEVOLENCE!
YOU HAVE EARNED THE IRE OF DOOM!
LORD DOOM?!
I WHUH-- I WASN'T--I DIDN'T--
IS THIS GOOD OR BAD?
IT'S WORSE.

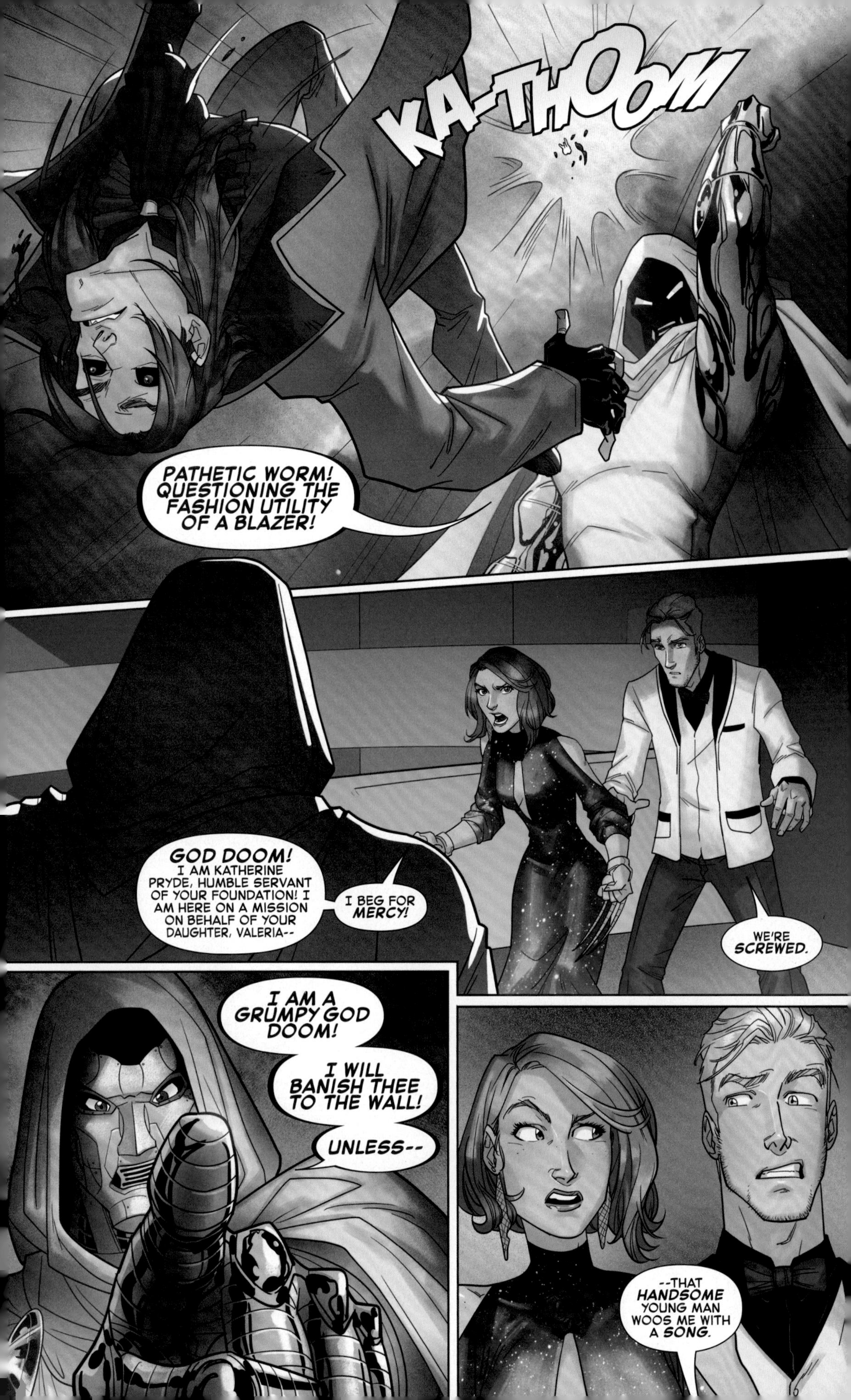

KA-THOOOM
PATHETIC WORM! QUESTIONING THE FASHION UTILITY OF A BLAZER!
GOD DOOM! I AM KATHERINE PRYDE, HUMBLE SERVANT OF YOUR FOUNDATION! I AM HERE ON A MISSION ON BEHALF OF YOUR DAUGHTER, VALERIA--
I BEG FOR MERCY!
WE'RE SCREWED.
I AM A GRUMPY GOD DOOM!
I WILL BANISH THEE TO THE WALL!
UNLESS--
--THAT HANDSOME YOUNG MAN WOOS ME WITH A SONG.

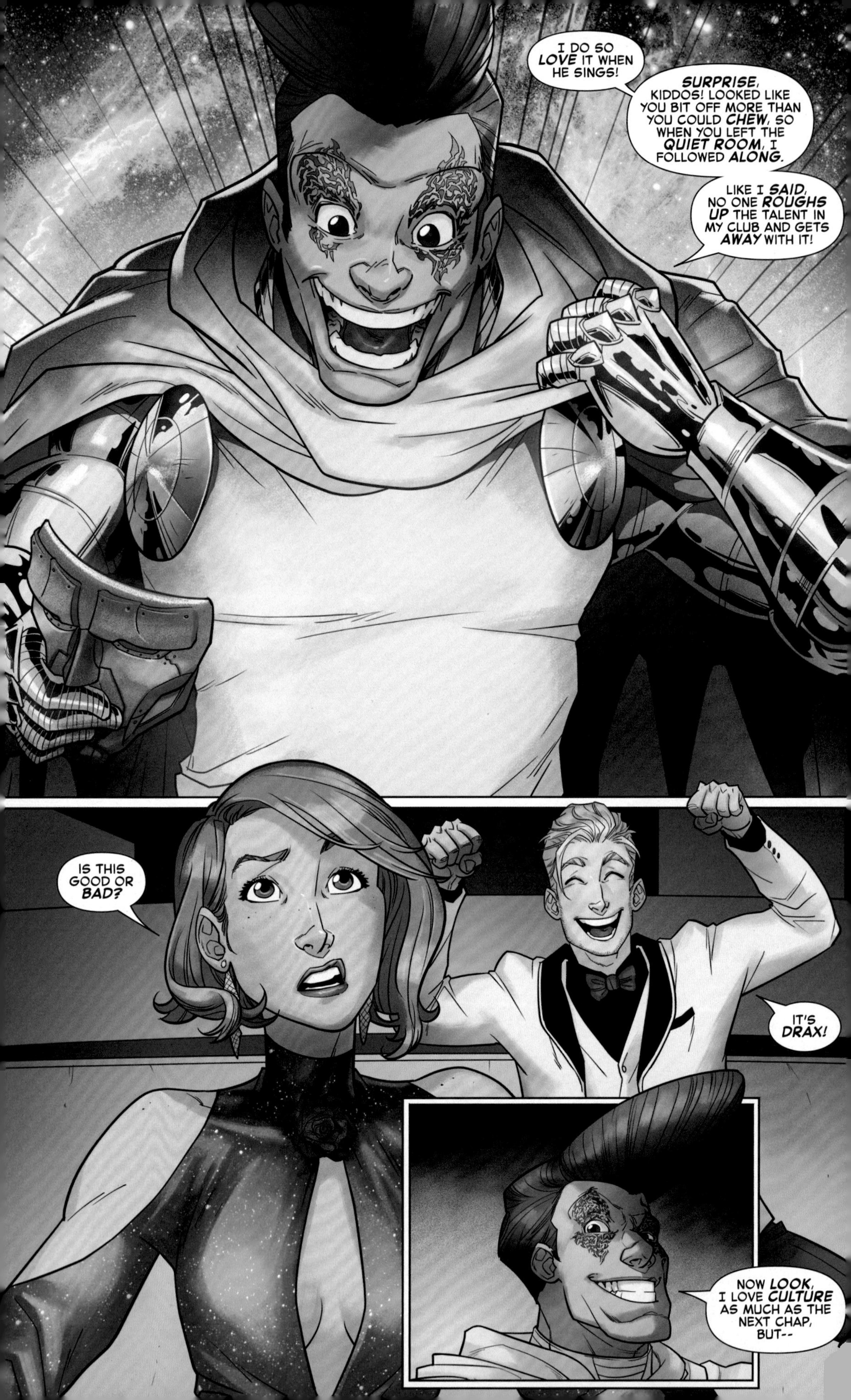
I DO SO LOVE IT WHEN HE SINGS!
SURPRISE, KIDDOS! LOOKED LIKE YOU BIT OFF MORE THAN YOU COULD CHEW, SO WHEN YOU LEFT THE QUIET ROOM, I FOLLOWED ALONG.
LIKE I SAID, NO ONE ROUGHS UP THE TALENT IN MY CLUB AND GETS AWAY WITH IT!
IS THIS GOOD OR BAD?
IT'S DRAX!
NOW LOOK, I LOVE CULTURE AS MUCH AS THE NEXT CHAP, BUT--

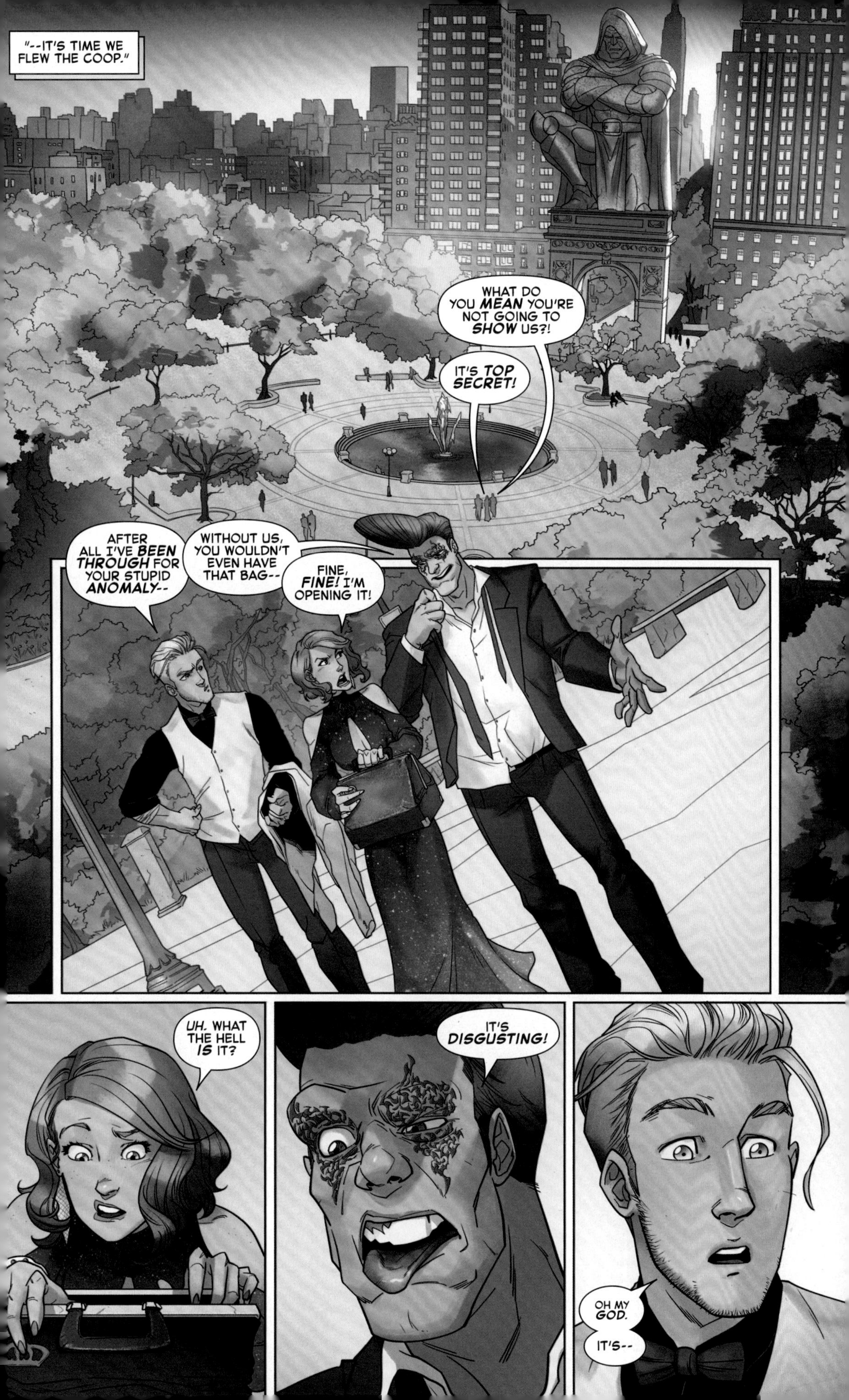
"--IT'S TIME WE FLEW THE COOP."
WHAT DO YOU MEAN YOU'RE NOT GOING TO SHOW US?!
IT'S TOP SECRET!
AFTER ALL I'VE BEEN THROUGH FOR YOUR STUPID ANOMALY--
WITHOUT US, YOU WOULDN'T EVEN HAVE THAT BAG--
FINE, FINE! I'M OPENING IT!
UH. WHAT THE HELL IS IT?
IT'S DISGUSTING!
OH MY GOD.
IT'S--

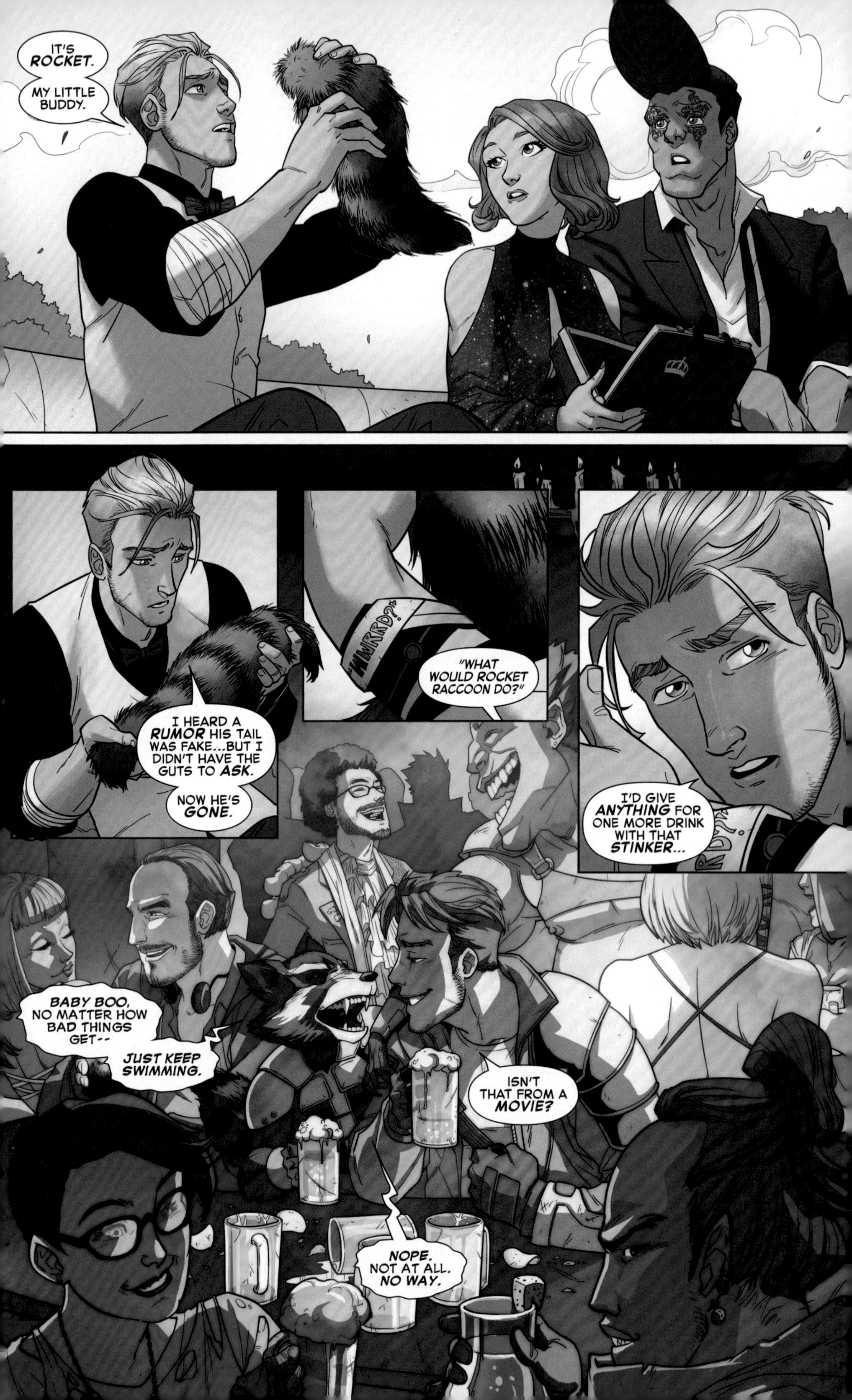
IT'S ROCKET.
MY LITTLE BUDDY.
I HEARD A RUMOR HIS TAIL WAS FAKE...BUT I DIDN'T HAVE THE GUTS TO ASK.
NOW HE'S GONE.
"WWRRD?"
"WHAT WOULD ROCKET RACCOON DO?"
I'D GIVE ANYTHING FOR ONE MORE DRINK WITH THAT STINKER...
BABY BOO, NO MATTER HOW BAD THINGS GET--
JUST KEEP SWIMMING.
ISN'T THAT FROM A MOVIE?
NOPE. NOT AT ALL. NO WAY.

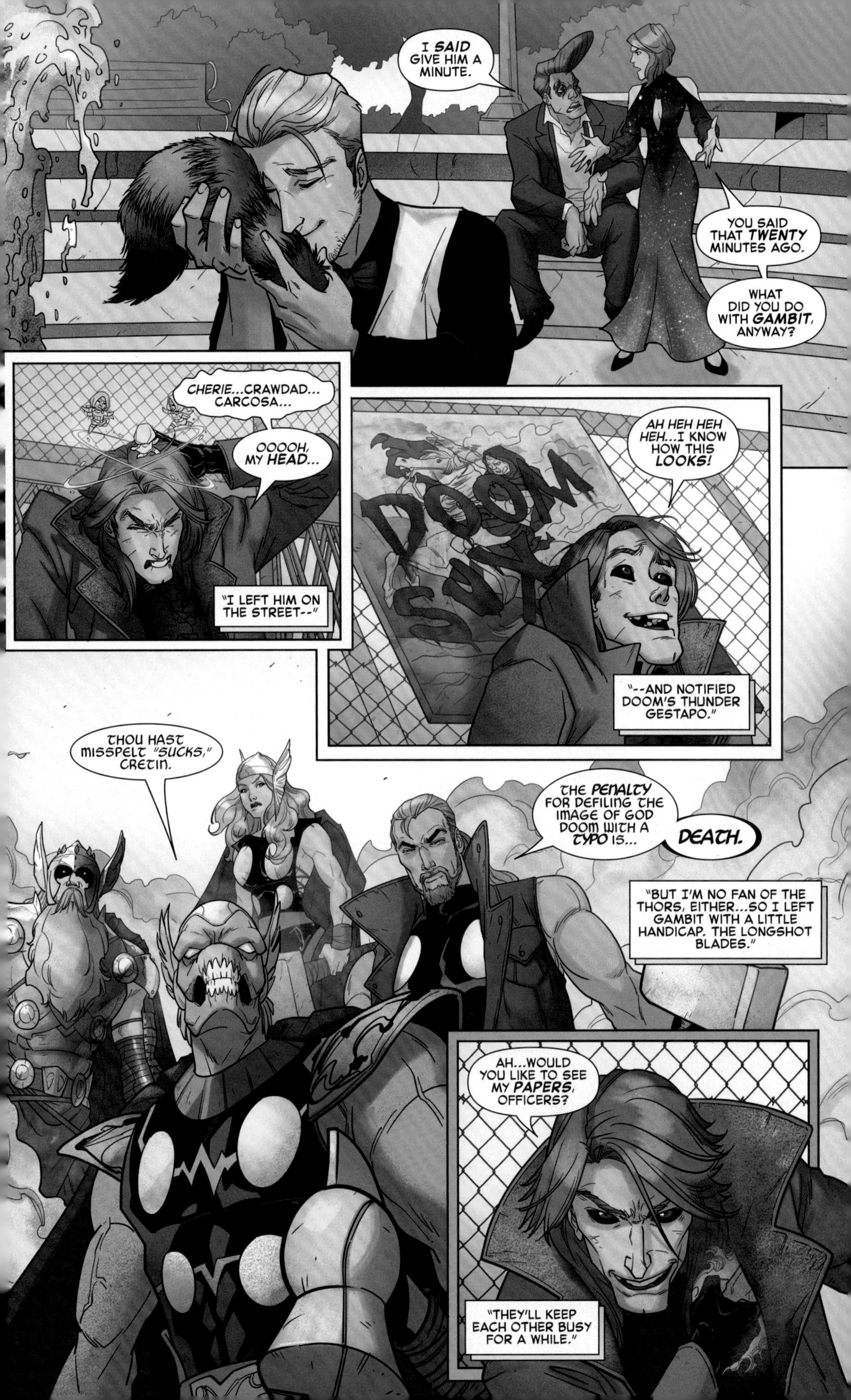
I SAID GIVE HIM A MINUTE.
YOU SAID THAT TWENTY MINUTES AGO.
WHAT DID YOU DO WITH GAMBIT, ANYWAY?
CHERIE...CRAWDAD... CARCOSA...
OOOOH, MY HEAD...
"I LEFT HIM ON THE STREET--"
AH HEH HEH HEH...I KNOW HOW THIS LOOKS!
DOOM SUX
"--AND NOTIFIED DOOM'S THUNDER GESTAPO."
THOU HAST MISSPELT "SUCKS," CRETIN.
THE PENALTY FOR DEFILING THE IMAGE OF GOD DOOM WITH A TYPO IS...
DEATH.
"BUT I'M NO FAN OF THE THORS, EITHER...SO I LEFT GAMBIT WITH A LITTLE HANDICAP. THE LONGSHOT BLADES."
AH...WOULD YOU LIKE TO SEE MY PAPERS, OFFICERS?
"THEY'LL KEEP EACH OTHER BUSY FOR A WHILE."

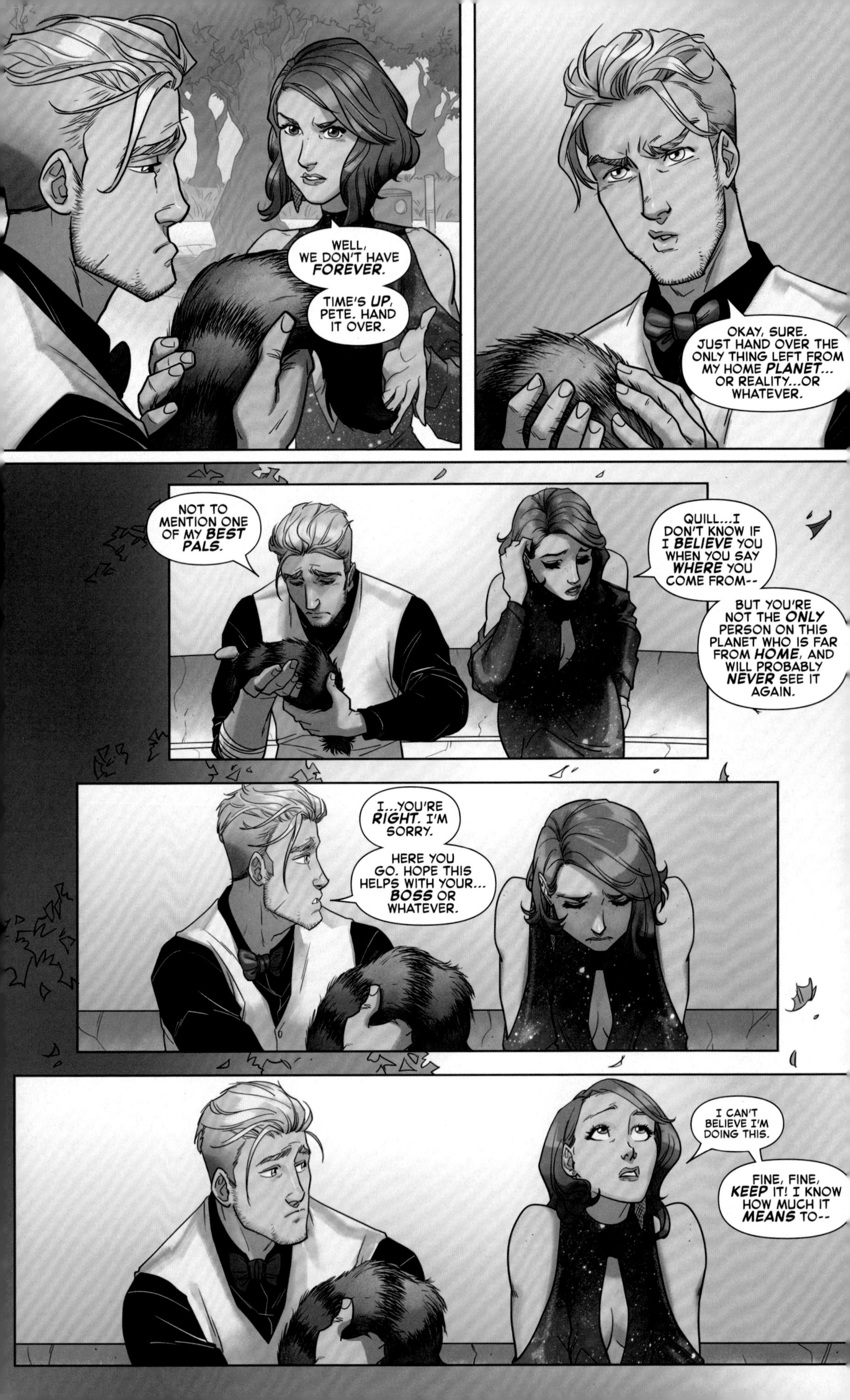
WELL, WE DON'T HAVE FOREVER.
TIME'S UP, PETE. HAND IT OVER.
OKAY, SURE. JUST HAND OVER THE ONLY THING LEFT FROM MY HOME PLANET... OR REALITY...OR WHATEVER.
NOT TO MENTION ONE OF MY BEST PALS.
QUILL...I DON'T KNOW IF I BELIEVE YOU WHEN YOU SAY WHERE YOU COME FROM--
BUT YOU'RE NOT THE ONLY PERSON ON THIS PLANET WHO IS FAR FROM HOME, AND WILL PROBABLY NEVER SEE IT AGAIN.
I...YOU'RE RIGHT. I'M SORRY.
HERE YOU GO. HOPE THIS HELPS WITH YOUR... BOSS OR WHATEVER.
I CAN'T BELIEVE I'M DOING THIS.
FINE, FINE, KEEP IT! I KNOW HOW MUCH IT MEANS TO--

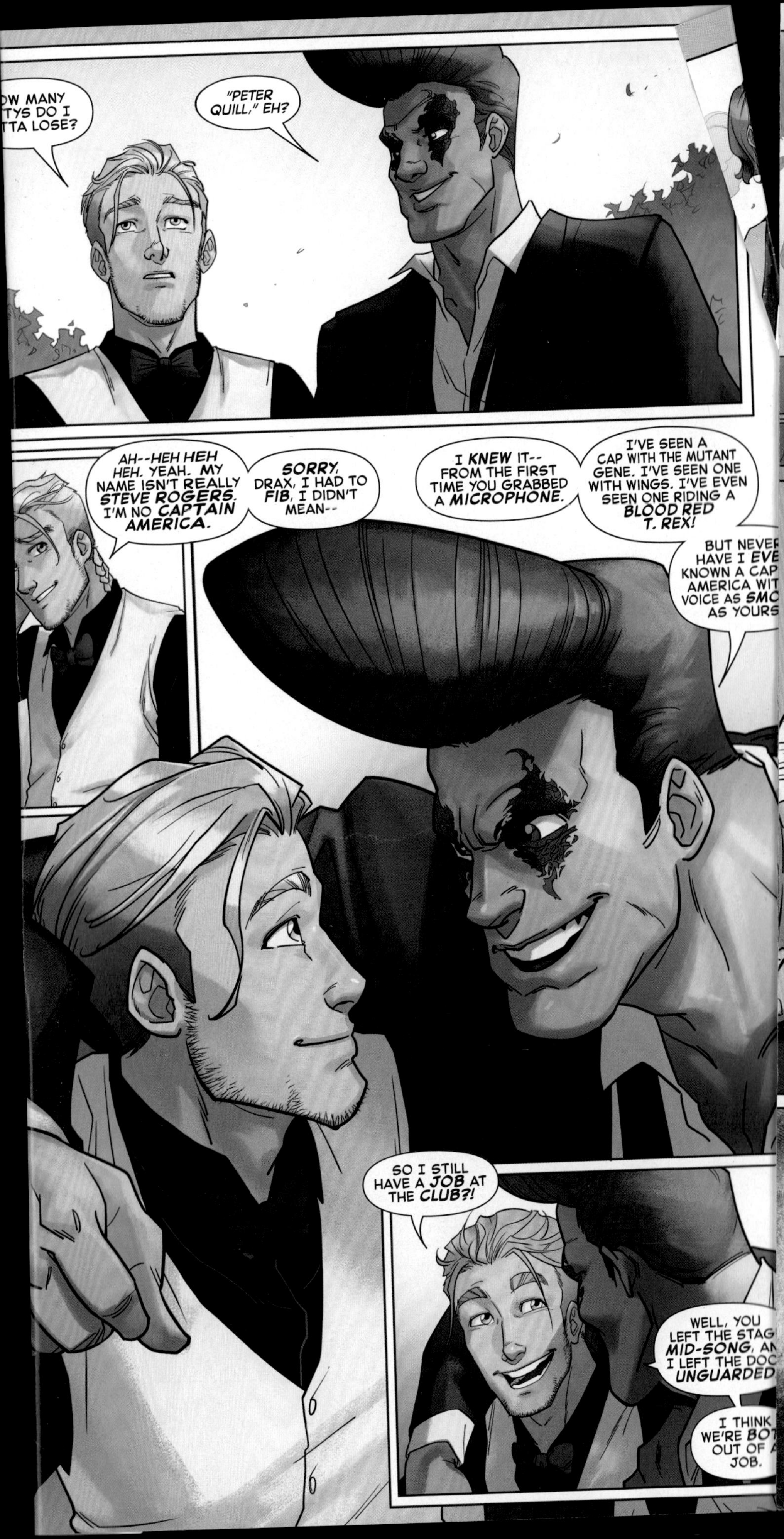
OW MANY TTYS DO I TTA LOSE?
"PETER QUILL," EH?
AH--HEH HEH HEH. YEAH. MY NAME ISN'T REALLY STEVE ROGERS. I'M NO CAPTAIN AMERICA.
SORRY, DRAX, I HAD TO FIB, I DIDN'T MEAN--
I KNEW IT-- FROM THE FIRST TIME YOU GRABBED A MICROPHONE.
I'VE SEEN A CAP WITH THE MUTANT GENE. I'VE SEEN ONE WITH WINGS. I'VE EVEN SEEN ONE RIDING A BLOOD RED T. REX!
BUT NEVER HAVE I EVE KNOWN A CAP AMERICA WIT VOICE AS SMO AS YOURS
SO I STILL HAVE A JOB AT THE CLUB?!
WELL, YOU LEFT THE STAG MID-SONG, AN I LEFT THE DOO UNGUARDED
I THINK WE'RE BOT OUT OF A JOB.
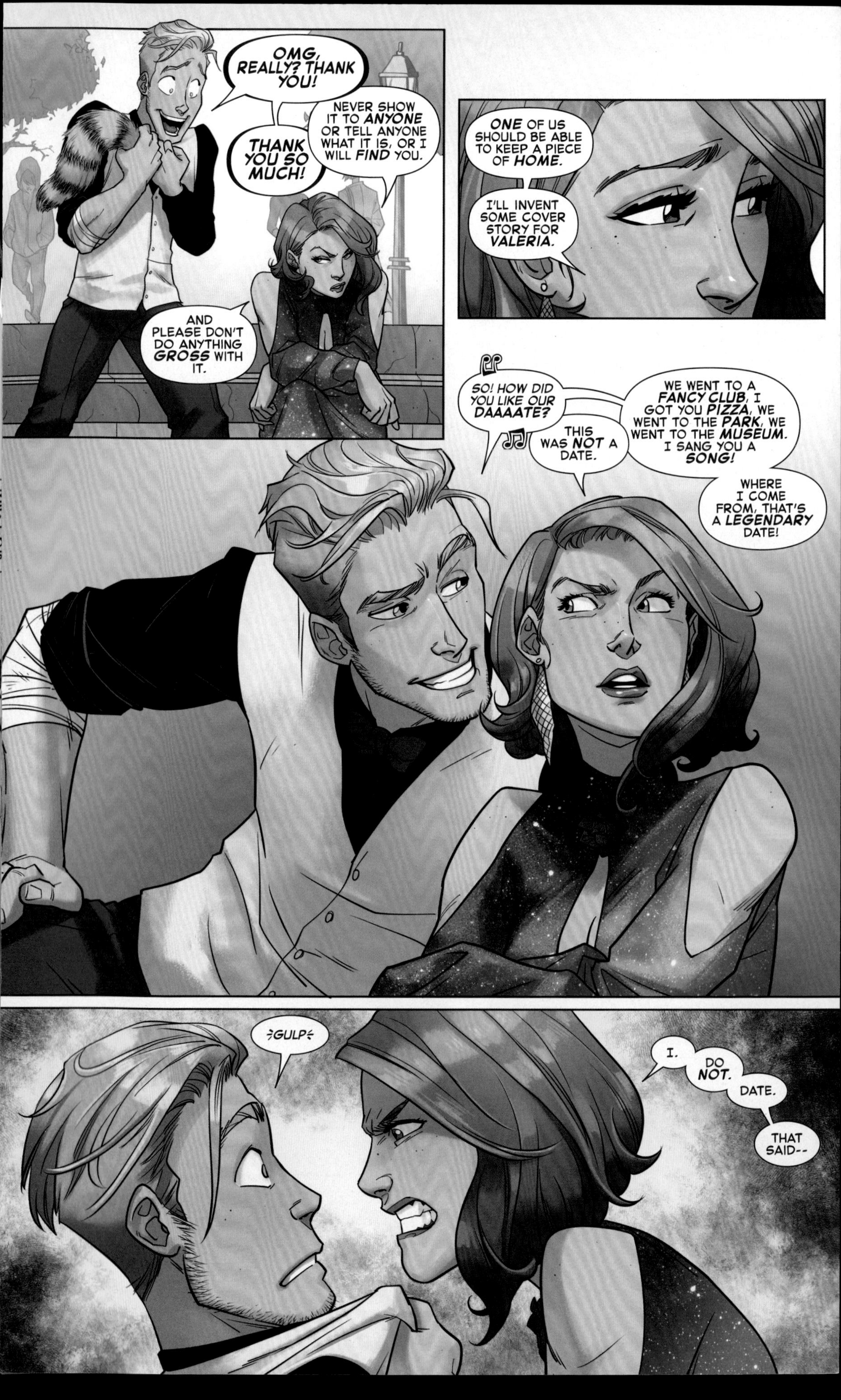
OMG, REALLY? THANK YOU!
THANK YOU SO MUCH!
NEVER SHOW IT TO ANYONE OR TELL ANYONE WHAT IT IS, OR I WILL FIND YOU.
AND PLEASE DON'T DO ANYTHING GROSS WITH IT.
ONE OF US SHOULD BE ABLE TO KEEP A PIECE OF HOME.
I'LL INVENT SOME COVER STORY FOR VALERIA.
SO! HOW DID YOU LIKE OUR DAAAATE?
THIS WAS NOT A DATE.
WE WENT TO A FANCY CLUB, I GOT YOU PIZZA, WE WENT TO THE PARK, WE WENT TO THE MUSEUM. I SANG YOU A SONG!
WHERE I COME FROM, THAT'S A LEGENDARY DATE!
GULP
I.
DO NOT.
DATE.
THAT SAID--

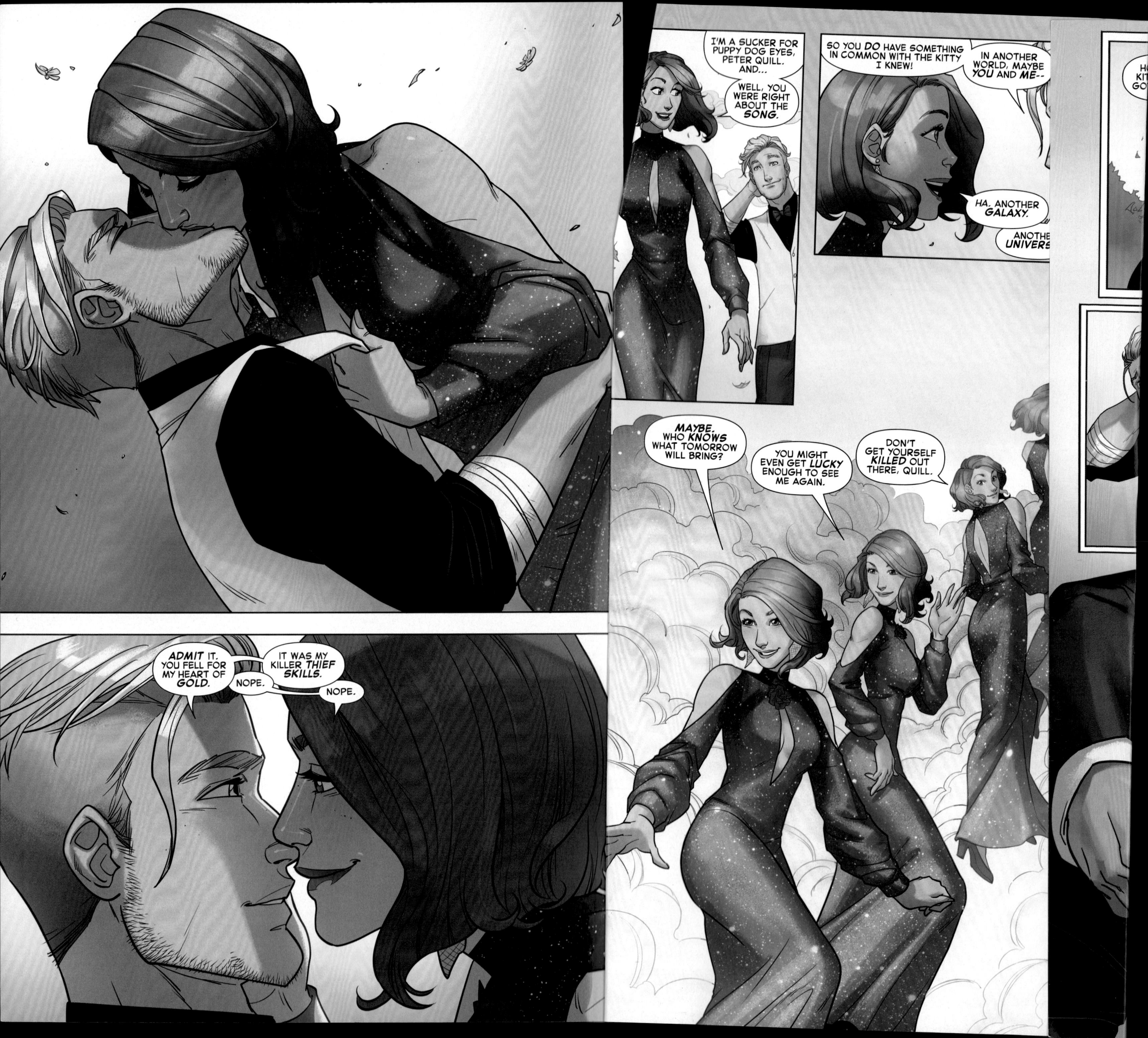
ADMIT IT. YOU FELL FOR MY HEART OF GOLD.
IT WAS MY KILLER THIEF SKILLS.
NOPE.
NOPE.
I'M A SUCKER FOR PUPPY DOG EYES, PETER QUILL. AND...
WELL, YOU WERE RIGHT ABOUT THE SONG.
SO YOU DO HAVE SOMETHING IN COMMON WITH THE KITTY I KNEW!
IN ANOTHER WORLD, MAYBE YOU AND ME--
HA. ANOTHER GALAXY.
ANOTHE UNIVERS
MAYBE. WHO KNOWS WHAT TOMORROW WILL BRING?
YOU MIGHT EVEN GET LUCKY ENOUGH TO SEE ME AGAIN.
DON'T GET YOURSELF KILLED OUT THERE, QUILL.

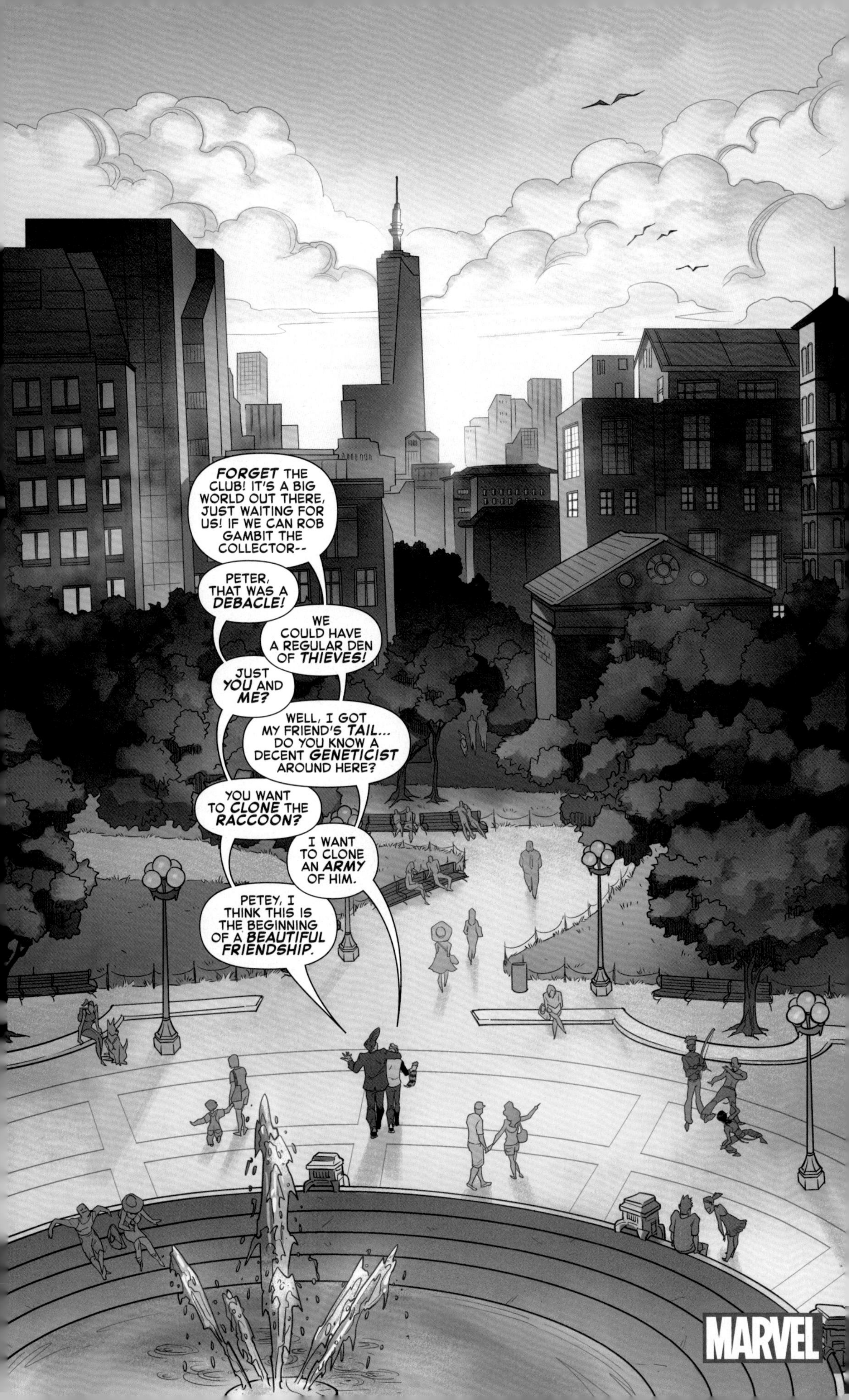
FORGET THE CLUB! IT'S A BIG WORLD OUT THERE, JUST WAITING FOR US! IF WE CAN ROB GAMBIT THE COLLECTOR--
PETER, THAT WAS A DEBACLE!
WE COULD HAVE A REGULAR DEN OF THIEVES!
JUST YOU AND ME?
WELL, I GOT MY FRIEND'S TAIL... DO YOU KNOW A DECENT GENETICIST AROUND HERE?
YOU WANT TO CLONE THE RACCOON?
I WANT TO CLONE AN ARMY OF HIM.
PETEY, I THINK THIS IS THE BEGINNING OF A BEAUTIFUL FRIENDSHIP.
MARVEL

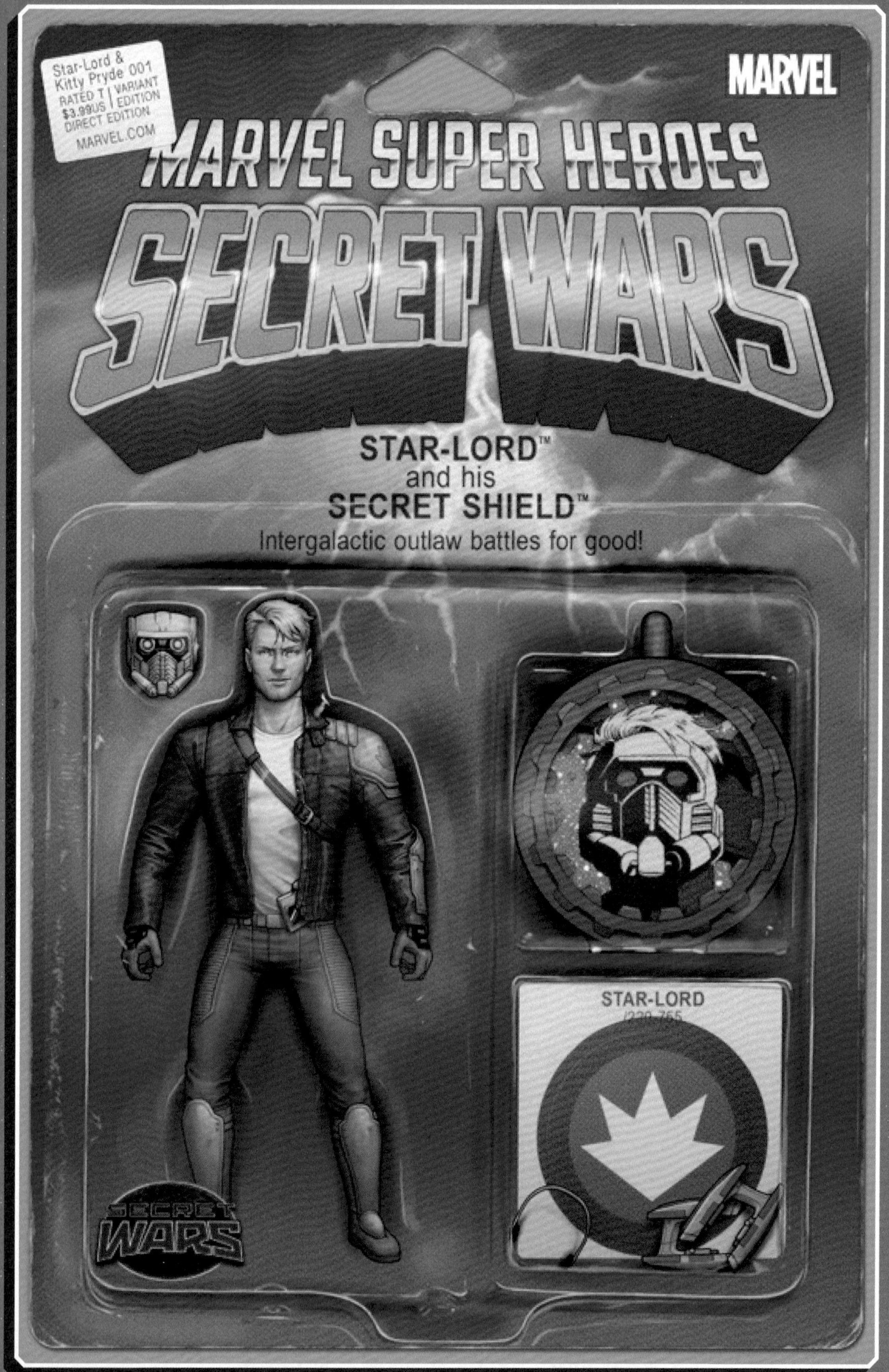
Star-Lord & Kitty Pryde 001
RATED T
$3.99US
DIRECT EDITION
VARIANT EDITION
MARVEL.COM
MARVEL
MARVEL SUPER HEROES
SECRET WARS
STAR-LORD™
and his
SECRET SHIELD™
Intergalactic outlaw battles for good!
STAR-LORD
SECRET WARS

STAR LORD & KITTY PRYDE #1 action figure variant
by JOHN TYLER CHRISTOPHER

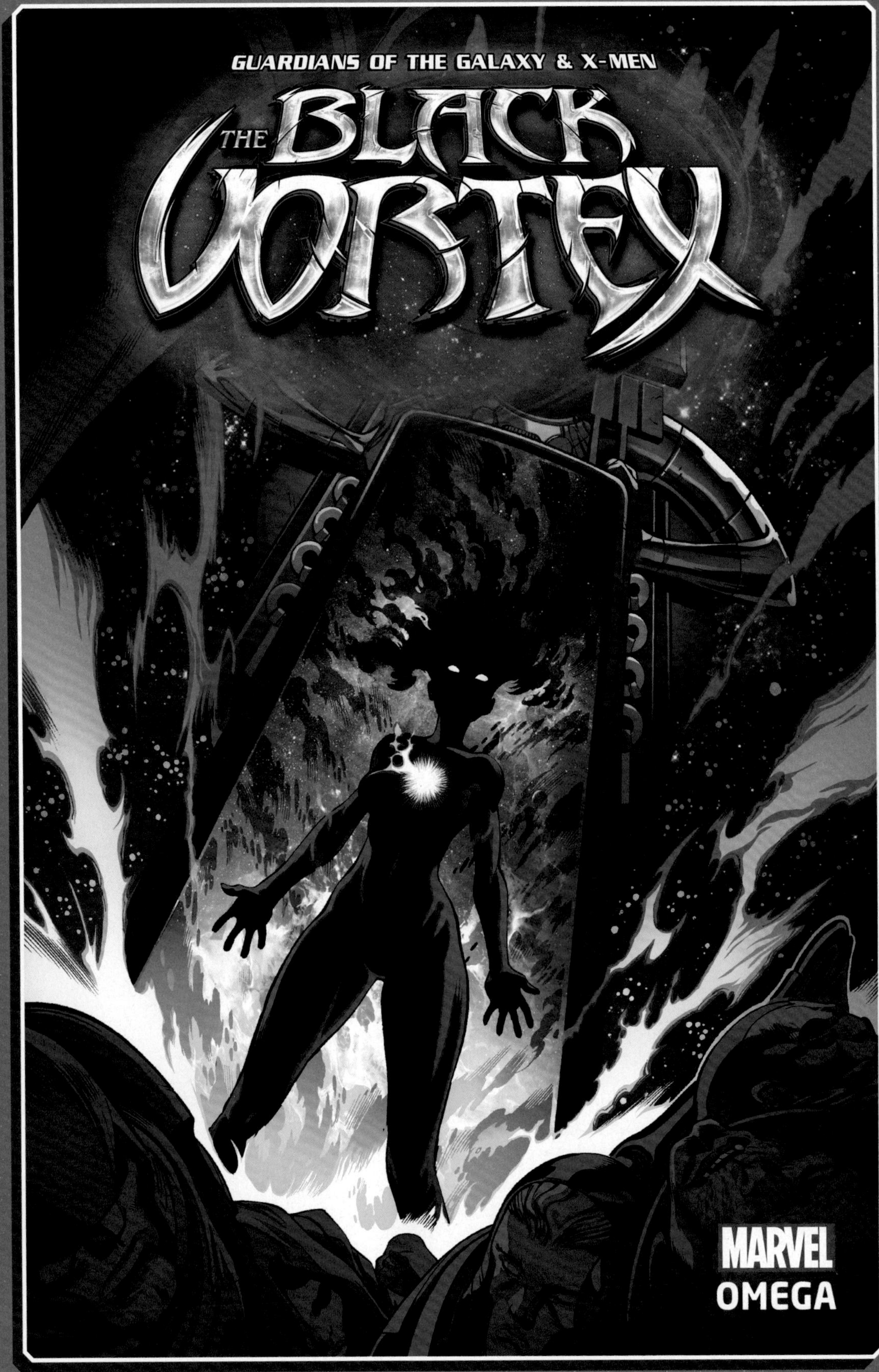
GUARDIANS OF THE GALAXY & X-MEN
THE BLACK VORTEX
MARVEL
OMEGA

GUARDIANS OF THE GALAXY & X-MEN

THE BLACK VORTEX

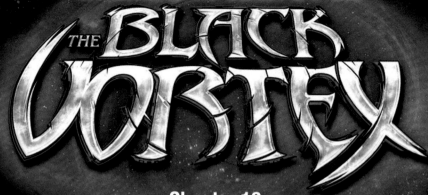

Chapter 13

Previously in *The Black Vortex*...

Billions of years ago, an ancient race named the Viscardi were gifted an object of immense cosmic power by a Celestial. This artifact, known as the Black Vortex, transformed the user, imbuing them with cosmic energy. However, the power of this object caused the Viscardi to turn on each other, annihilating their own race from within.

When J'Son, Peter Quill's father, obtained the Black Vortex, Peter and Kitty Pryde stole the artifact and recruited the Guardians of the Galaxy and the X-Men for help. Some of the heroes submitted to the Black Vortex, gaining cosmic powers in an effort to save the galaxy from the hands of Mister Knife.

Spartax has been encased in amber by the cosmically empowered Thane, son of Thanos. Knife intends to partner with the Brood in order to rebuild his galactic empire. The Brood would burrow into the amber, implanting eggs into the trapped citizens of Spartax. Should the eggs hatch, a massive new Brood armada, billions strong, would be born.

With the threat posed by the Brood compounding their need to save Spartax, the group knew that one of them would have to submit to the Vortex to stop them. One who could resist the corruption often caused by the Vortex's power. Someone like Kitty Pryde, who stepped forward and accepted her cosmic mantle, submitting to the Black Vortex...

SAM HUMPHRIES
WRITER

ED McGUINNESS AND JAVIER GARRON
PENCILS

MARK FARMER, JAVIER GARRON AND ED MCGUINNESS
INKERS

MARTE GRACIA
COLORS

TRAVIS LANHAM
LETTERER

ED McGUINNESS, MARK FARMER AND MARTE GRACIA
COVER ARTISTS

XANDER JAROWEY
ASSISTANT EDITOR

MIKE MARTS
EDITOR

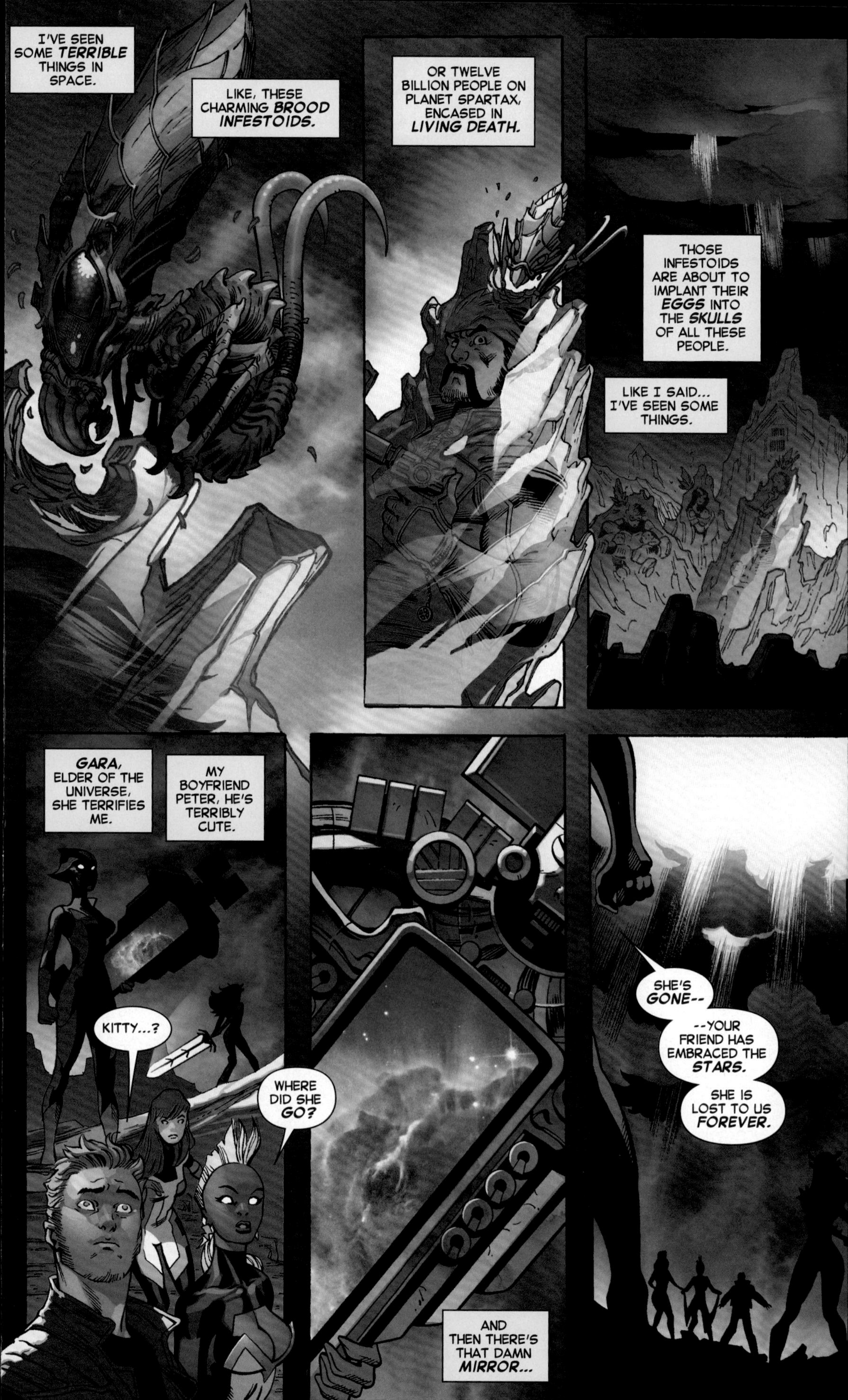

I'VE SEEN SOME TERRIBLE THINGS IN SPACE.
LIKE, THESE CHARMING BROOD INFESTOIDS.
OR TWELVE BILLION PEOPLE ON PLANET SPARTAX, ENCASED IN LIVING DEATH.
THOSE INFESTOIDS ARE ABOUT TO IMPLANT THEIR EGGS INTO THE SKULLS OF ALL THESE PEOPLE.
LIKE I SAID... I'VE SEEN SOME THINGS.
GARA, ELDER OF THE UNIVERSE, SHE TERRIFIES ME.
MY BOYFRIEND PETER, HE'S TERRIBLY CUTE.
KITTY...?
WHERE DID SHE GO?
AND THEN THERE'S THAT DAMN MIRROR...
SHE'S GONE--
--YOUR FRIEND HAS EMBRACED THE STARS.
SHE IS LOST TO US FOREVER.

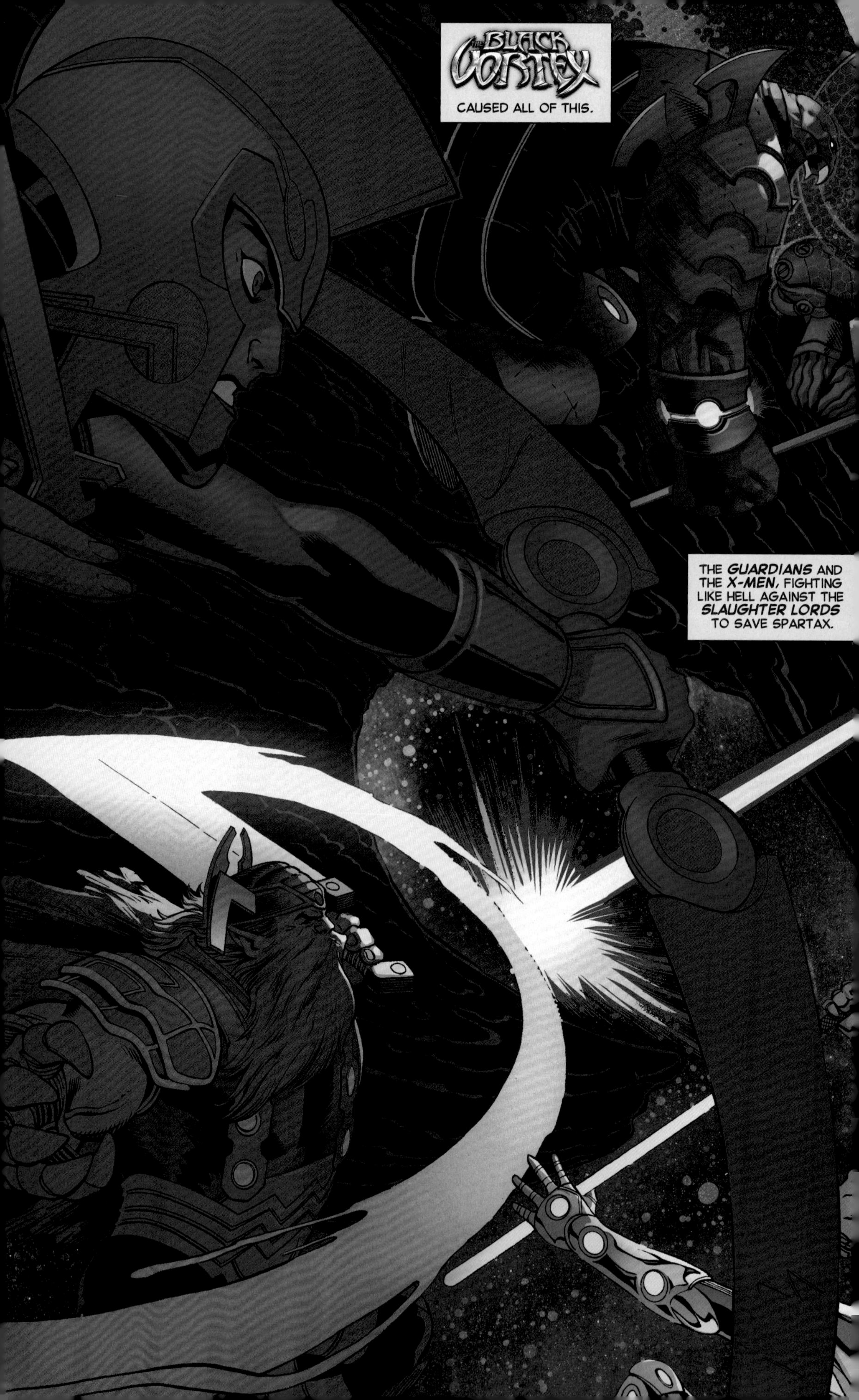
THE BLACK VORTEX
CAUSED ALL OF THIS.
THE GUARDIANS AND THE X-MEN, FIGHTING LIKE HELL AGAINST THE SLAUGHTER LORDS TO SAVE SPARTAX.

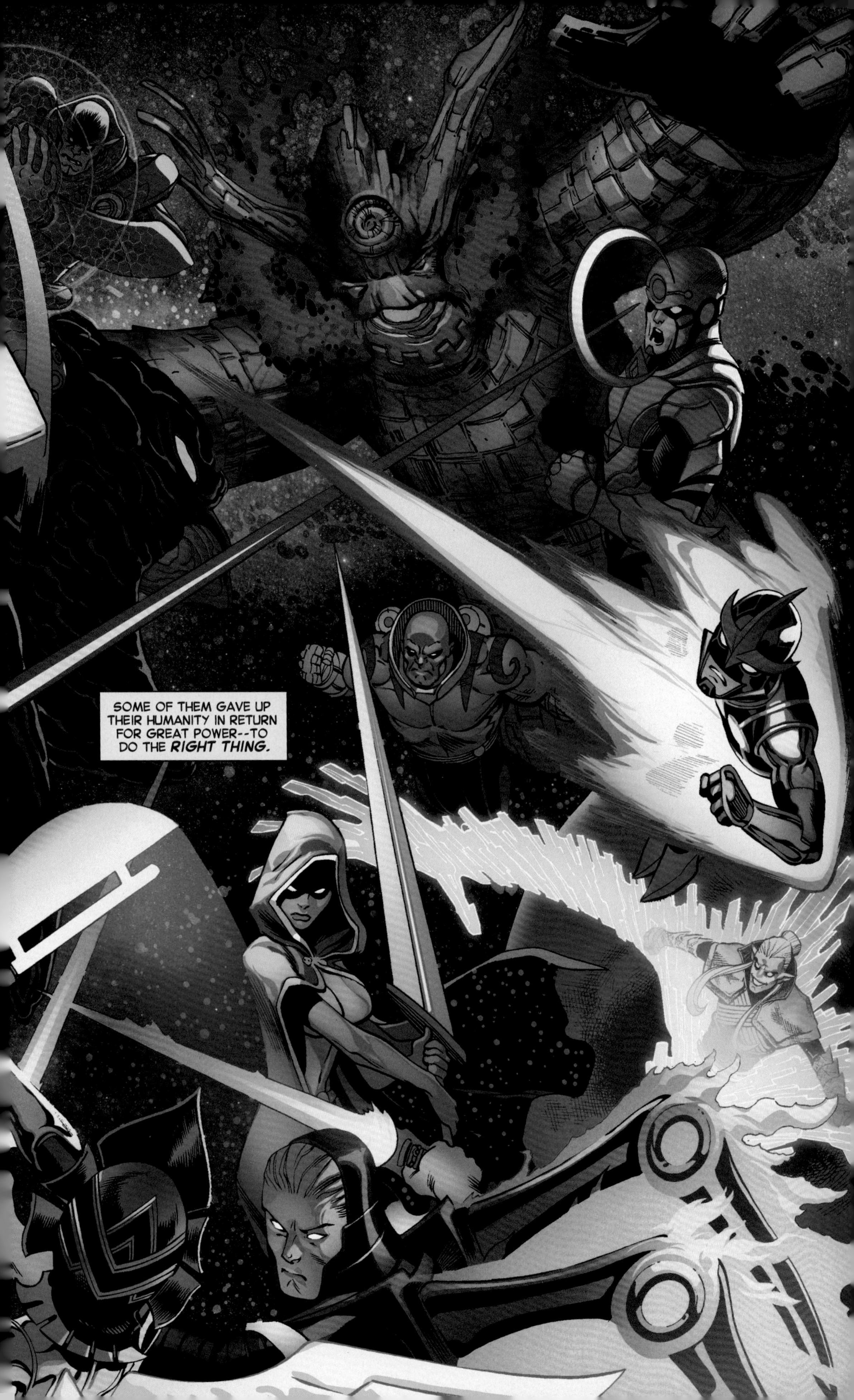
SOME OF THEM GAVE UP THEIR HUMANITY IN RETURN FOR GREAT POWER--TO DO THE *RIGHT THING.*

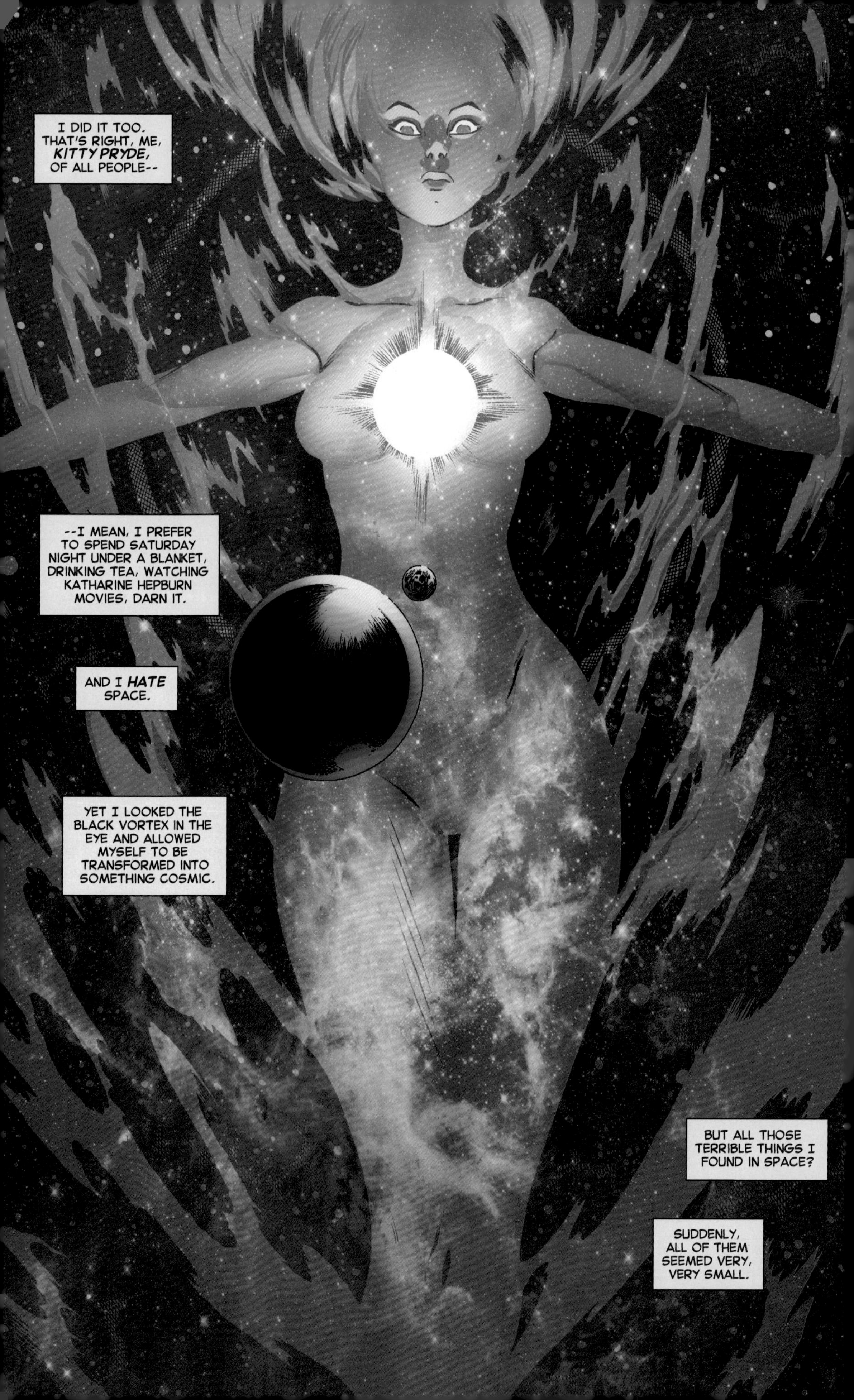
I DID IT TOO. THAT'S RIGHT, ME, KITTY PRYDE, OF ALL PEOPLE--
--I MEAN, I PREFER TO SPEND SATURDAY NIGHT UNDER A BLANKET, DRINKING TEA, WATCHING KATHARINE HEPBURN MOVIES, DARN IT.
AND I HATE SPACE.
YET I LOOKED THE BLACK VORTEX IN THE EYE AND ALLOWED MYSELF TO BE TRANSFORMED INTO SOMETHING COSMIC.
BUT ALL THOSE TERRIBLE THINGS I FOUND IN SPACE?
SUDDENLY, ALL OF THEM SEEMED VERY, VERY SMALL.

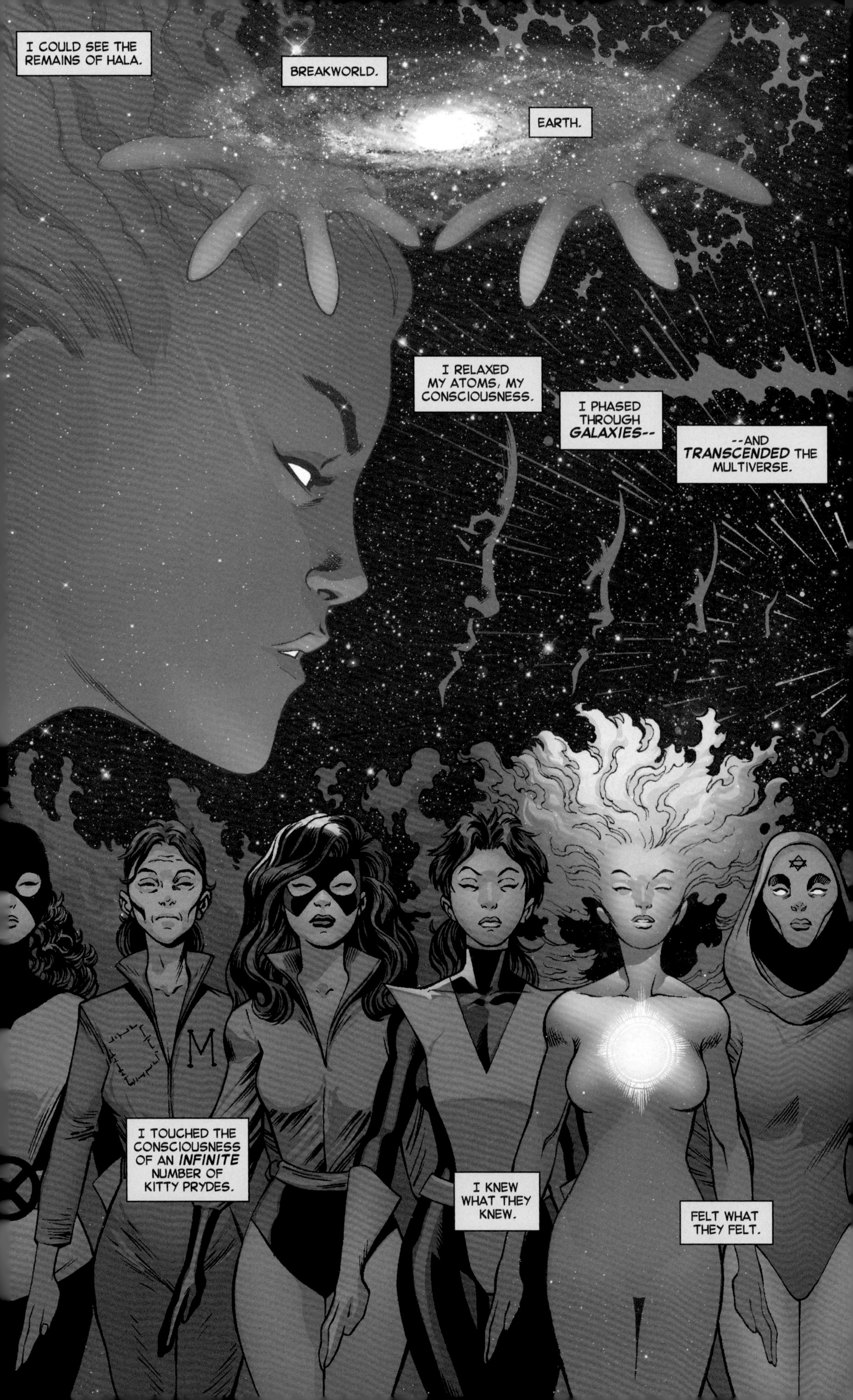
I COULD SEE THE REMAINS OF HALA.
BREAKWORLD.
EARTH.
I RELAXED MY ATOMS, MY CONSCIOUSNESS.
I PHASED THROUGH *GALAXIES*--
--AND *TRANSCENDED* THE MULTIVERSE.
I TOUCHED THE CONSCIOUSNESS OF AN *INFINITE* NUMBER OF KITTY PRYDES.
I KNEW WHAT THEY KNEW.
FELT WHAT THEY FELT.

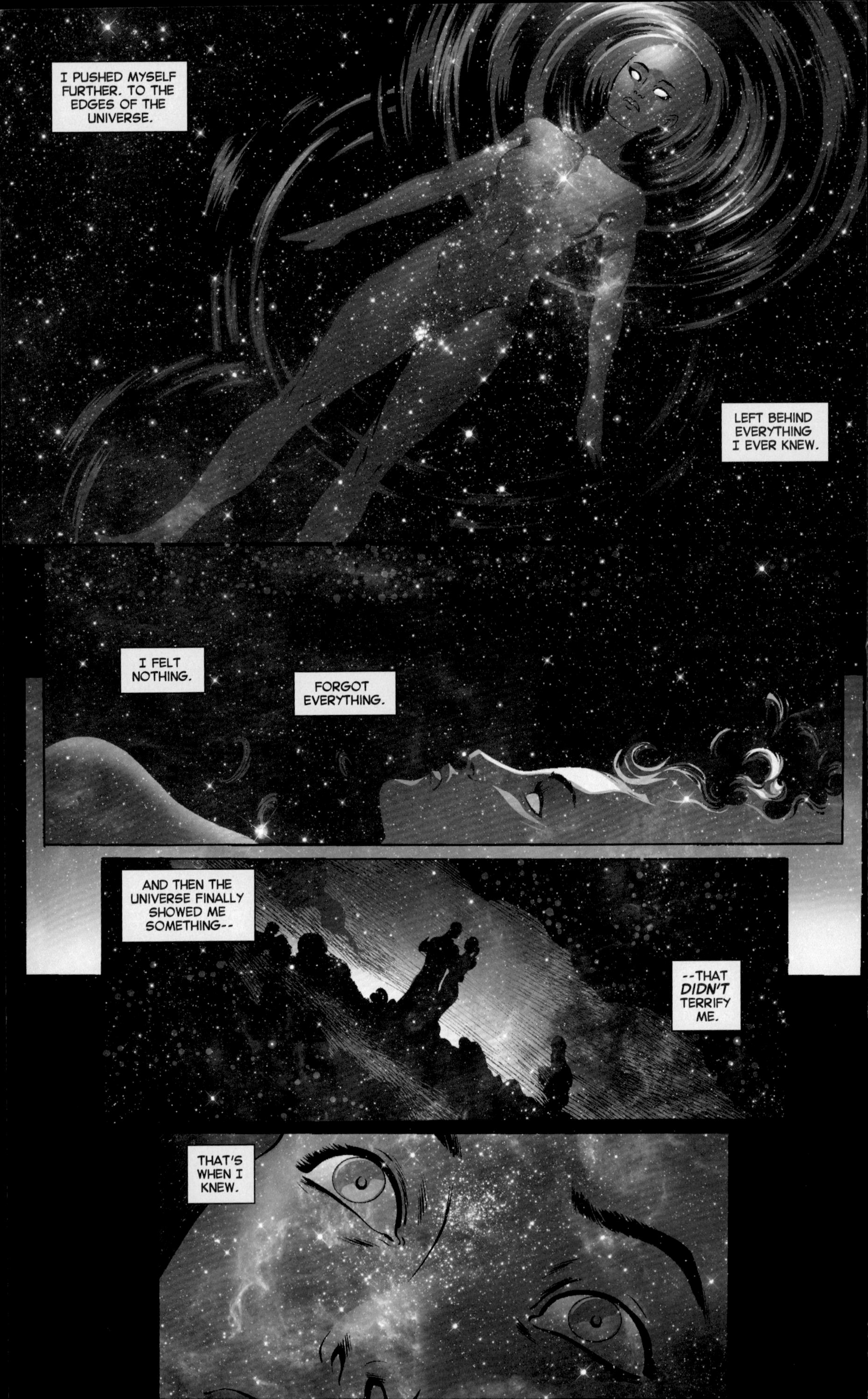

I PUSHED MYSELF FURTHER. TO THE EDGES OF THE UNIVERSE.
LEFT BEHIND EVERYTHING I EVER KNEW.
I FELT NOTHING.
FORGOT EVERYTHING.
AND THEN THE UNIVERSE FINALLY SHOWED ME SOMETHING--
--THAT *DIDN'T* TERRIFY ME.
THAT'S WHEN I KNEW.

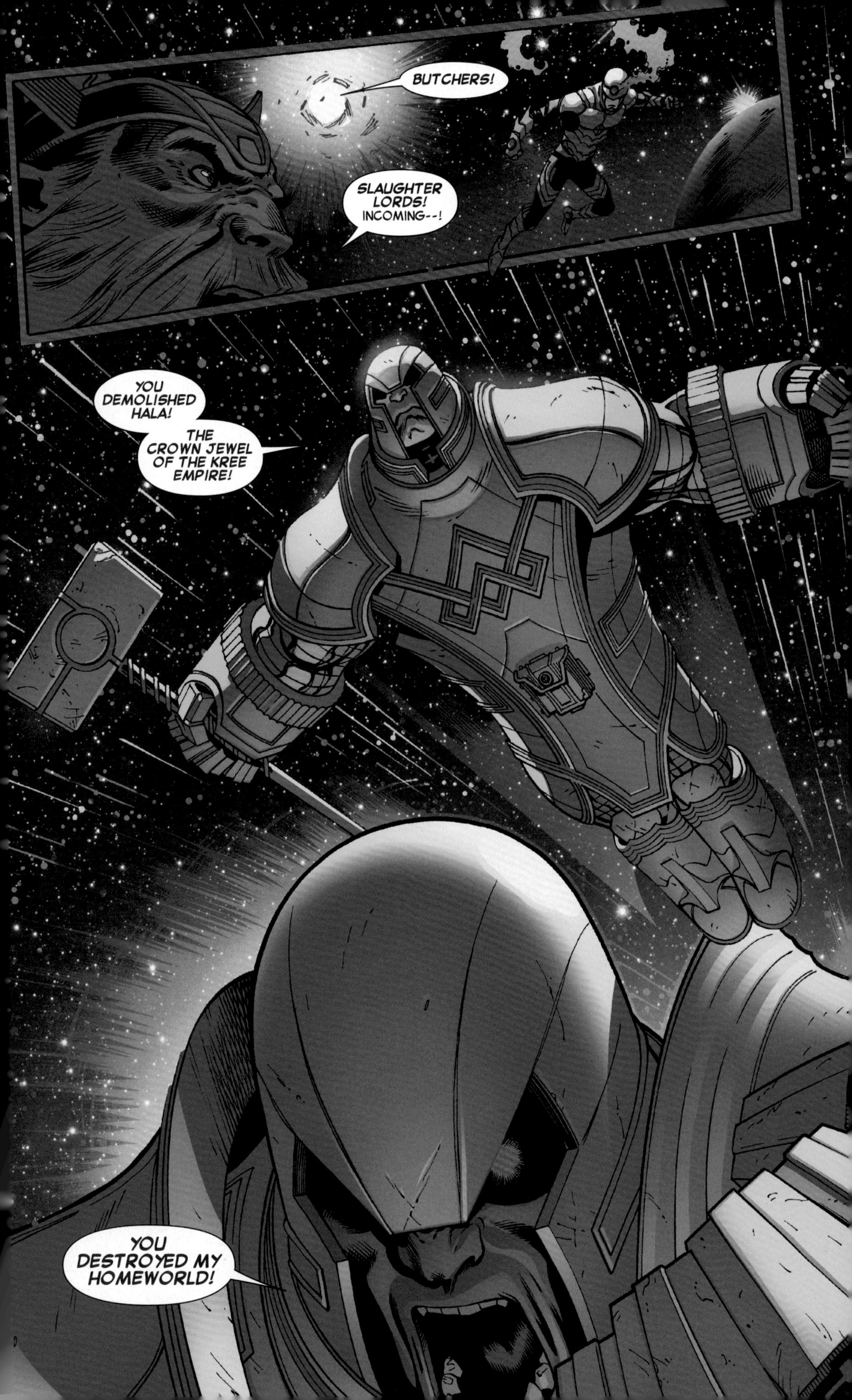
BUTCHERS!
SLAUGHTER LORDS! INCOMING--!
YOU DEMOLISHED HALA!
THE CROWN JEWEL OF THE KREE EMPIRE!
YOU DESTROYED MY HOMEWORLD!

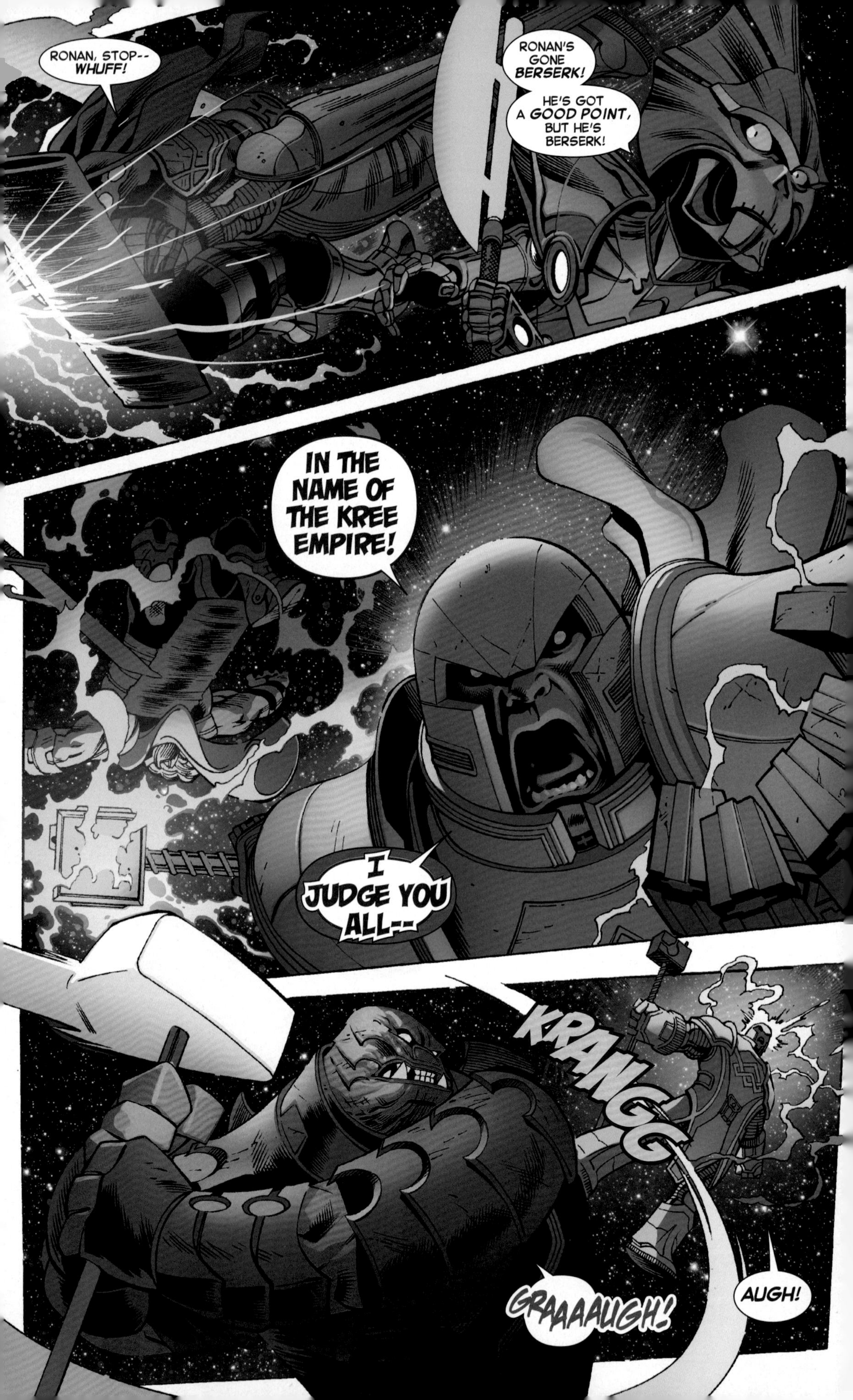
RONAN, STOP-- WHUFF!
RONAN'S GONE BERSERK!
HE'S GOT A GOOD POINT, BUT HE'S BERSERK!
IN THE NAME OF THE KREE EMPIRE!
I JUDGE YOU ALL--
KRANGG
GRAAAAUGH!
AUGH!

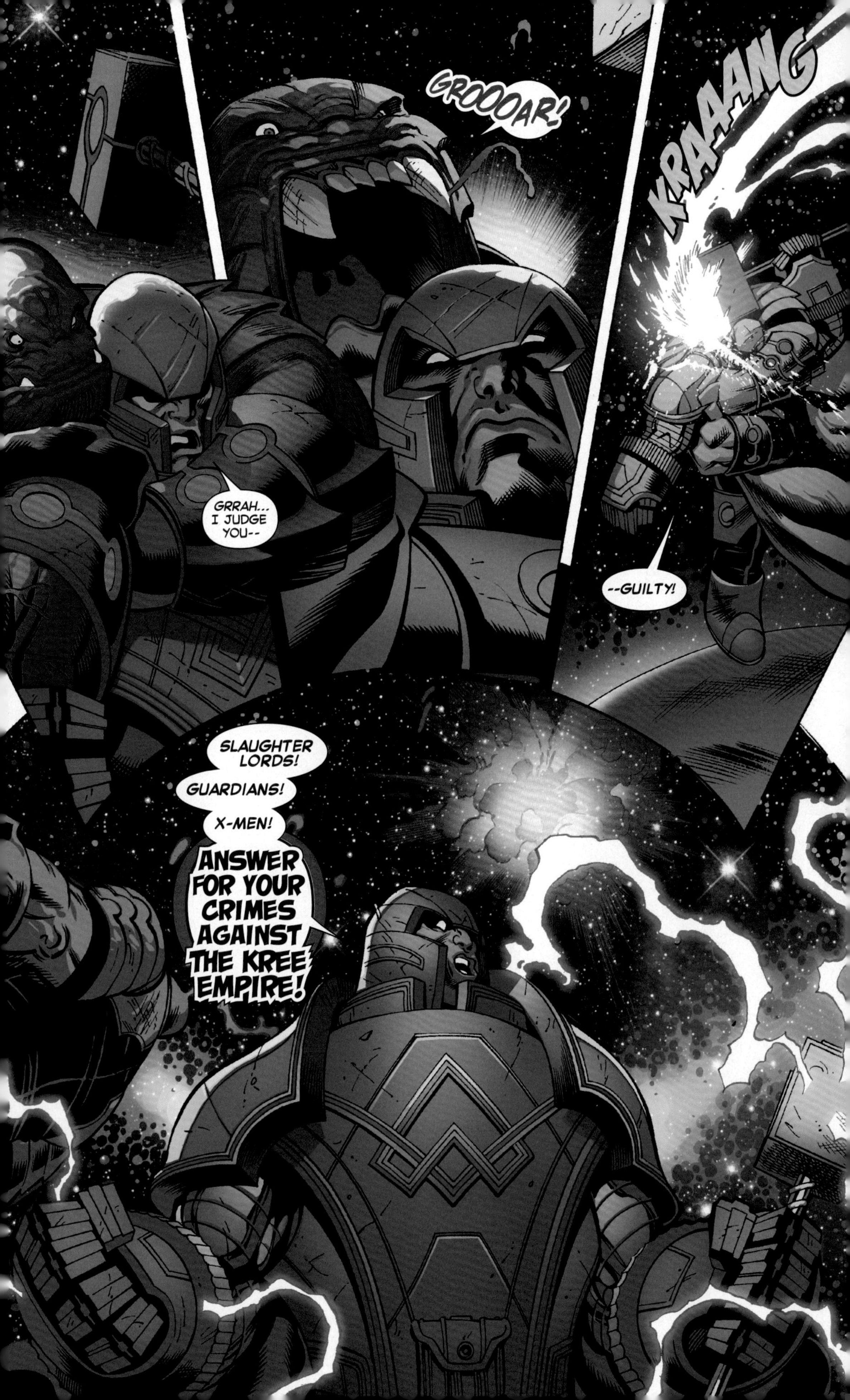
GROOOAR!
KRAAANG
GRRAH... I JUDGE YOU--
--GUILTY!
SLAUGHTER LORDS!
GUARDIANS!
X-MEN!
ANSWER FOR YOUR CRIMES AGAINST THE KREE EMPIRE!

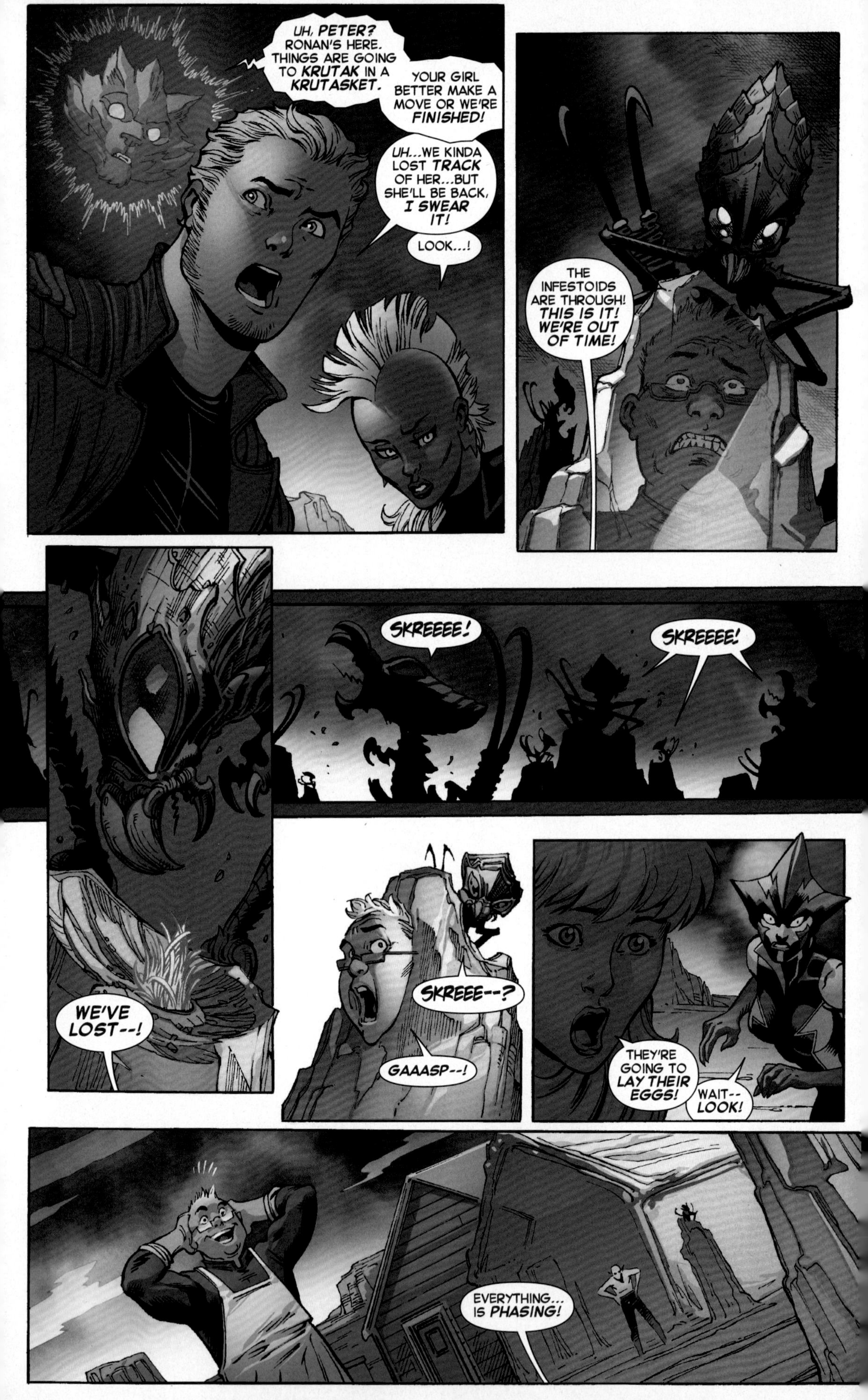
UH, PETER? RONAN'S HERE. THINGS ARE GOING TO KRUTAK IN A KRUTASKET.
YOUR GIRL BETTER MAKE A MOVE OR WE'RE FINISHED!
UH...WE KINDA LOST TRACK OF HER...BUT SHE'LL BE BACK, I SWEAR IT!
LOOK...!
THE INFESTOIDS ARE THROUGH! THIS IS IT! WE'RE OUT OF TIME!
SKREEEE!
SKREEEE!
WE'VE LOST--!
SKREEE--?
GAAASP--!
THEY'RE GOING TO LAY THEIR EGGS!
WAIT-- LOOK!
EVERYTHING... IS PHASING!

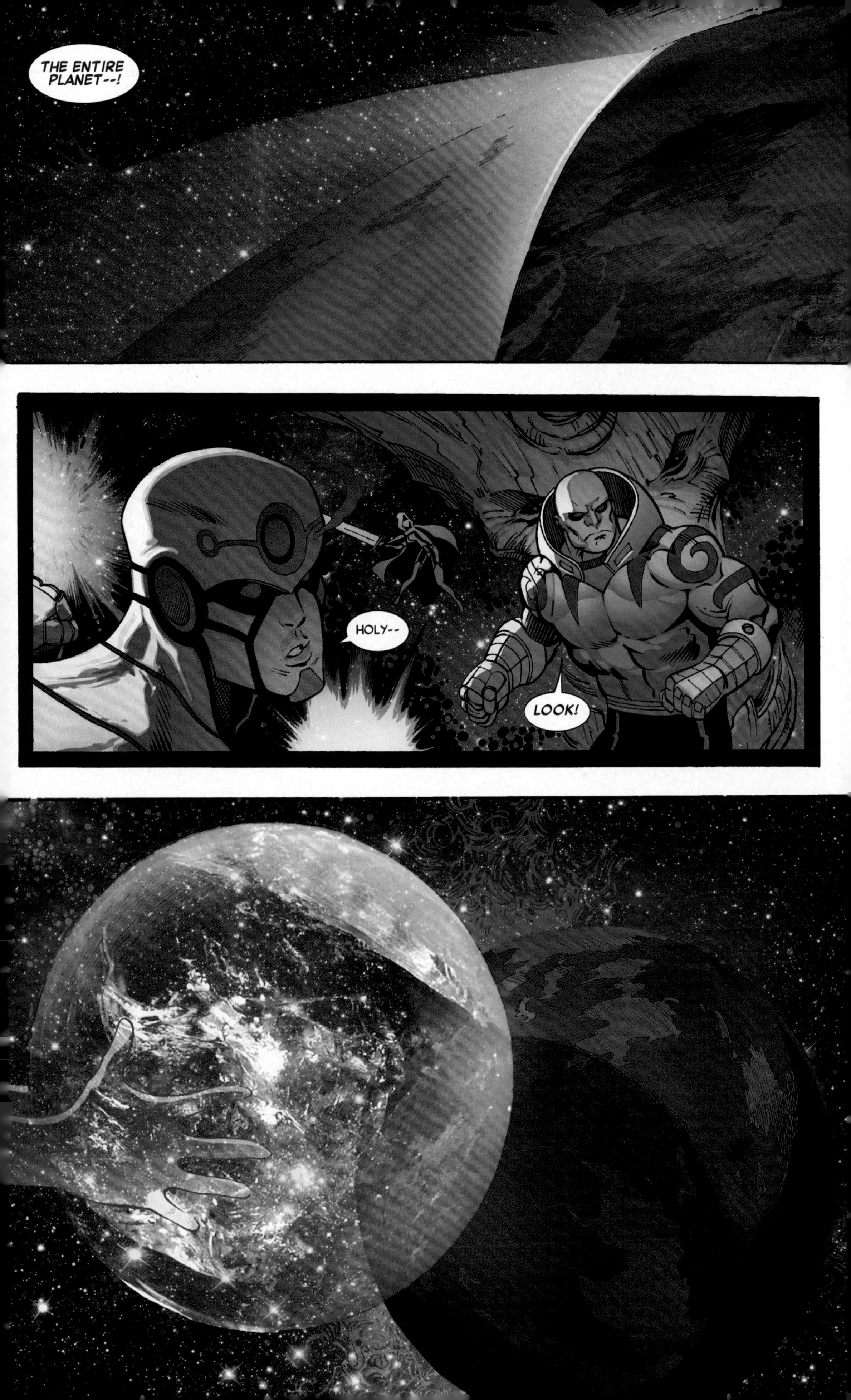
THE ENTIRE PLANET--!
HOLY--
LOOK!

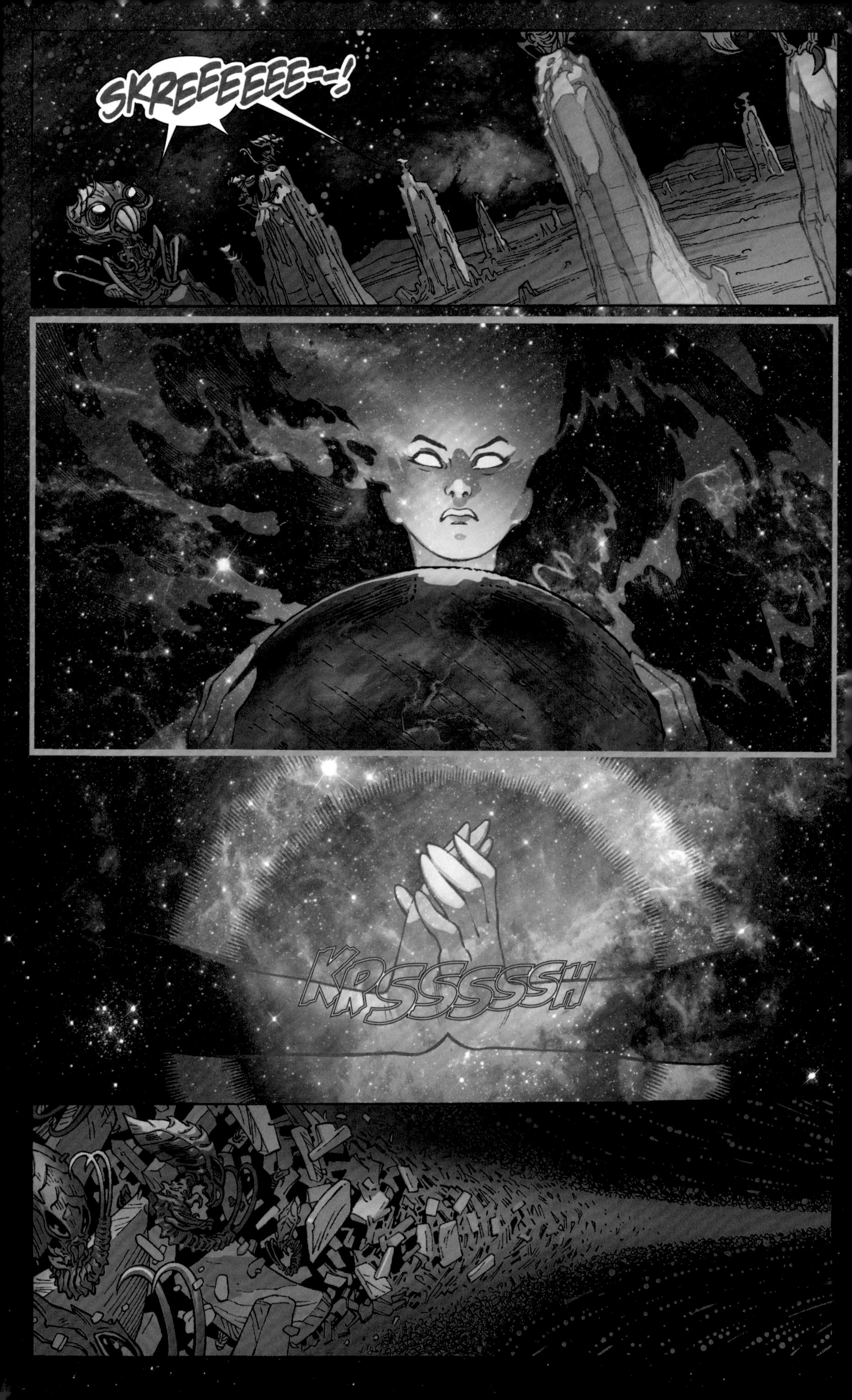
SKREEEEEEE--!
KRSSSSSSH

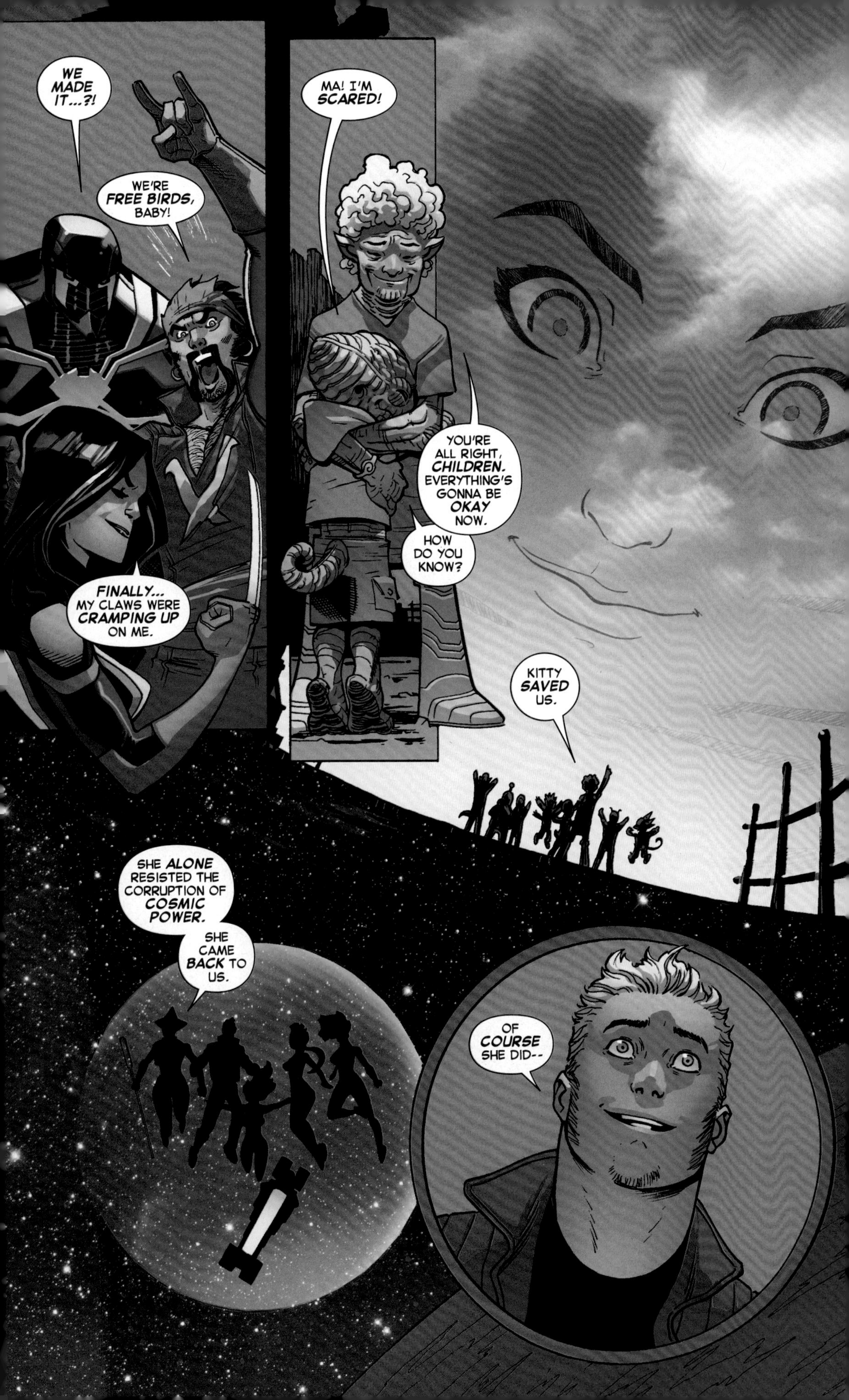
WE MADE IT...?!
WE'RE FREE BIRDS, BABY!
FINALLY... MY CLAWS WERE CRAMPING UP ON ME.
MA! I'M SCARED!
YOU'RE ALL RIGHT, CHILDREN. EVERYTHING'S GONNA BE OKAY NOW.
HOW DO YOU KNOW?
KITTY SAVED US.
SHE ALONE RESISTED THE CORRUPTION OF COSMIC POWER.
SHE CAME BACK TO US.
OF COURSE SHE DID--

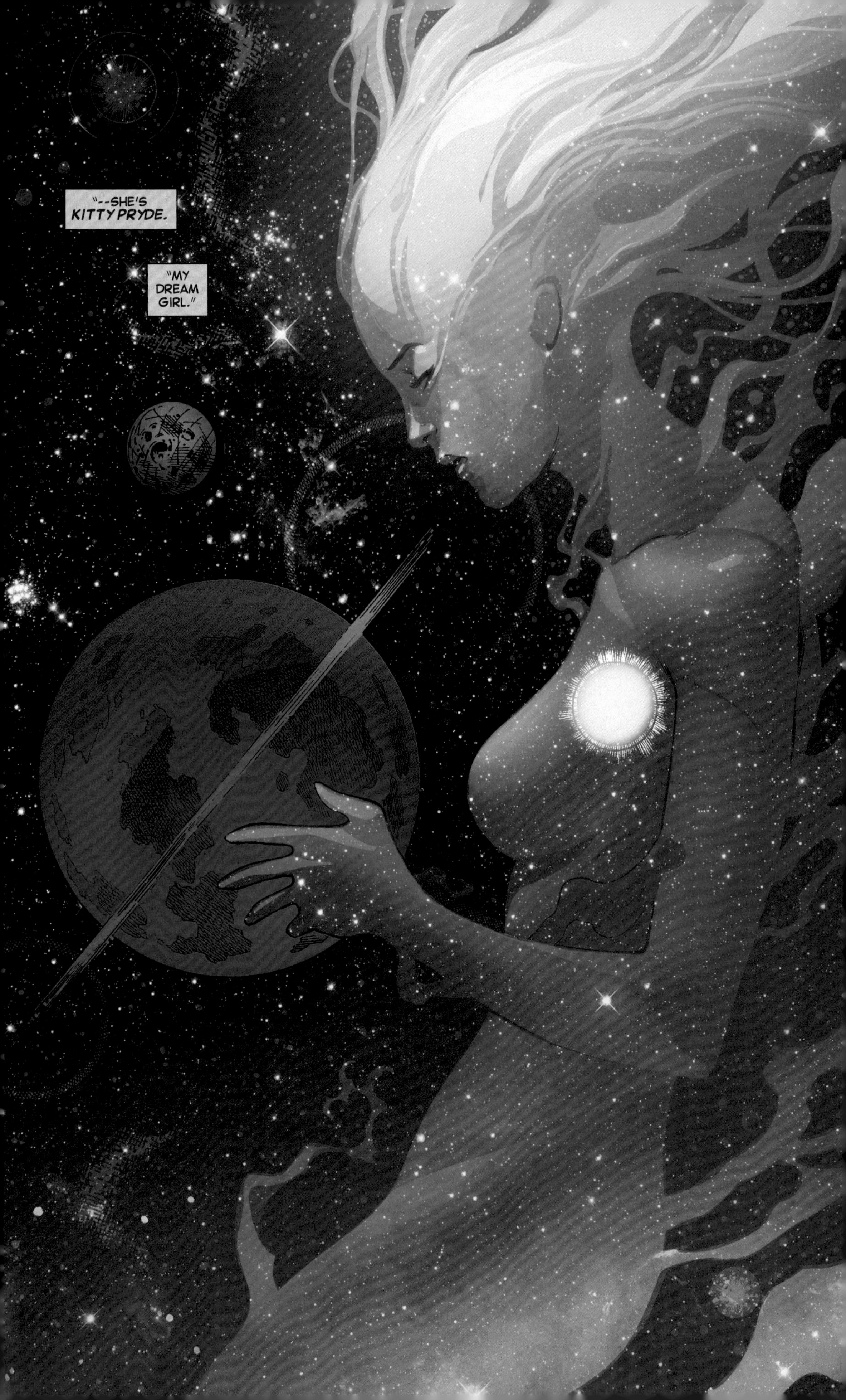
"--SHE'S KITTY PRYDE.
"MY DREAM GIRL."

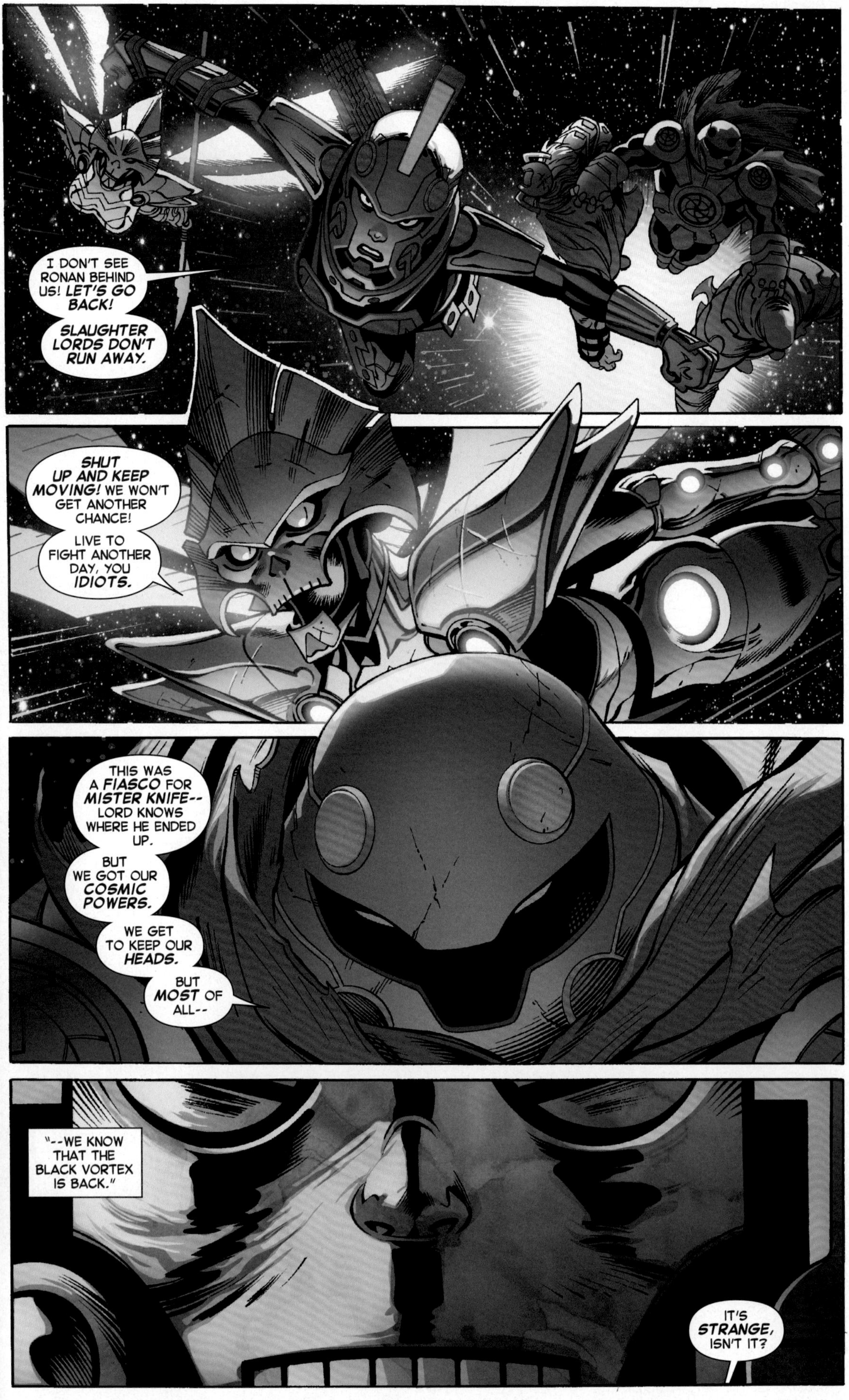
I DON'T SEE RONAN BEHIND US! LET'S GO BACK!
SLAUGHTER LORDS DON'T RUN AWAY.
SHUT UP AND KEEP MOVING! WE WON'T GET ANOTHER CHANCE!
LIVE TO FIGHT ANOTHER DAY, YOU IDIOTS.
THIS WAS A FIASCO FOR MISTER KNIFE-- LORD KNOWS WHERE HE ENDED UP.
BUT WE GOT OUR COSMIC POWERS.
WE GET TO KEEP OUR HEADS.
BUT MOST OF ALL--
"--WE KNOW THAT THE BLACK VORTEX IS BACK."
IT'S STRANGE, ISN'T IT?

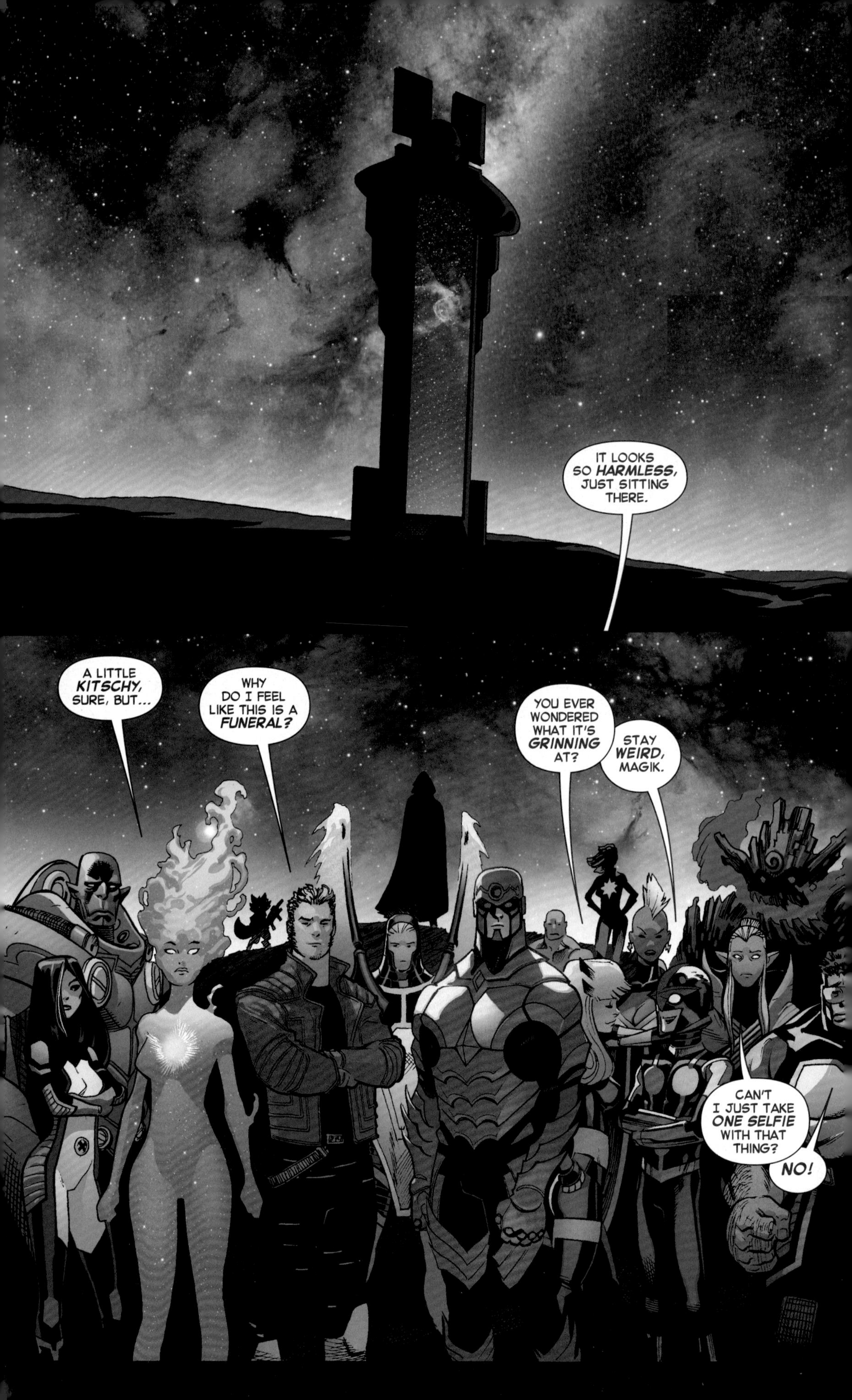
IT LOOKS SO HARMLESS, JUST SITTING THERE.
A LITTLE KITSCHY, SURE, BUT...
WHY DO I FEEL LIKE THIS IS A FUNERAL?
YOU EVER WONDERED WHAT IT'S GRINNING AT?
STAY WEIRD, MAGIK.
CAN'T I JUST TAKE ONE SELFIE WITH THAT THING?
NO!

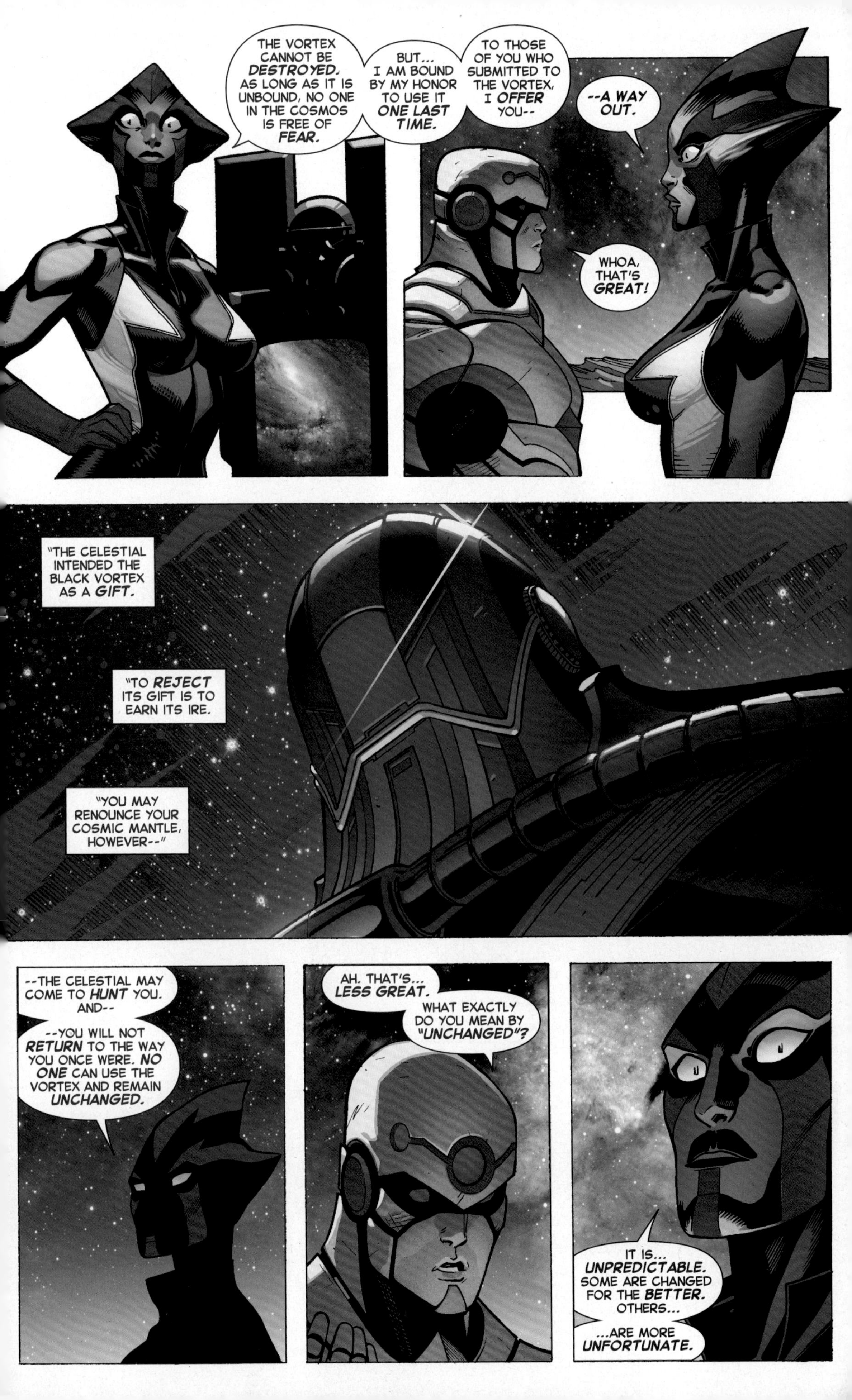

THE VORTEX CANNOT BE DESTROYED. AS LONG AS IT IS UNBOUND, NO ONE IN THE COSMOS IS FREE OF FEAR.
BUT... I AM BOUND BY MY HONOR TO USE IT ONE LAST TIME.
TO THOSE OF YOU WHO SUBMITTED TO THE VORTEX, I OFFER YOU--
--A WAY OUT.
WHOA, THAT'S GREAT!
"THE CELESTIAL INTENDED THE BLACK VORTEX AS A GIFT.
"TO REJECT ITS GIFT IS TO EARN ITS IRE.
"YOU MAY RENOUNCE YOUR COSMIC MANTLE, HOWEVER--"
--THE CELESTIAL MAY COME TO HUNT YOU. AND--
--YOU WILL NOT RETURN TO THE WAY YOU ONCE WERE. NO ONE CAN USE THE VORTEX AND REMAIN UNCHANGED.
AH. THAT'S... LESS GREAT.
WHAT EXACTLY DO YOU MEAN BY "UNCHANGED"?
IT IS... UNPREDICTABLE. SOME ARE CHANGED FOR THE BETTER. OTHERS...
...ARE MORE UNFORTUNATE.

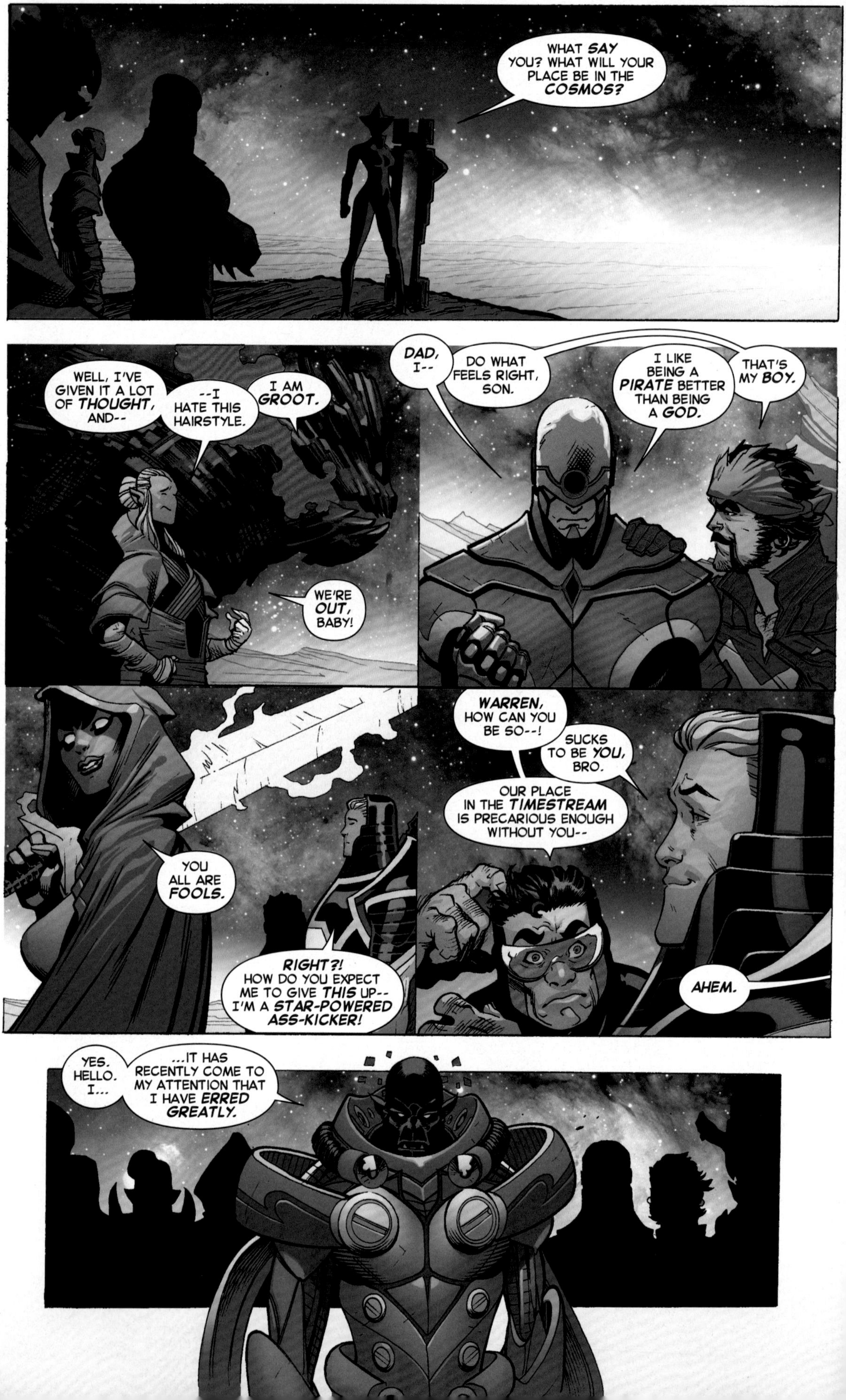
WHAT SAY YOU? WHAT WILL YOUR PLACE BE IN THE COSMOS?
WELL, I'VE GIVEN IT A LOT OF THOUGHT, AND--
--I HATE THIS HAIRSTYLE.
I AM GROOT.
WE'RE OUT, BABY!
DAD, I--
DO WHAT FEELS RIGHT, SON.
I LIKE BEING A PIRATE BETTER THAN BEING A GOD.
THAT'S MY BOY.
YOU ALL ARE FOOLS.
RIGHT?! HOW DO YOU EXPECT ME TO GIVE THIS UP-- I'M A STAR-POWERED ASS-KICKER!
WARREN, HOW CAN YOU BE SO--!
SUCKS TO BE YOU, BRO.
OUR PLACE IN THE TIMESTREAM IS PRECARIOUS ENOUGH WITHOUT YOU--
AHEM.
YES. HELLO. I...
...IT HAS RECENTLY COME TO MY ATTENTION THAT I HAVE ERRED GREATLY.

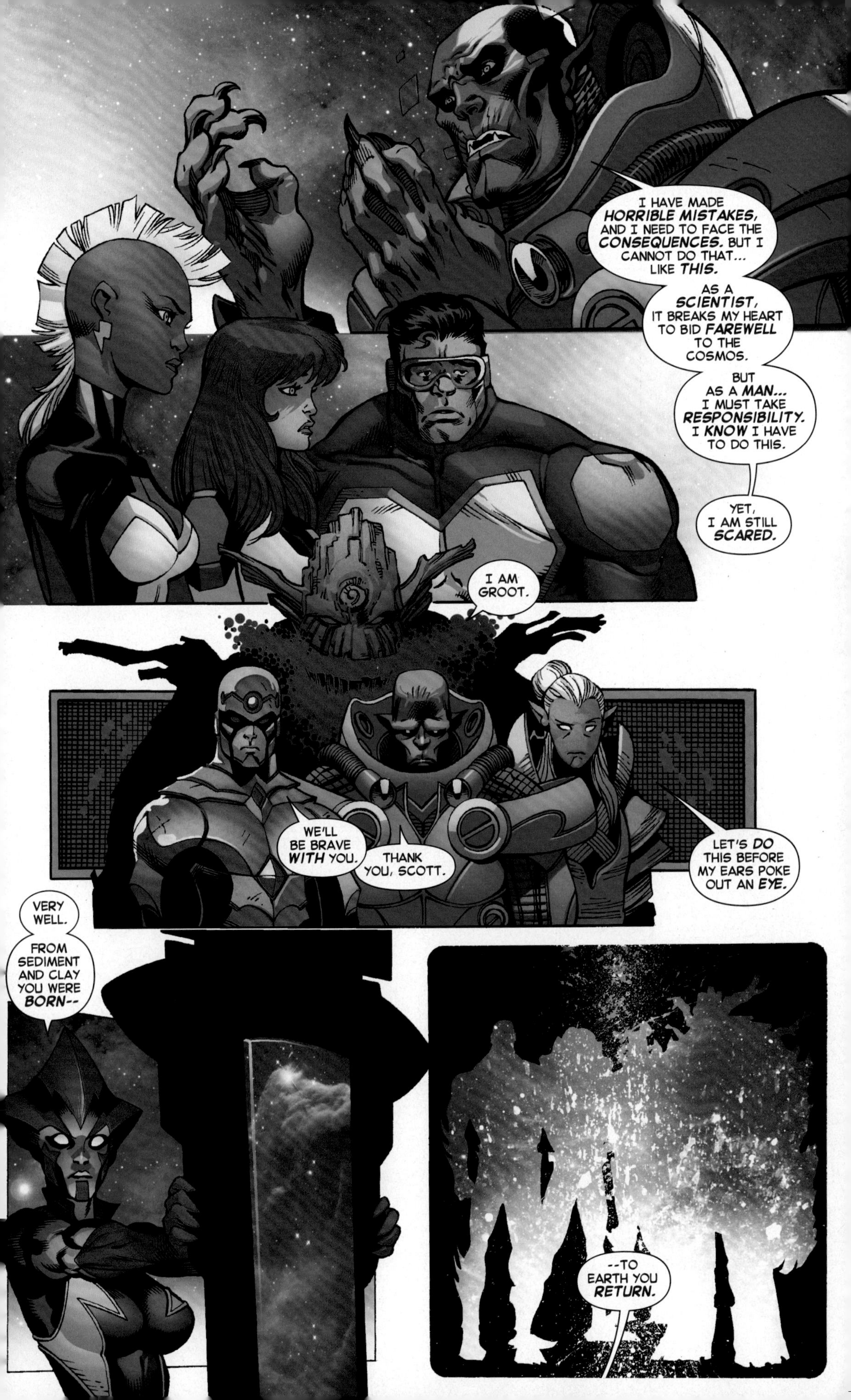

I HAVE MADE HORRIBLE MISTAKES, AND I NEED TO FACE THE CONSEQUENCES. BUT I CANNOT DO THAT... LIKE THIS.
AS A SCIENTIST, IT BREAKS MY HEART TO BID FAREWELL TO THE COSMOS.
BUT AS A MAN... I MUST TAKE RESPONSIBILITY. I KNOW I HAVE TO DO THIS.
YET, I AM STILL SCARED.
I AM GROOT.
WE'LL BE BRAVE WITH YOU.
THANK YOU, SCOTT.
LET'S DO THIS BEFORE MY EARS POKE OUT AN EYE.
VERY WELL.
FROM SEDIMENT AND CLAY YOU WERE BORN--
--TO EARTH YOU RETURN.

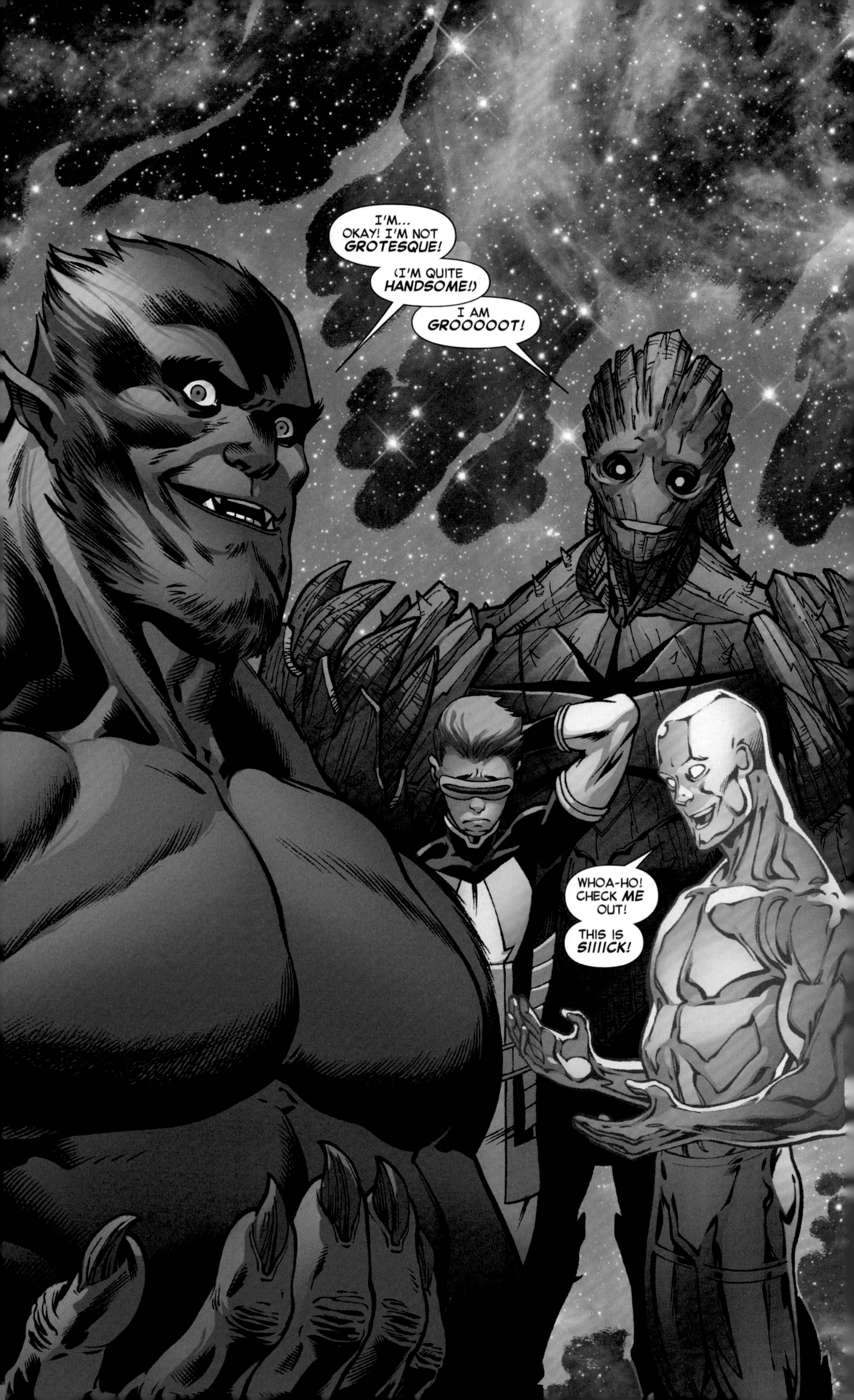
I'M... OKAY! I'M NOT GROTESQUE!
(I'M QUITE HANDSOME!)
I AM GROOOOOT!
WHOA-HO! CHECK ME OUT!
THIS IS SIIIICK!

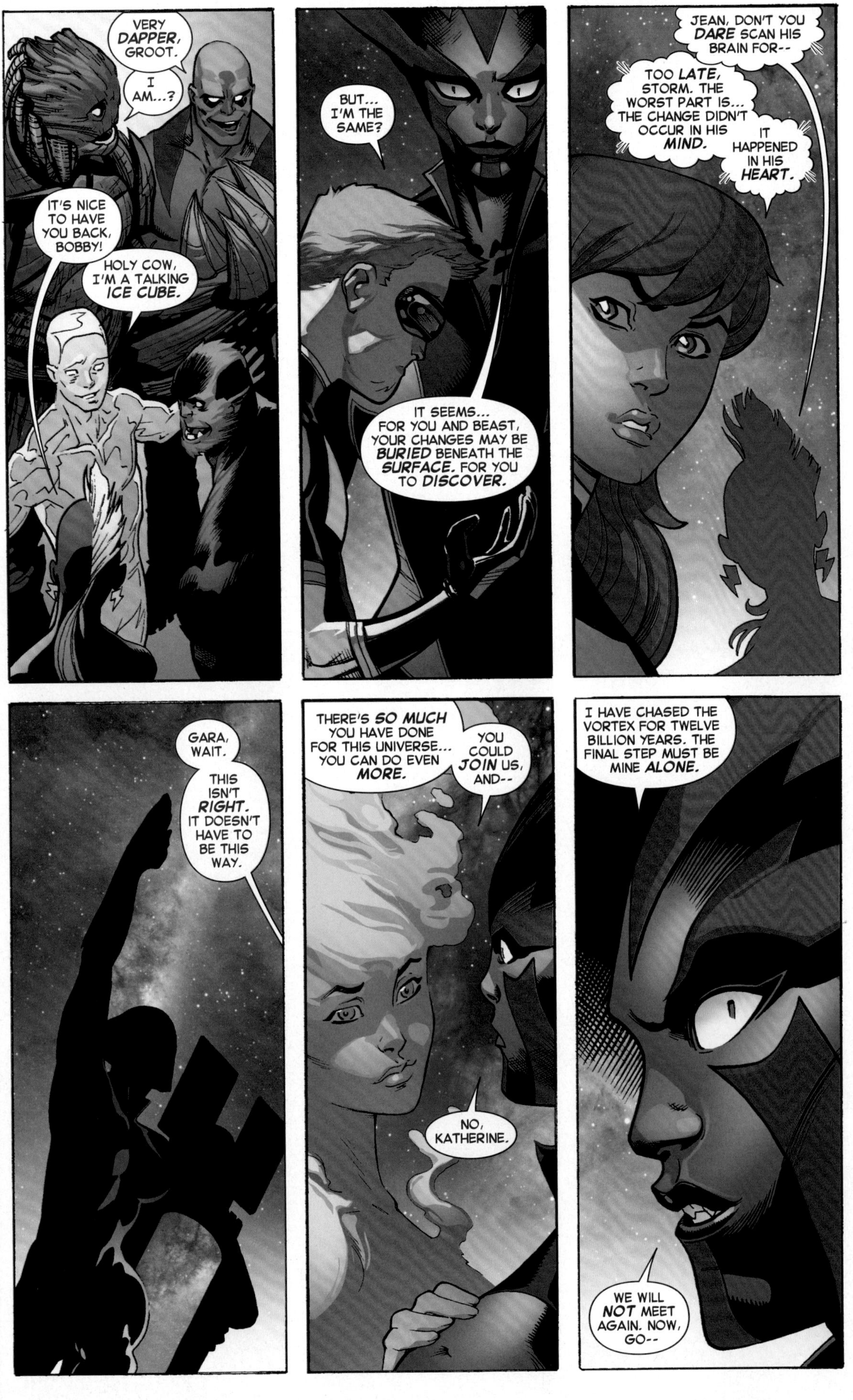
VERY DAPPER, GROOT.
I AM...?
IT'S NICE TO HAVE YOU BACK, BOBBY!
HOLY COW, I'M A TALKING ICE CUBE.
BUT... I'M THE SAME?
IT SEEMS... FOR YOU AND BEAST, YOUR CHANGES MAY BE BURIED BENEATH THE SURFACE. FOR YOU TO DISCOVER.
JEAN, DON'T YOU DARE SCAN HIS BRAIN FOR--
TOO LATE, STORM. THE WORST PART IS... THE CHANGE DIDN'T OCCUR IN HIS MIND.
IT HAPPENED IN HIS HEART.
GARA, WAIT.
THIS ISN'T RIGHT. IT DOESN'T HAVE TO BE THIS WAY.
THERE'S SO MUCH YOU HAVE DONE FOR THIS UNIVERSE... YOU CAN DO EVEN MORE.
YOU COULD JOIN US, AND--
NO, KATHERINE.
I HAVE CHASED THE VORTEX FOR TWELVE BILLION YEARS. THE FINAL STEP MUST BE MINE ALONE.
WE WILL NOT MEET AGAIN. NOW, GO--

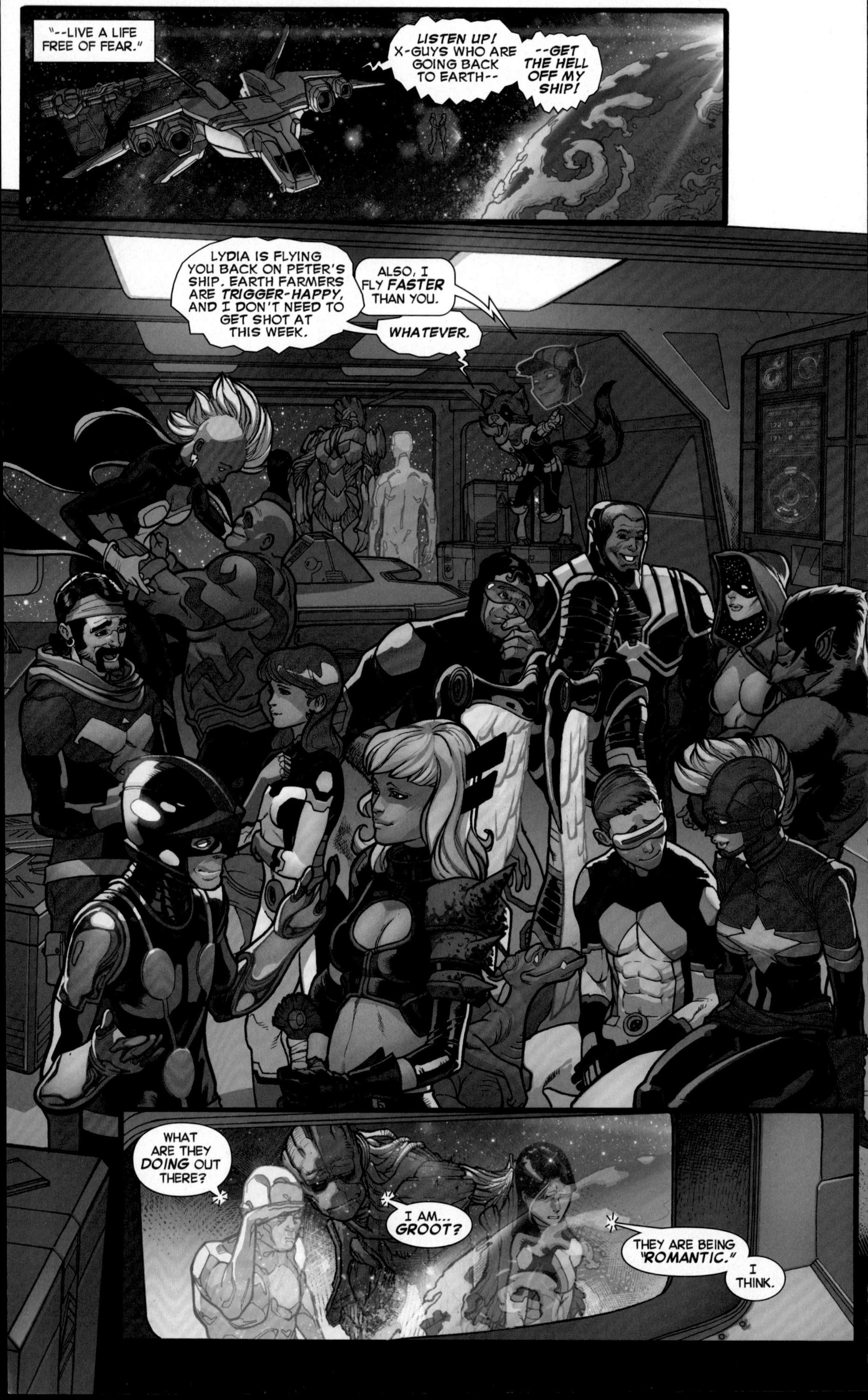
"--LIVE A LIFE FREE OF FEAR."
LISTEN UP! X-GUYS WHO ARE GOING BACK TO EARTH--
--GET THE HELL OFF MY SHIP!
LYDIA IS FLYING YOU BACK ON PETER'S SHIP. EARTH FARMERS ARE TRIGGER-HAPPY, AND I DON'T NEED TO GET SHOT AT THIS WEEK.
ALSO, I FLY FASTER THAN YOU.
WHATEVER.
WHAT ARE THEY DOING OUT THERE?
I AM... GROOT?
THEY ARE BEING "ROMANTIC."
I THINK.

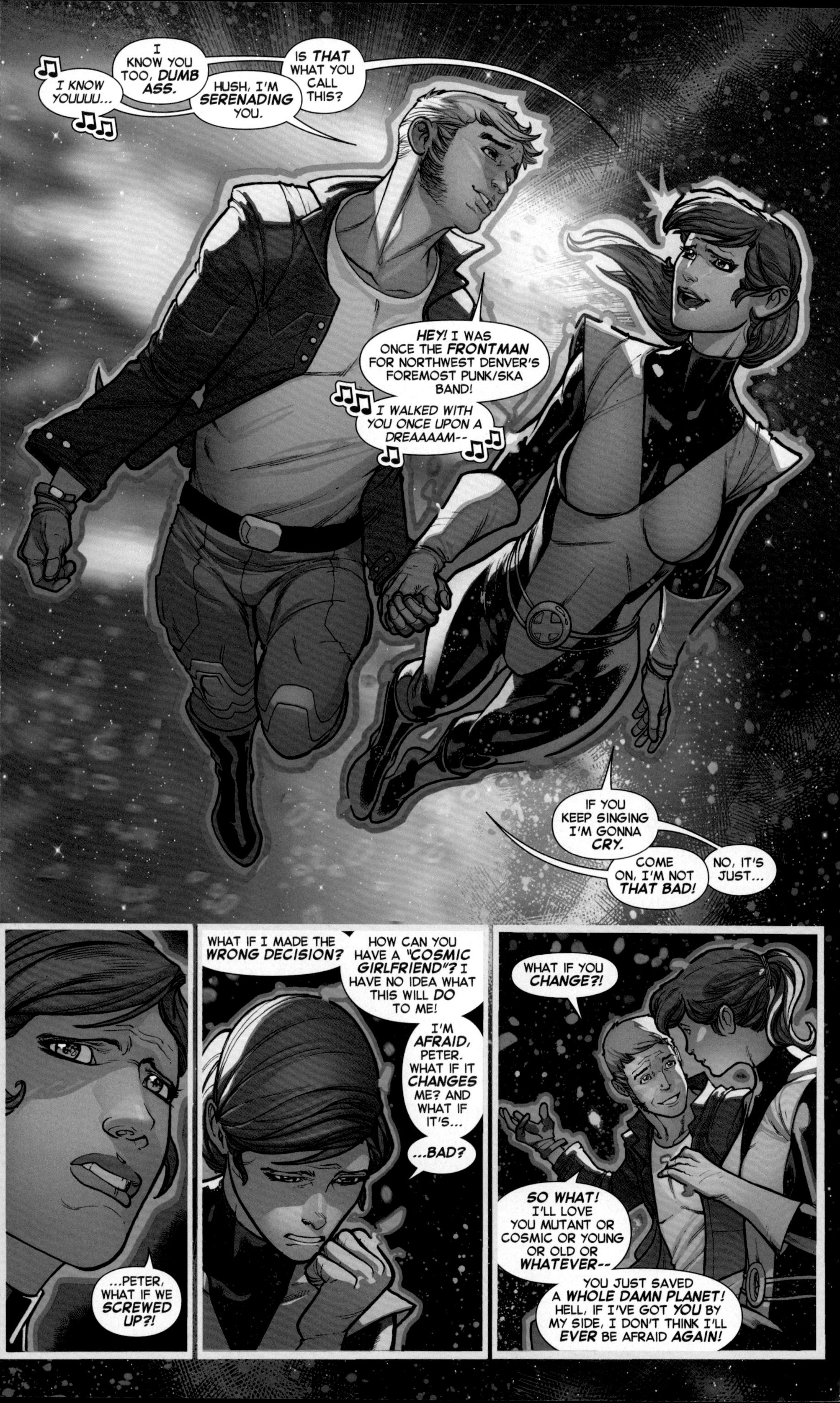
I KNOW YOUUUU...
I KNOW YOU TOO, DUMB ASS.
HUSH, I'M SERENADING YOU.
IS THAT WHAT YOU CALL THIS?
HEY! I WAS ONCE THE FRONTMAN FOR NORTHWEST DENVER'S FOREMOST PUNK/SKA BAND!
I WALKED WITH YOU ONCE UPON A DREAAAAM--
IF YOU KEEP SINGING I'M GONNA CRY.
COME ON, I'M NOT THAT BAD!
NO, IT'S JUST...
...PETER, WHAT IF WE SCREWED UP?!
WHAT IF I MADE THE WRONG DECISION?
HOW CAN YOU HAVE A "COSMIC GIRLFRIEND"? I HAVE NO IDEA WHAT THIS WILL DO TO ME!
I'M AFRAID, PETER. WHAT IF IT CHANGES ME? AND WHAT IF IT'S...
...BAD?
WHAT IF YOU CHANGE?!
SO WHAT! I'LL LOVE YOU MUTANT OR COSMIC OR YOUNG OR OLD OR WHATEVER--
YOU JUST SAVED A WHOLE DAMN PLANET! HELL, IF I'VE GOT YOU BY MY SIDE, I DON'T THINK I'LL EVER BE AFRAID AGAIN!

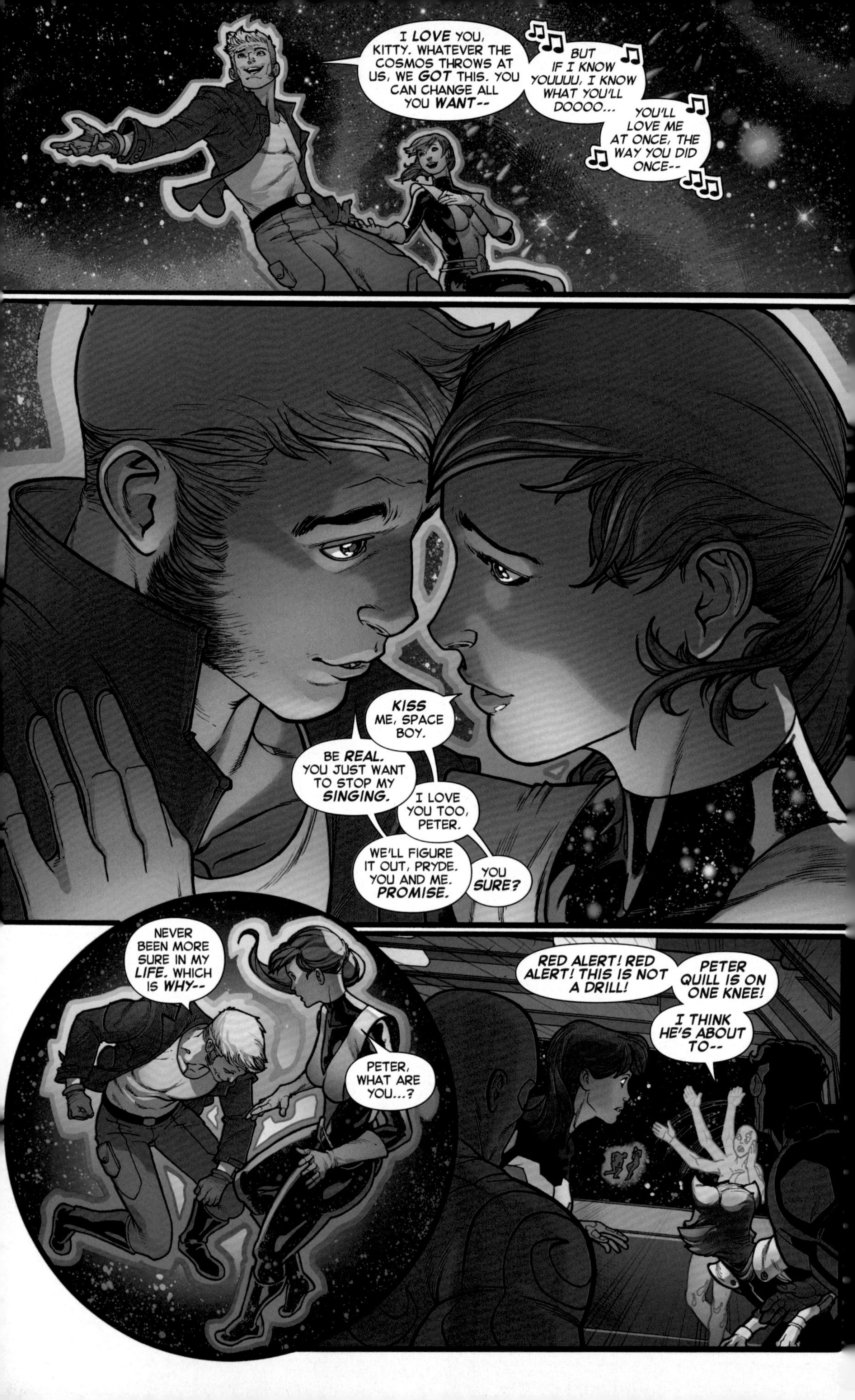

I LOVE YOU, KITTY. WHATEVER THE COSMOS THROWS AT US, WE GOT THIS. YOU CAN CHANGE ALL YOU WANT--
BUT IF I KNOW YOUUUU, I KNOW WHAT YOU'LL DOOOO...
YOU'LL LOVE ME AT ONCE, THE WAY YOU DID ONCE--
KISS ME, SPACE BOY.
BE REAL. YOU JUST WANT TO STOP MY SINGING.
I LOVE YOU TOO, PETER.
WE'LL FIGURE IT OUT, PRYDE. YOU AND ME. PROMISE.
YOU SURE?
NEVER BEEN MORE SURE IN MY LIFE. WHICH IS WHY--
PETER, WHAT ARE YOU...?
RED ALERT! RED ALERT! THIS IS NOT A DRILL!
PETER QUILL IS ON ONE KNEE!
I THINK HE'S ABOUT TO--

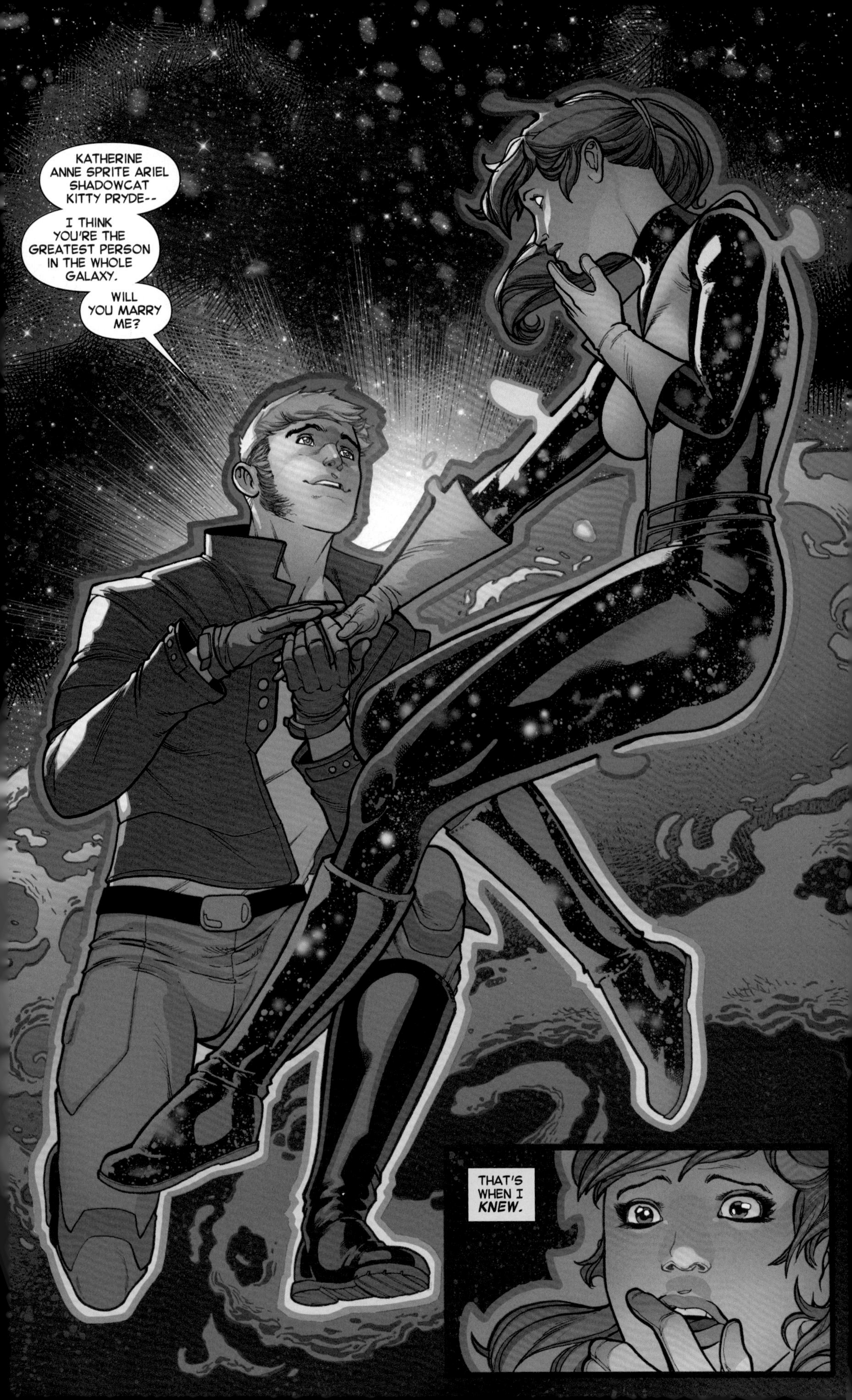
KATHERINE ANNE SPRITE ARIEL SHADOWCAT KITTY PRYDE--
I THINK YOU'RE THE GREATEST PERSON IN THE WHOLE GALAXY.
WILL YOU MARRY ME?
THAT'S WHEN I *KNEW.*

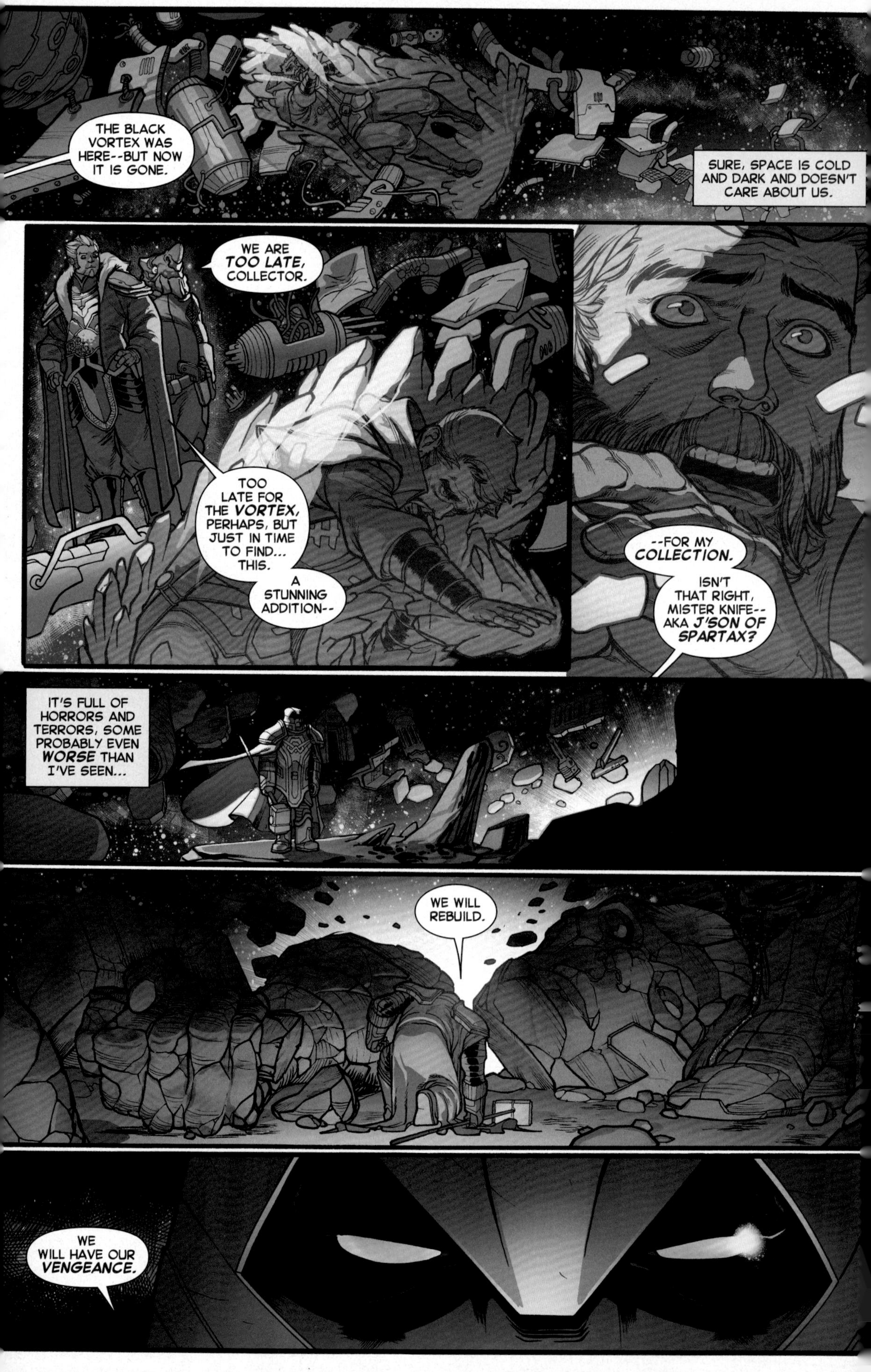
THE BLACK VORTEX WAS HERE--BUT NOW IT IS GONE.
SURE, SPACE IS COLD AND DARK AND DOESN'T CARE ABOUT US.
WE ARE TOO LATE, COLLECTOR.
TOO LATE FOR THE VORTEX, PERHAPS, BUT JUST IN TIME TO FIND... THIS.
A STUNNING ADDITION--
--FOR MY COLLECTION.
ISN'T THAT RIGHT, MISTER KNIFE--AKA J'SON OF SPARTAX?
IT'S FULL OF HORRORS AND TERRORS, SOME PROBABLY EVEN WORSE THAN I'VE SEEN...
WE WILL REBUILD.
WE WILL HAVE OUR VENGEANCE.

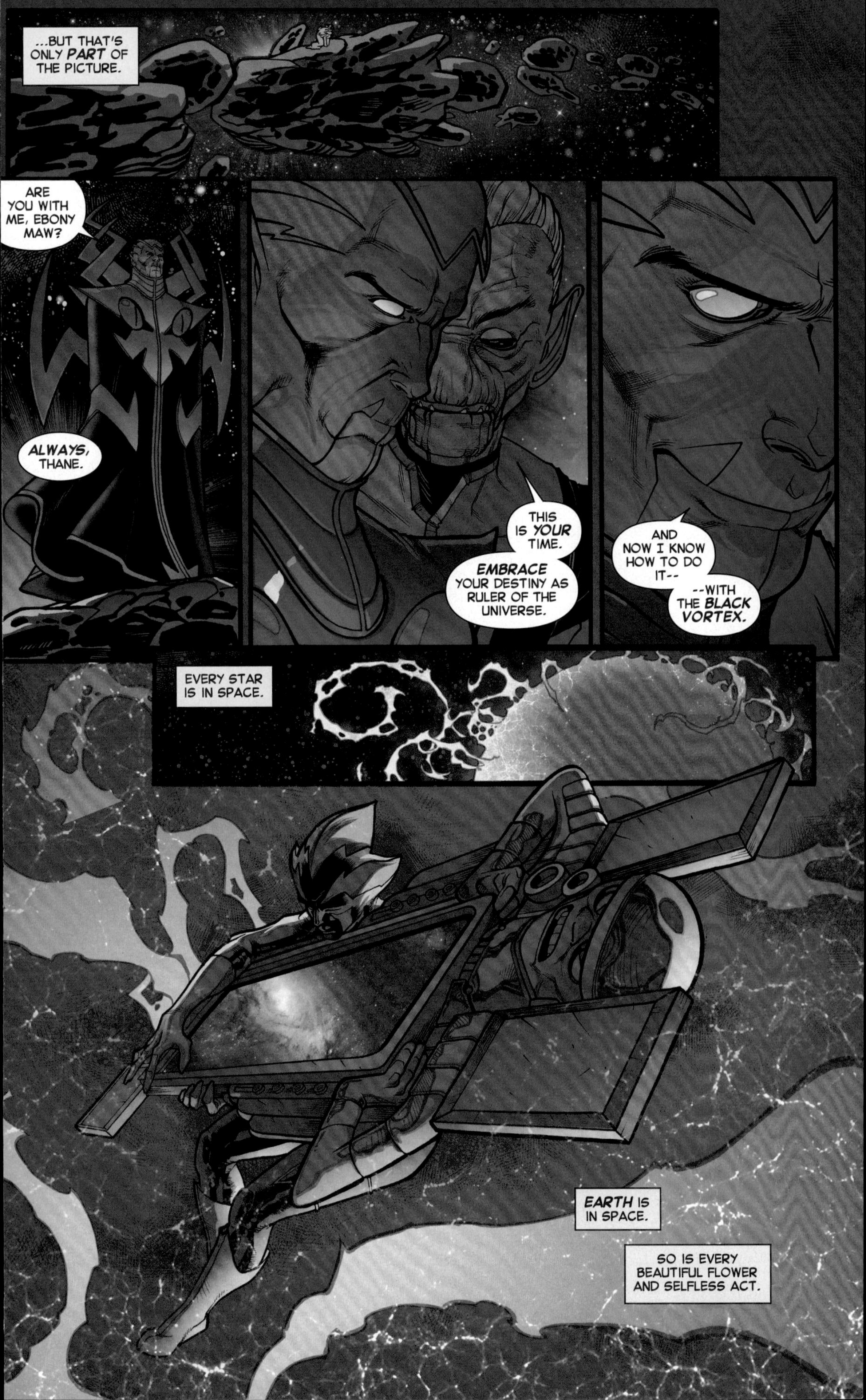
...BUT THAT'S ONLY PART OF THE PICTURE.
ARE YOU WITH ME, EBONY MAW?
ALWAYS, THANE.
THIS IS YOUR TIME.
EMBRACE YOUR DESTINY AS RULER OF THE UNIVERSE.
AND NOW I KNOW HOW TO DO IT--
--WITH THE BLACK VORTEX.
EVERY STAR IS IN SPACE.
EARTH IS IN SPACE.
SO IS EVERY BEAUTIFUL FLOWER AND SELFLESS ACT.

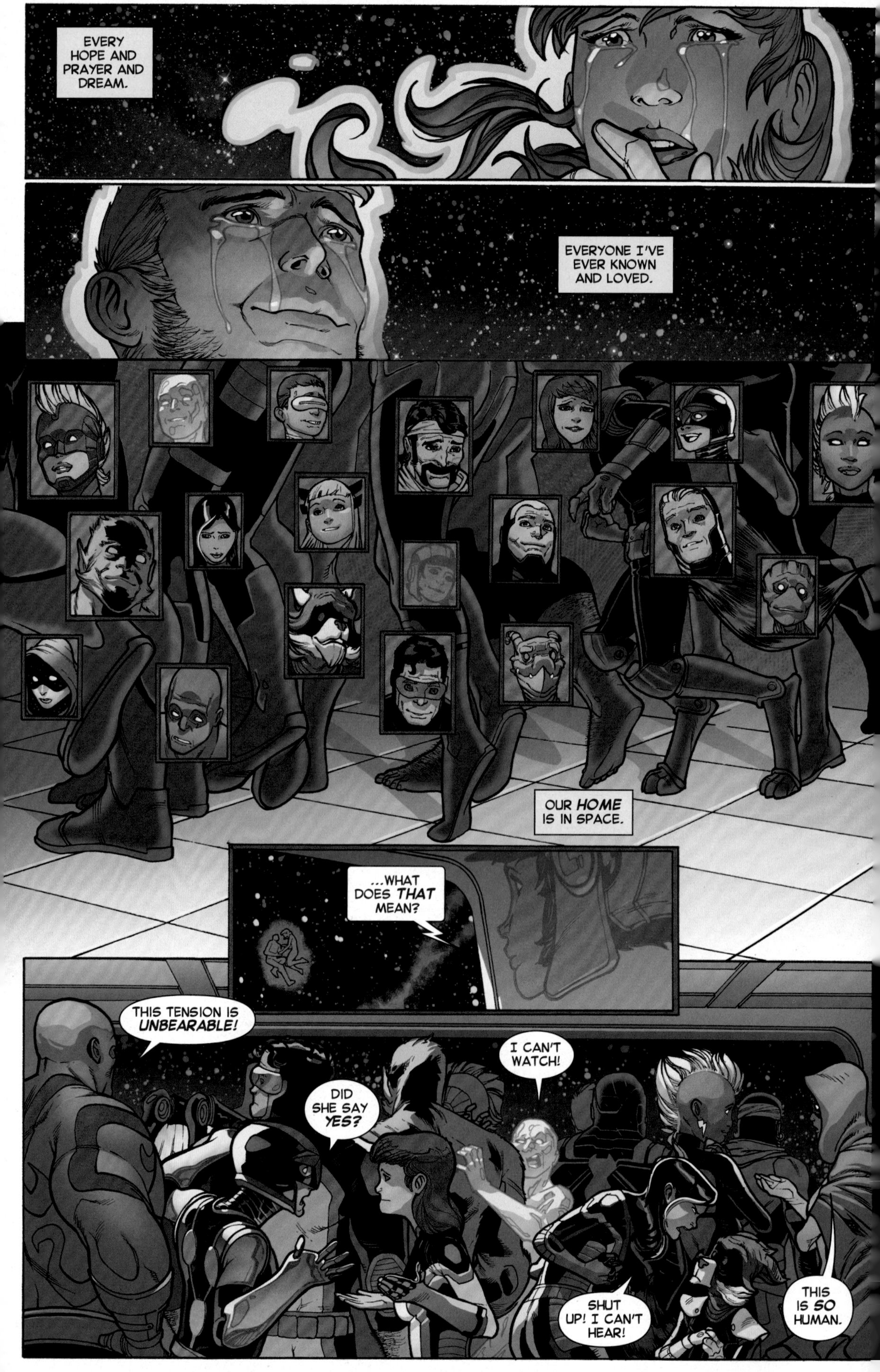

EVERY HOPE AND PRAYER AND DREAM.
EVERYONE I'VE EVER KNOWN AND LOVED.
OUR *HOME* IS IN SPACE.
...WHAT DOES *THAT* MEAN?
THIS TENSION IS *UNBEARABLE!*
DID SHE SAY *YES?*
I CAN'T WATCH!
SHUT UP! I CAN'T HEAR!
THIS IS *SO* HUMAN.

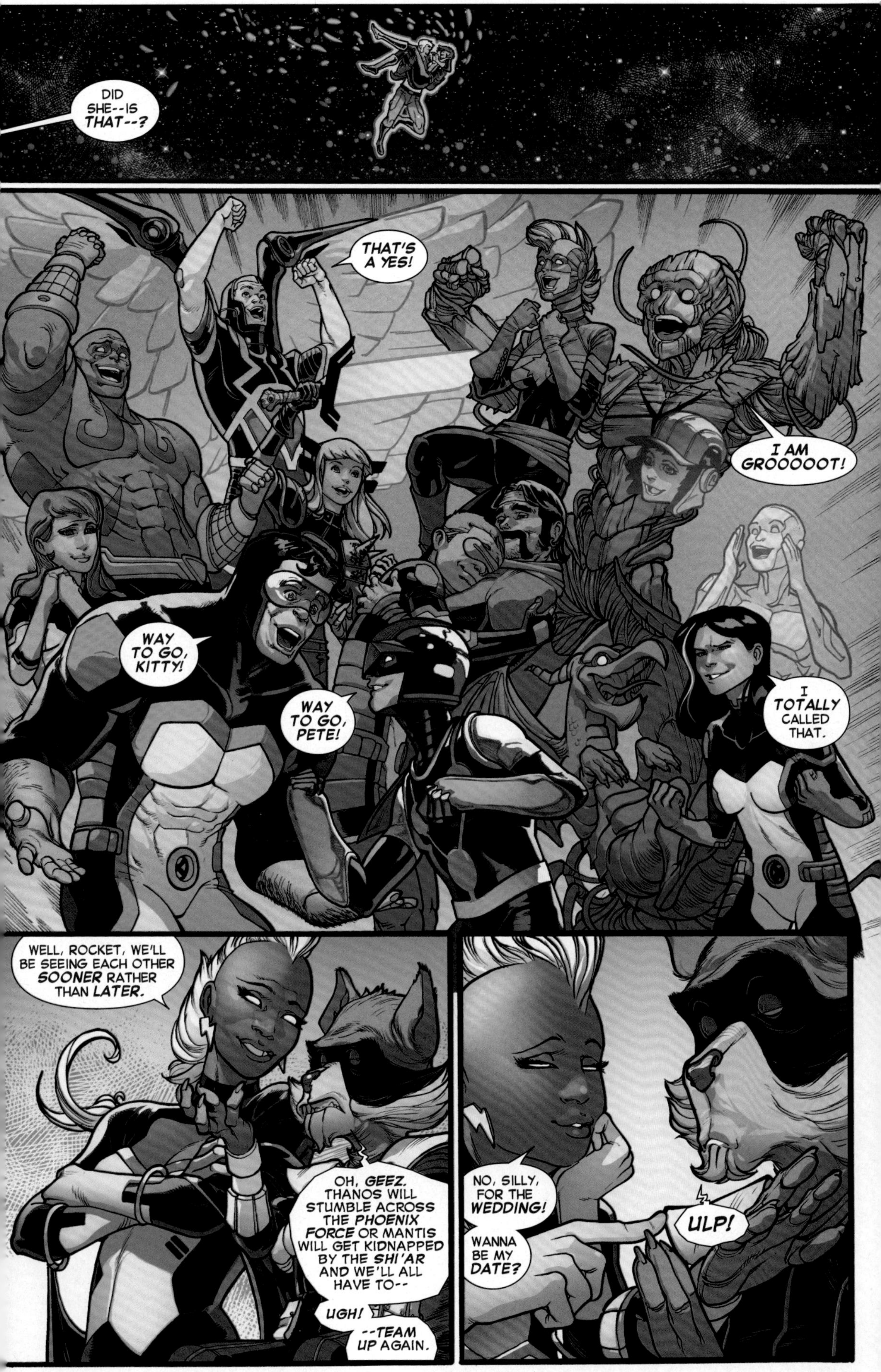
DID SHE--IS THAT--?
THAT'S A YES!
I AM GROOOOOT!
WAY TO GO, KITTY!
WAY TO GO, PETE!
I TOTALLY CALLED THAT.
WELL, ROCKET, WE'LL BE SEEING EACH OTHER SOONER RATHER THAN LATER.
OH, GEEZ. THANOS WILL STUMBLE ACROSS THE PHOENIX FORCE OR MANTIS WILL GET KIDNAPPED BY THE SHI'AR AND WE'LL ALL HAVE TO--
UGH!
--TEAM UP AGAIN.
NO, SILLY, FOR THE WEDDING!
WANNA BE MY DATE?
ULP!

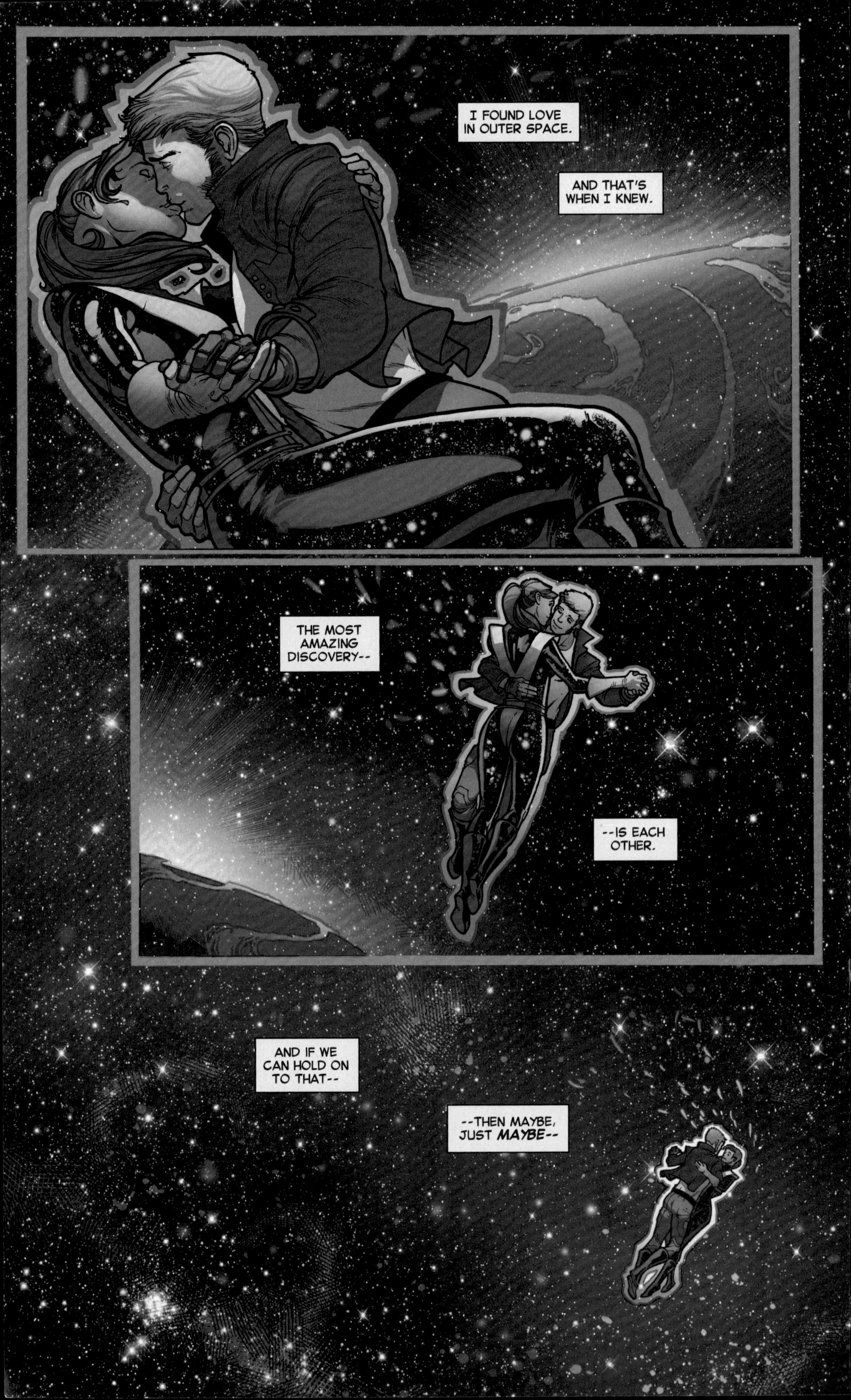
I FOUND LOVE IN OUTER SPACE.
AND THAT'S WHEN I KNEW.
THE MOST AMAZING DISCOVERY--
--IS EACH OTHER.
AND IF WE CAN HOLD ON TO THAT--
--THEN MAYBE, JUST *MAYBE*--

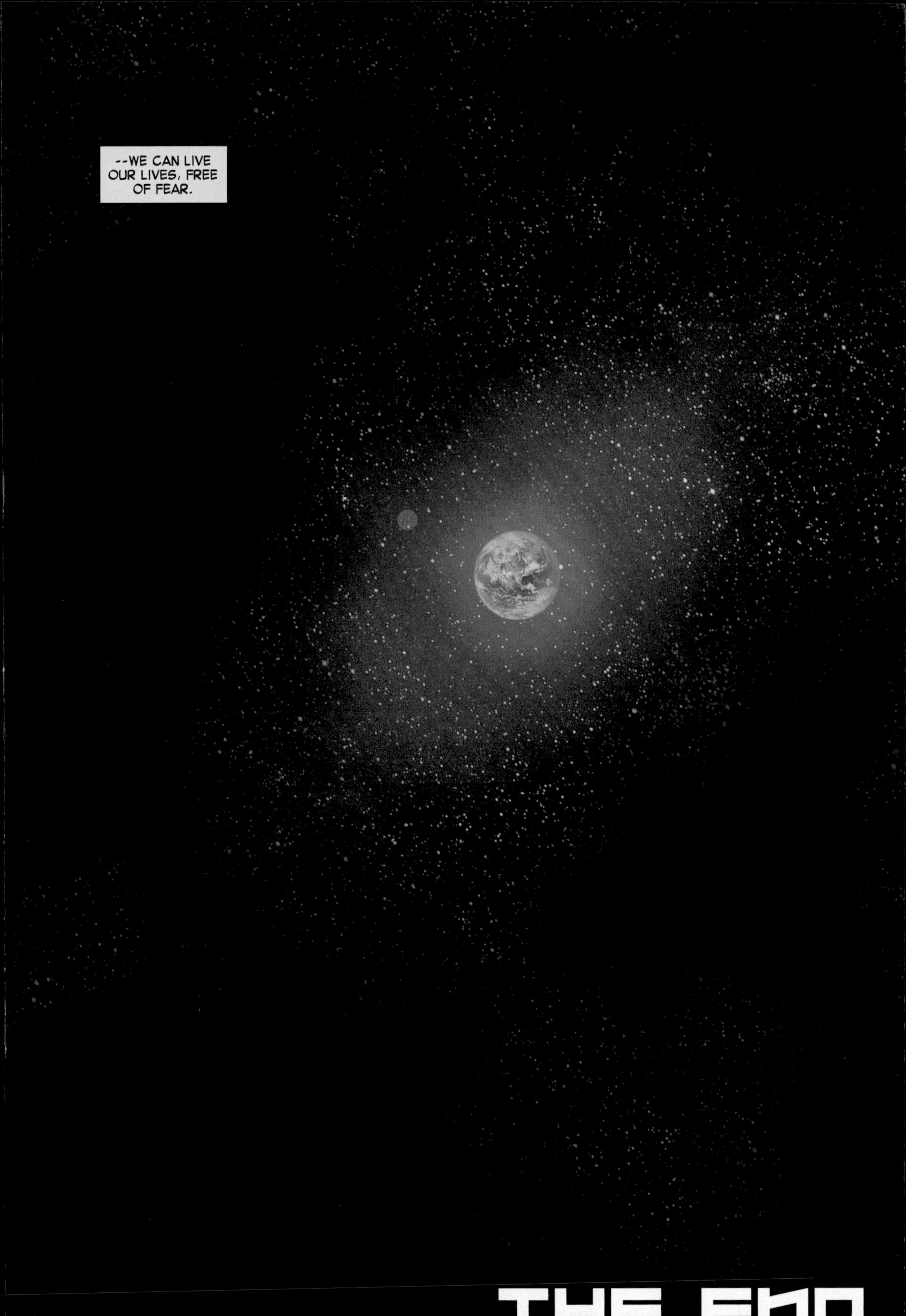
--WE CAN LIVE OUR LIVES, FREE OF FEAR.

THE END

GET THE FULL STORY IN
GUARDIANS OF THE GALAXY & X-MEN: THE BLACK VORTEX HC!

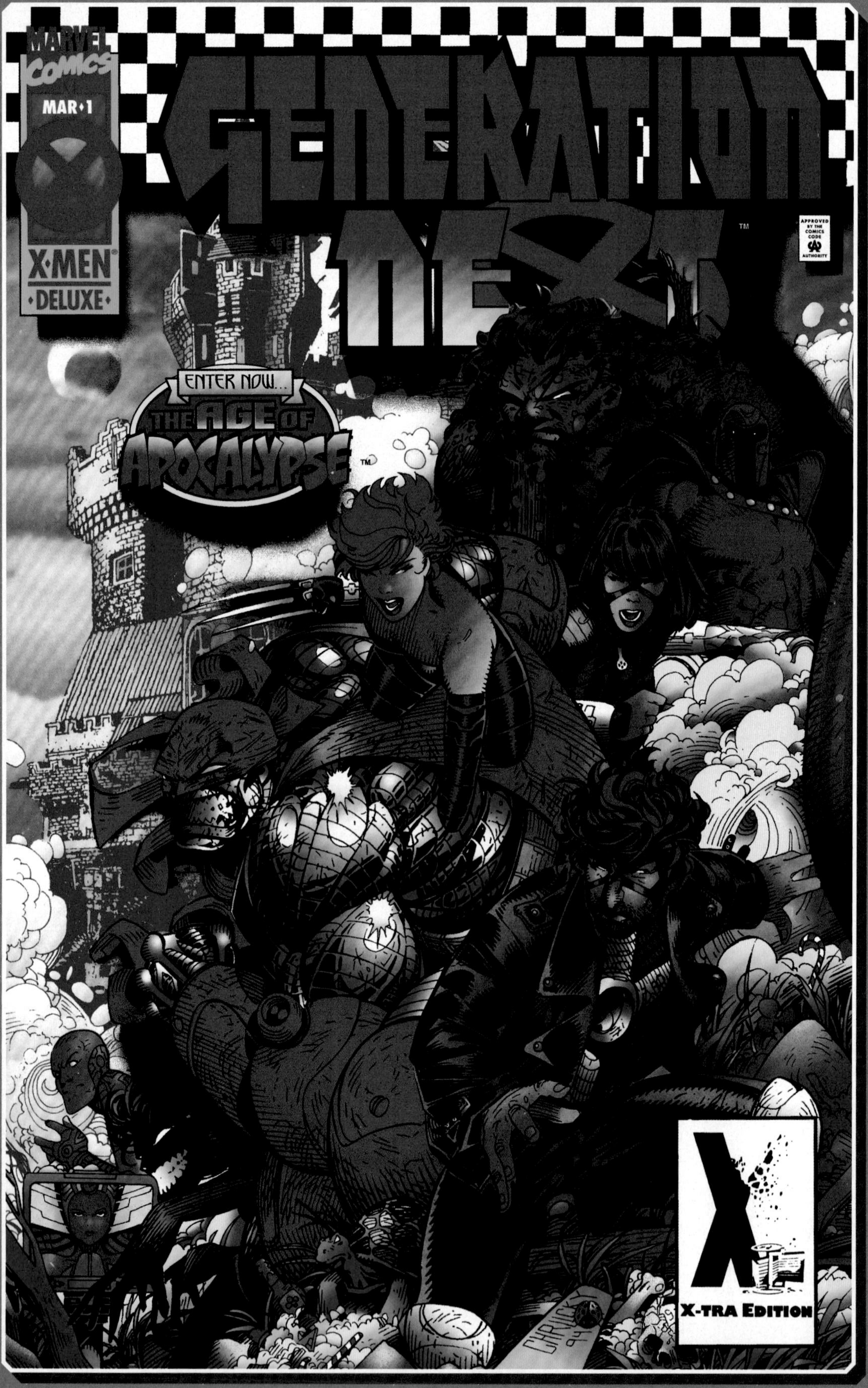
MARVEL COMICS
MAR 1
X-MEN
DELUXE
GENERATION NEXT
APPROVED BY THE COMICS CODE AUTHORITY
ENTER NOW...
THE AGE OF APOCALYPSE
X-TRA EDITION

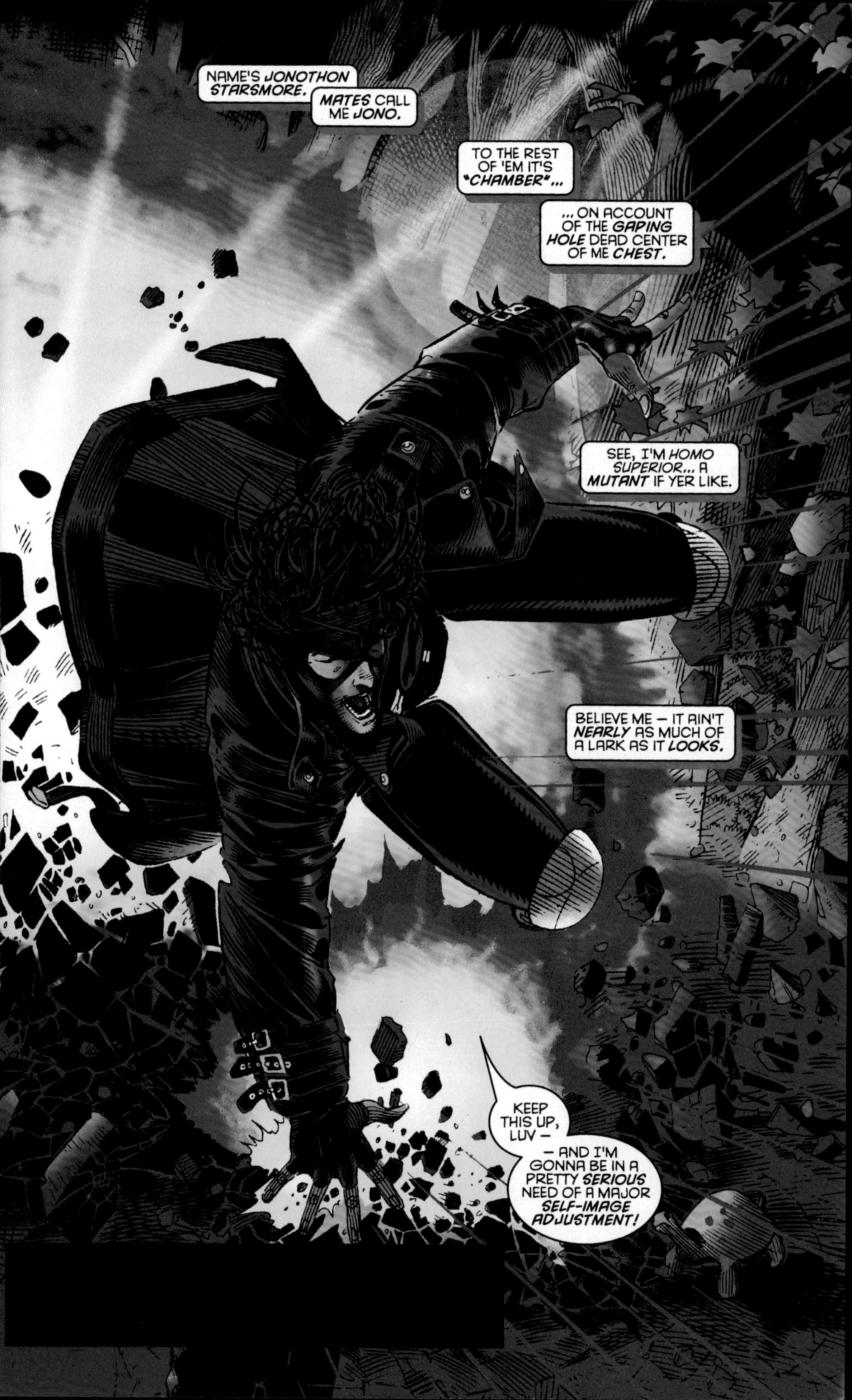
NAME'S JONOTHON STARSMORE.
MATES CALL ME JONO.
TO THE REST OF 'EM IT'S "CHAMBER"...
...ON ACCOUNT OF THE GAPING HOLE DEAD CENTER OF ME CHEST.
SEE, I'M HOMO SUPERIOR... A MUTANT IF YER LIKE.
BELIEVE ME — IT AIN'T NEARLY AS MUCH OF A LARK AS IT LOOKS.
KEEP THIS UP, LUV —
— AND I'M GONNA BE IN A PRETTY SERIOUS NEED OF A MAJOR SELF-IMAGE ADJUSTMENT!

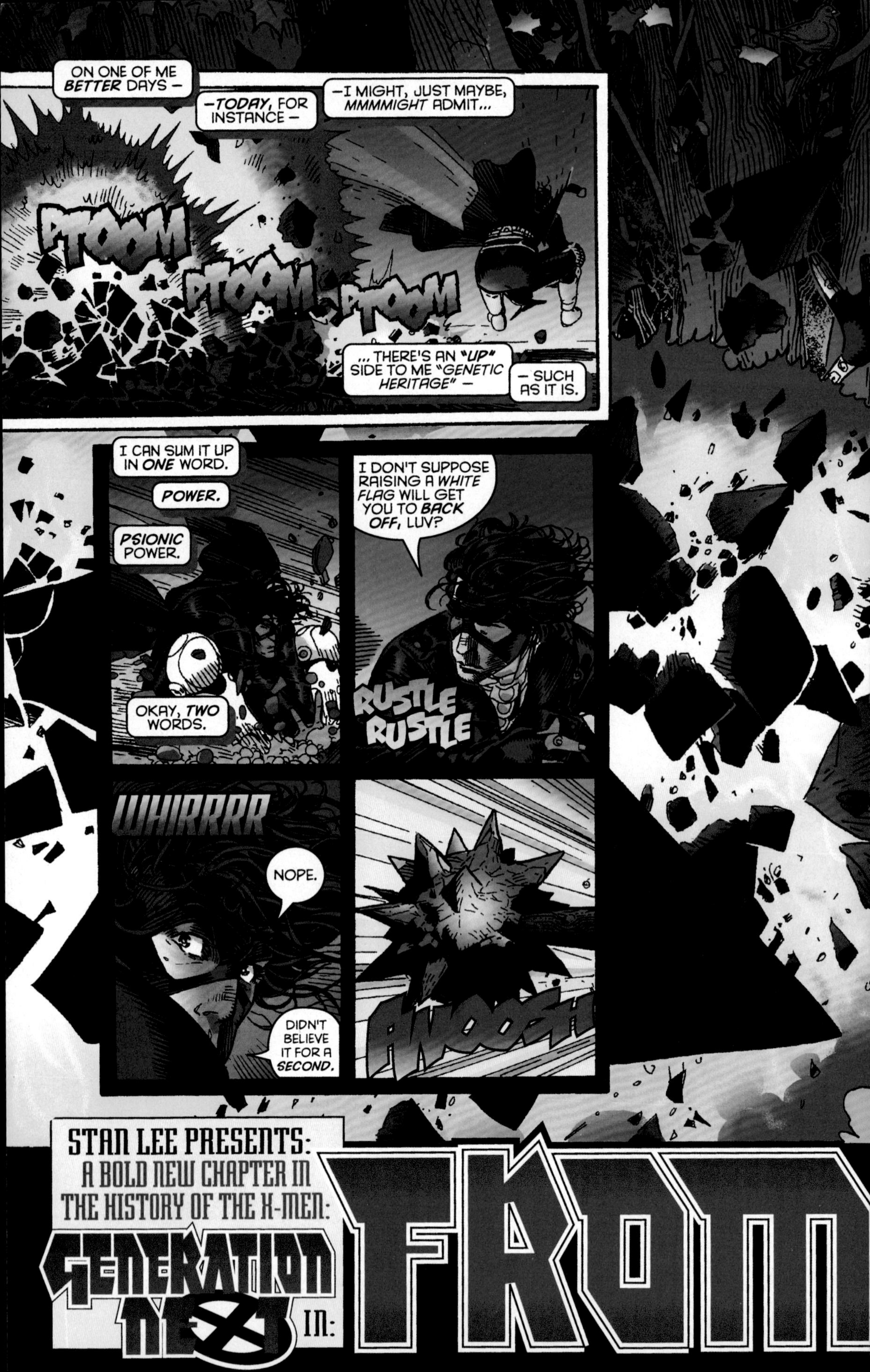
ON ONE OF ME BETTER DAYS —
—TODAY, FOR INSTANCE —
—I MIGHT, JUST MAYBE, MMMMIGHT ADMIT...
PTOOM
PTOOM
PTOOM
... THERE'S AN "UP" SIDE TO ME "GENETIC HERITAGE" —
— SUCH AS IT IS.
I CAN SUM IT UP IN ONE WORD.
POWER.
PSIONIC POWER.
OKAY, TWO WORDS.
I DON'T SUPPOSE RAISING A WHITE FLAG WILL GET YOU TO BACK OFF, LUV?
RUSTLE RUSTLE
WHIRRRR
NOPE.
DIDN'T BELIEVE IT FOR A SECOND.
AWOOSH
STAN LEE PRESENTS:
A BOLD NEW CHAPTER IN THE HISTORY OF THE X-MEN:
GENERATION NEXT IN:
FROM

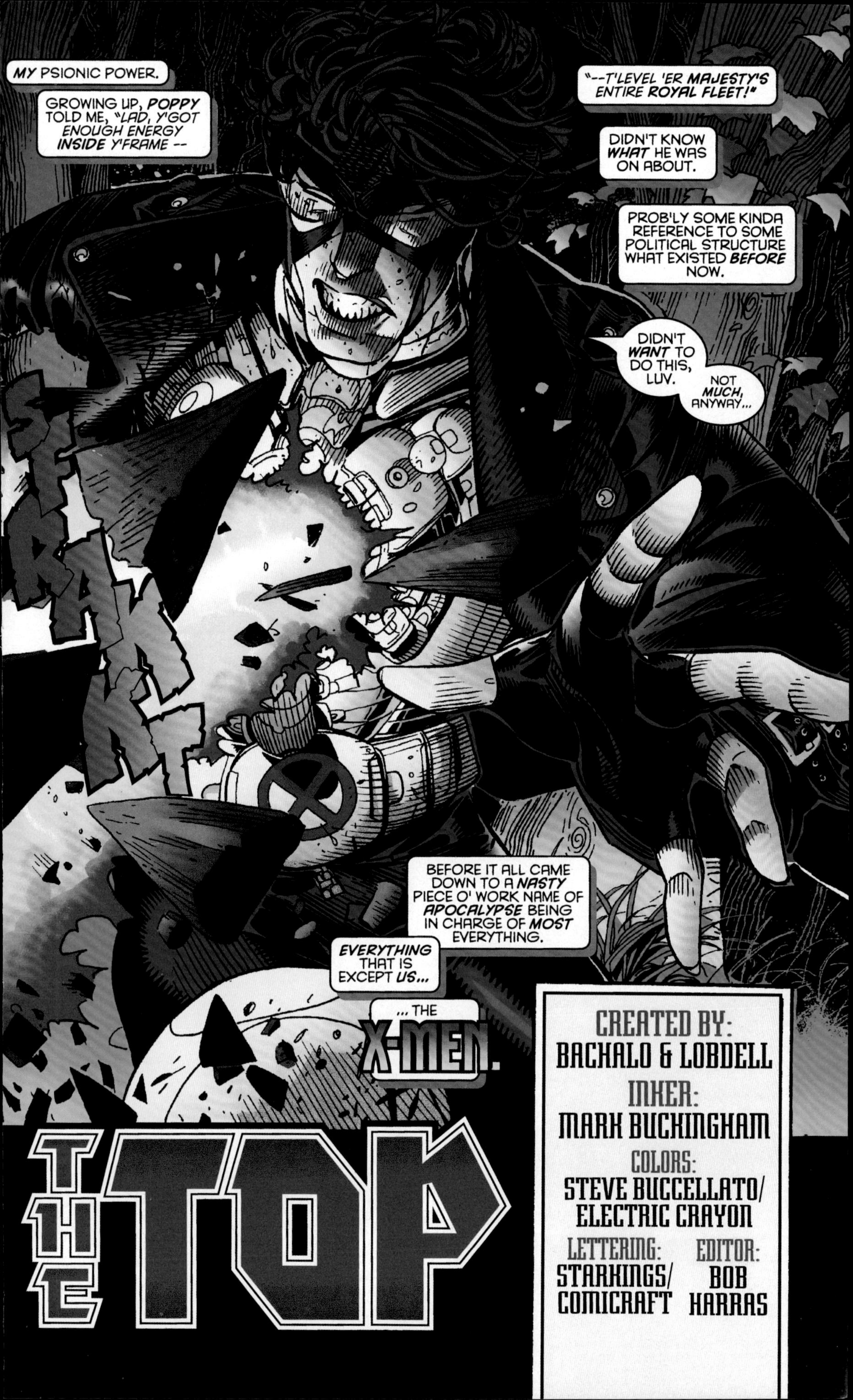
MY PSIONIC POWER.
GROWING UP, POPPY TOLD ME, "LAD, Y'GOT ENOUGH ENERGY INSIDE Y'FRAME --
"--T'LEVEL 'ER MAJESTY'S ENTIRE ROYAL FLEET!"
DIDN'T KNOW WHAT HE WAS ON ABOUT.
PROB'LY SOME KINDA REFERENCE TO SOME POLITICAL STRUCTURE WHAT EXISTED BEFORE NOW.
DIDN'T WANT TO DO THIS, LUV.
NOT MUCH, ANYWAY...
SHRAKKT
BEFORE IT ALL CAME DOWN TO A NASTY PIECE O' WORK NAME OF APOCALYPSE BEING IN CHARGE OF MOST EVERYTHING.
EVERYTHING THAT IS EXCEPT US...
... THE X-MEN.
THE TOP
CREATED BY: BACHALO & LOBDELL
INKER: MARK BUCKINGHAM
COLORS: STEVE BUCCELLATO/ ELECTRIC CRAYON
LETTERING: STARKINGS/ COMICRAFT
EDITOR: BOB HARRAS

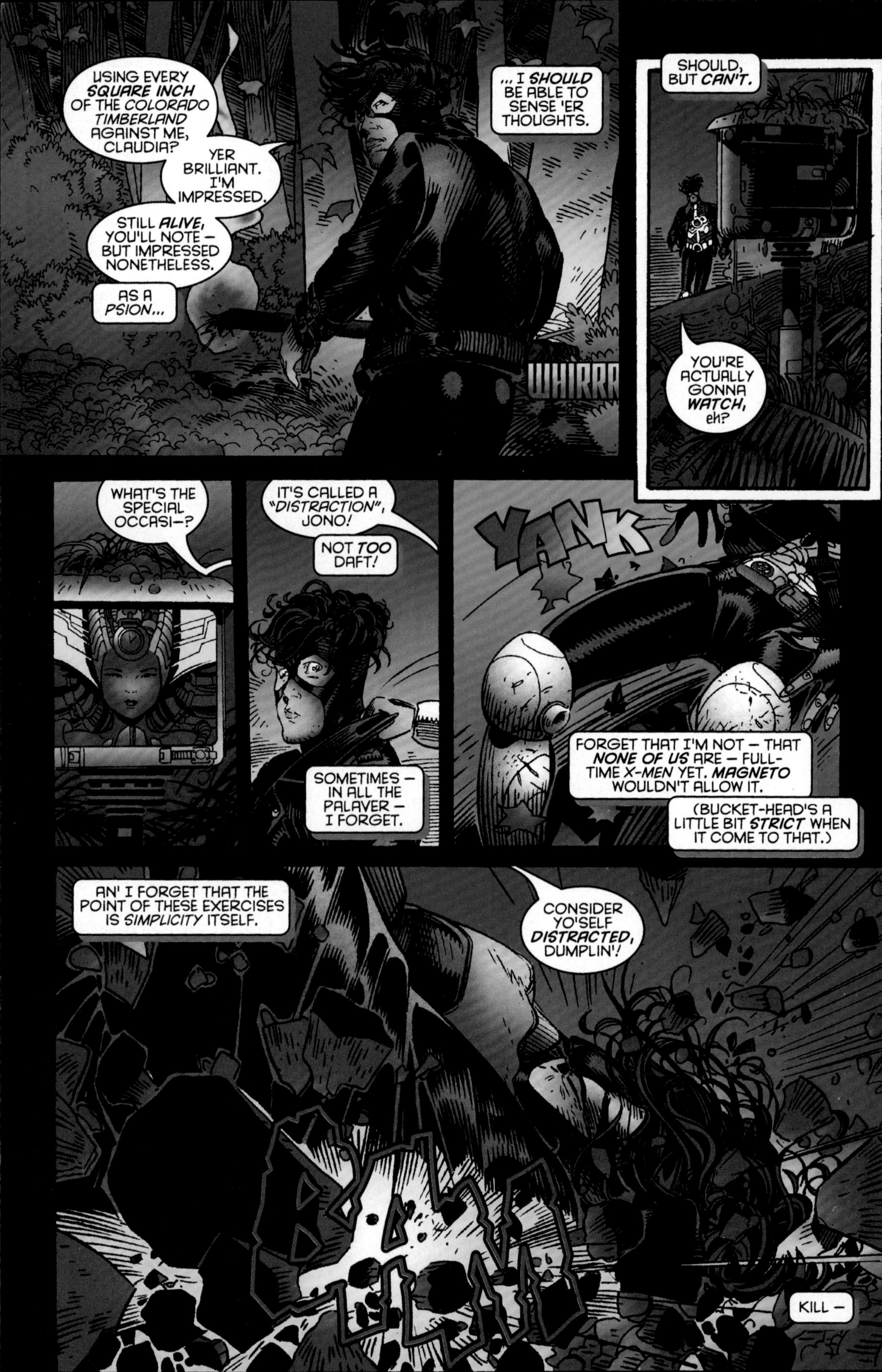
USING EVERY SQUARE INCH OF THE COLORADO TIMBERLAND AGAINST ME, CLAUDIA?
YER BRILLIANT. I'M IMPRESSED.
STILL ALIVE, YOU'LL NOTE — BUT IMPRESSED NONETHELESS.
AS A PSION...
...I SHOULD BE ABLE TO SENSE 'ER THOUGHTS.
WHIRRR
SHOULD, BUT CAN'T.
YOU'RE ACTUALLY GONNA WATCH, eh?
WHAT'S THE SPECIAL OCCASI—?
IT'S CALLED A "DISTRACTION", JONO!
NOT TOO DAFT!
SOMETIMES — IN ALL THE PALAVER — I FORGET.
YANK
FORGET THAT I'M NOT — THAT NONE OF US ARE — FULL-TIME X-MEN YET. MAGNETO WOULDN'T ALLOW IT.
(BUCKET-HEAD'S A LITTLE BIT STRICT WHEN IT COME TO THAT.)
AN' I FORGET THAT THE POINT OF THESE EXERCISES IS SIMPLICITY ITSELF.
CONSIDER YO'SELF DISTRACTED, DUMPLIN'!
KILL —

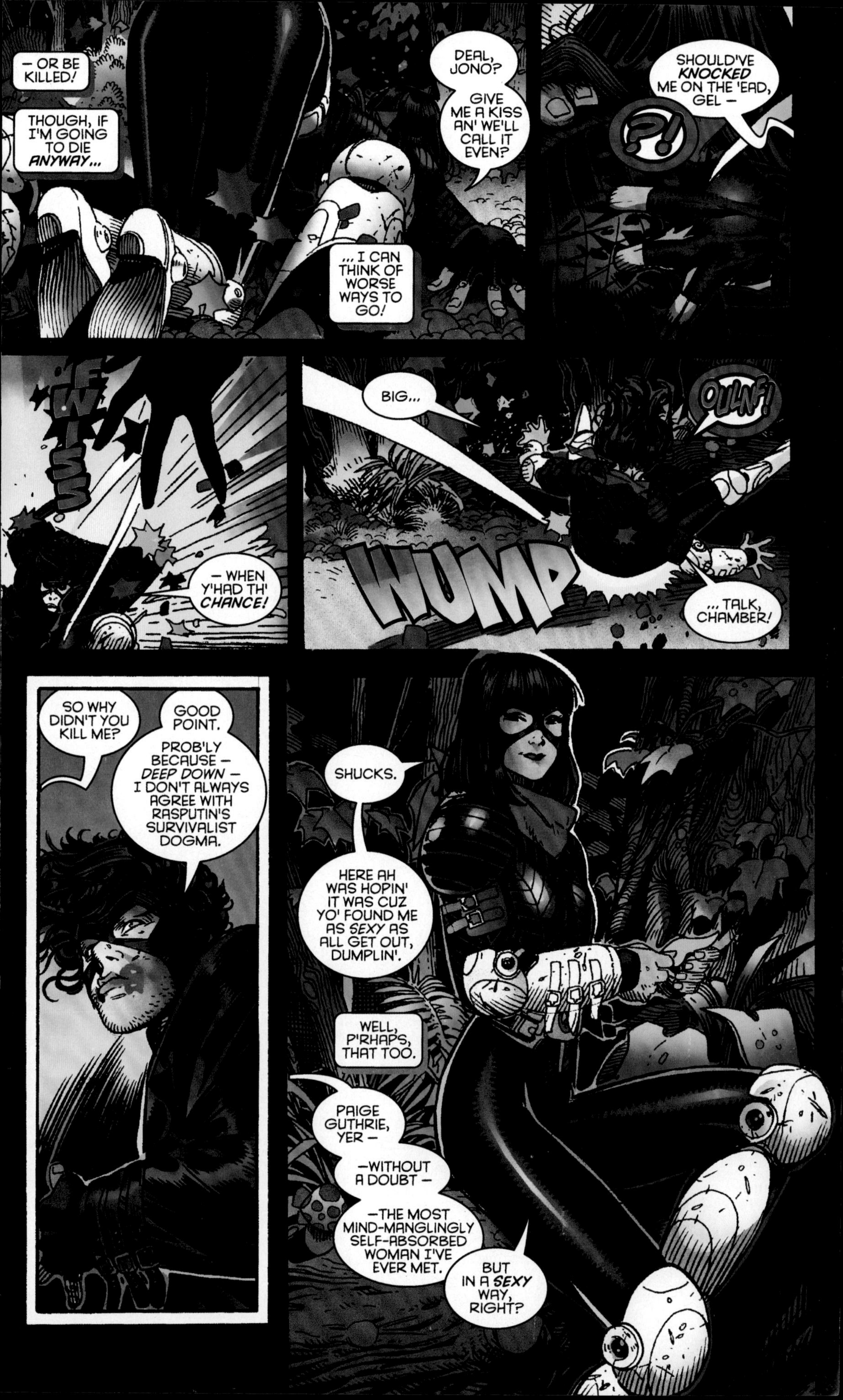

— OR BE KILLED!
THOUGH, IF I'M GOING TO DIE *ANYWAY*...
DEAL, JONO?
GIVE ME A KISS AN' WE'LL CALL IT EVEN?
...I CAN THINK OF WORSE WAYS TO GO!
SHOULD'VE *KNOCKED* ME ON THE 'EAD, GEL —
?!
FWISS
— WHEN Y'HAD TH' *CHANCE!*
BIG...
OULNF!
WUMP
...TALK, CHAMBER!
SO WHY DIDN'T YOU KILL ME?
GOOD POINT.
PROB'LY BECAUSE — *DEEP DOWN* — I DON'T ALWAYS AGREE WITH RASPUTIN'S SURVIVALIST DOGMA.
SHUCKS.
HERE AH WAS HOPIN' IT WAS CUZ YO' FOUND ME AS *SEXY* AS ALL GET OUT, DUMPLIN'.
WELL, P'RHAPS, THAT TOO.
PAIGE GUTHRIE, YER —
—WITHOUT A DOUBT —
—THE MOST MIND-MANGLINGLY SELF-ABSORBED WOMAN I'VE EVER MET.
BUT IN A *SEXY* WAY, RIGHT?

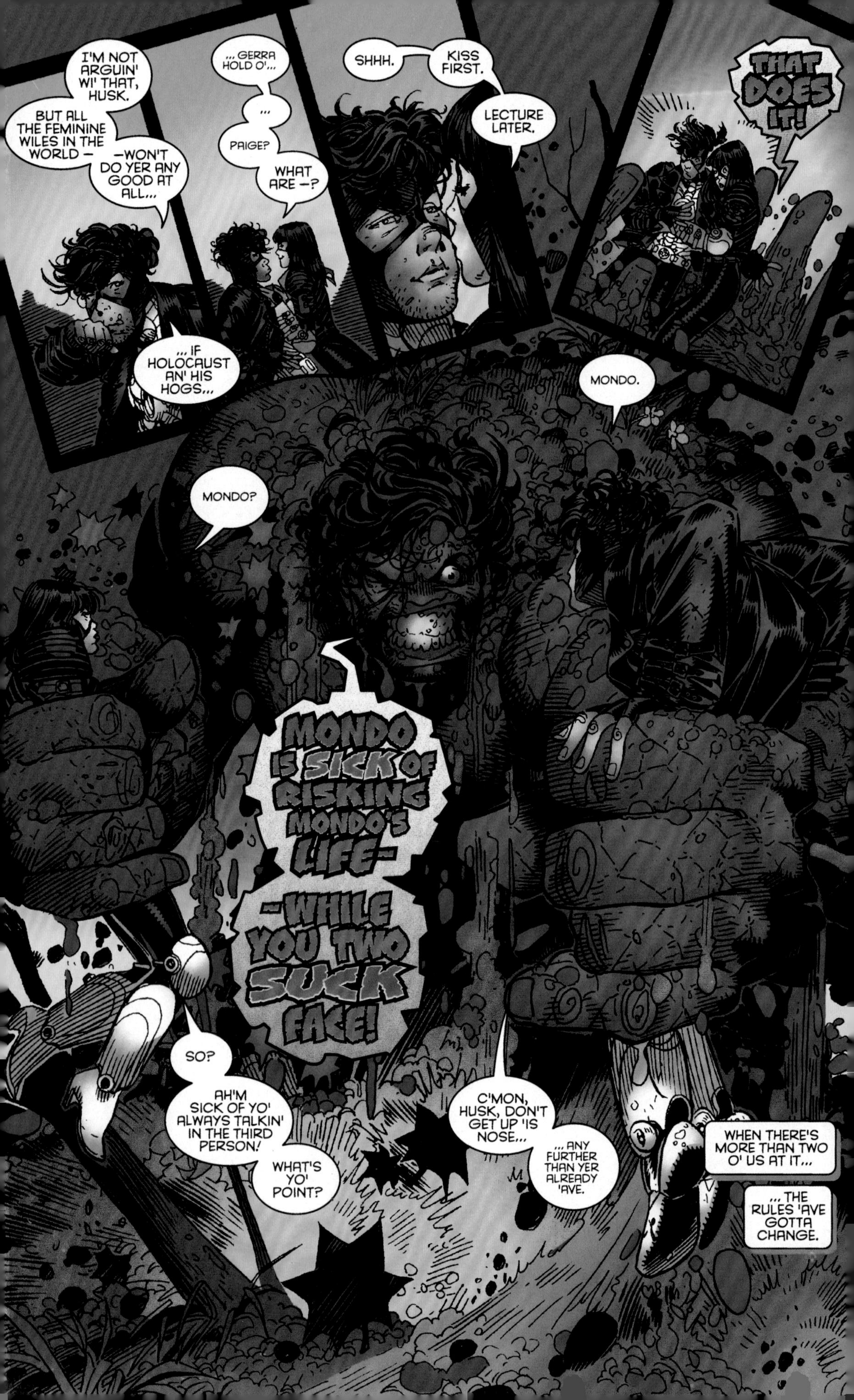

I'M NOT ARGUIN' WI' THAT, HUSK.
BUT ALL THE FEMININE WILES IN THE WORLD —
—WON'T DO YER ANY GOOD AT ALL...
...IF HOLOCAUST AN' HIS HOGS...
...GERRA HOLD O'...
...
PAIGE?
WHAT ARE —?
SHHH.
KISS FIRST.
LECTURE LATER.
THAT DOES IT!
MONDO.
MONDO?
MONDO IS SICK OF RISKING MONDO'S LIFE—
—WHILE YOU TWO SUCK FACE!
SO?
AH'M SICK OF YO' ALWAYS TALKIN' IN THE THIRD PERSON!
WHAT'S YO' POINT?
C'MON, HUSK, DON'T GET UP 'IS NOSE...
...ANY FURTHER THAN YER ALREADY 'AVE.
WHEN THERE'S MORE THAN TWO O' US AT IT...
...THE RULES 'AVE GOTTA CHANGE.

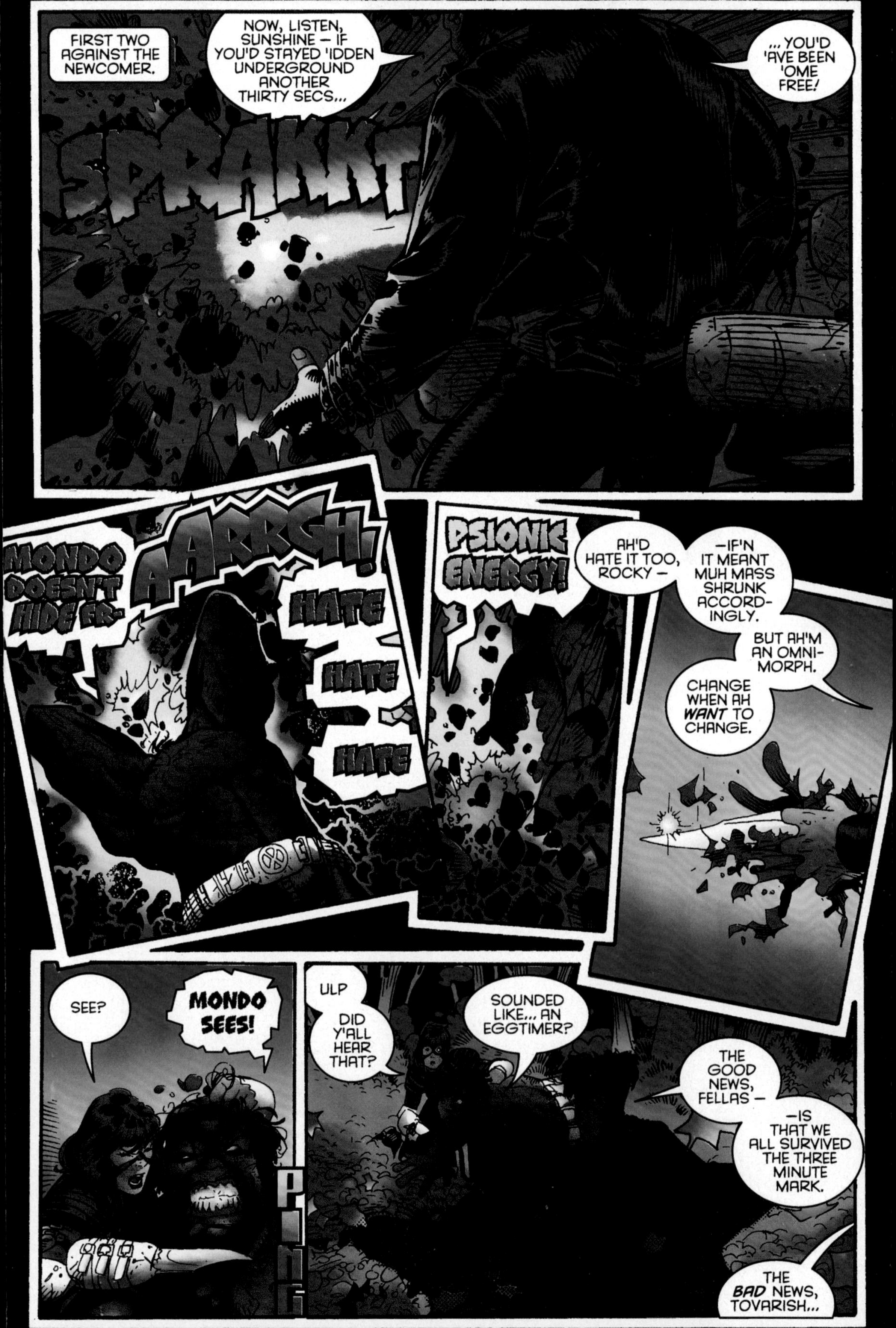
FIRST TWO AGAINST THE NEWCOMER.
NOW, LISTEN, SUNSHINE — IF YOU'D STAYED 'IDDEN UNDERGROUND ANOTHER THIRTY SECS...
...YOU'D 'AVE BEEN 'OME FREE!
SPRAKKT
MONDO DOESN'T HIDE FR-
AARRGH!
HATE
HATE
HATE
PSIONIC ENERGY!
AH'D HATE IT TOO, ROCKY —
—IF'N IT MEANT MUH MASS SHRUNK ACCORD-INGLY.
BUT AH'M AN OMNI-MORPH.
CHANGE WHEN AH WANT TO CHANGE.
SEE?
MONDO SEES!
PING
ULP
DID Y'ALL HEAR THAT?
SOUNDED LIKE... AN EGGTIMER?
THE GOOD NEWS, FELLAS —
—IS THAT WE ALL SURVIVED THE THREE MINUTE MARK.
THE BAD NEWS, TOVARISH...

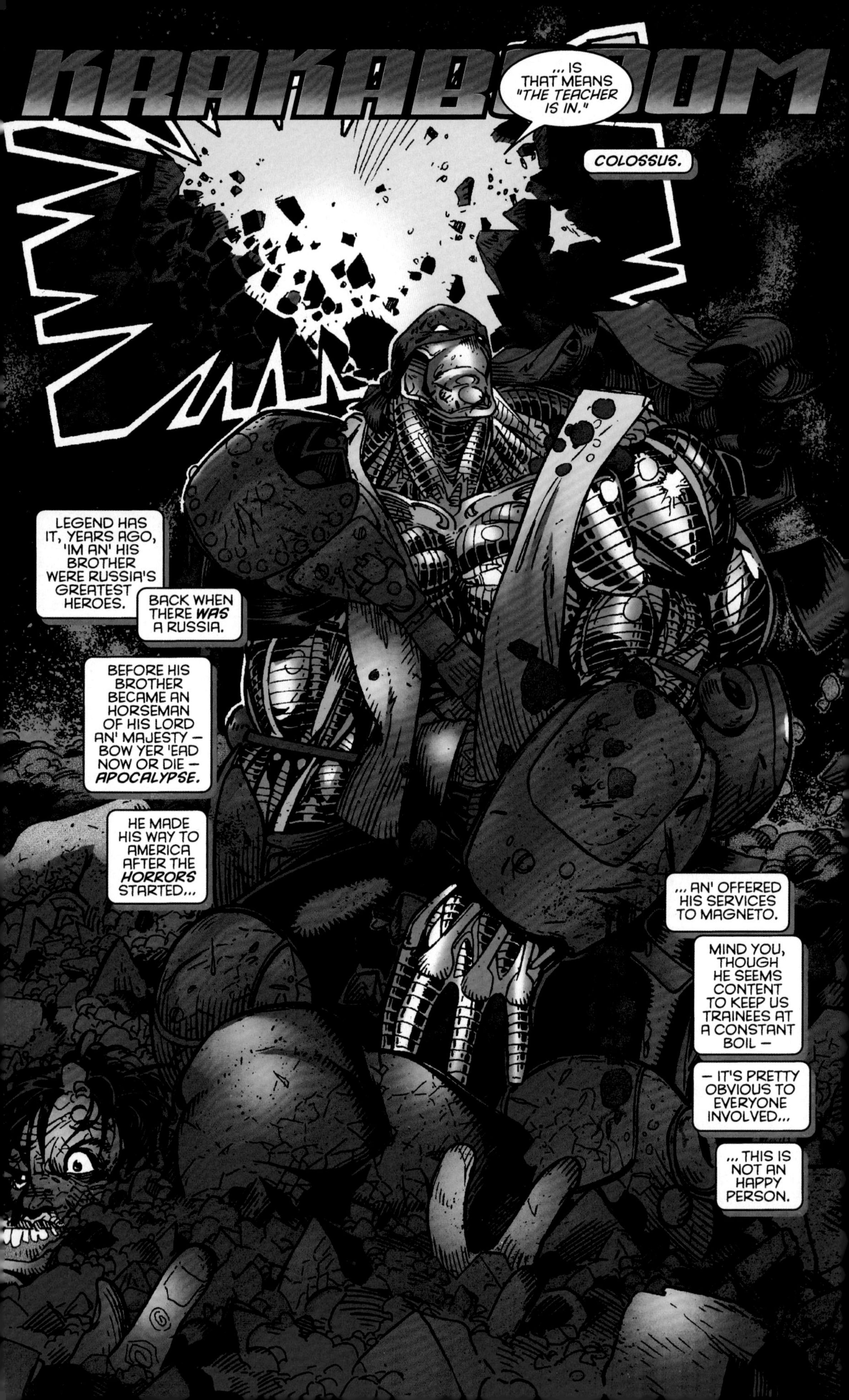
KRAKABOOOM
... IS THAT MEANS "THE TEACHER IS IN."
COLOSSUS.
LEGEND HAS IT, YEARS AGO, 'IM AN' HIS BROTHER WERE RUSSIA'S GREATEST HEROES.
BACK WHEN THERE WAS A RUSSIA.
BEFORE HIS BROTHER BECAME AN HORSEMAN OF HIS LORD AN' MAJESTY — BOW YER 'EAD NOW OR DIE — APOCALYPSE.
HE MADE HIS WAY TO AMERICA AFTER THE HORRORS STARTED...
... AN' OFFERED HIS SERVICES TO MAGNETO.
MIND YOU, THOUGH HE SEEMS CONTENT TO KEEP US TRAINEES AT A CONSTANT BOIL —
— IT'S PRETTY OBVIOUS TO EVERYONE INVOLVED...
... THIS IS NOT AN HAPPY PERSON.

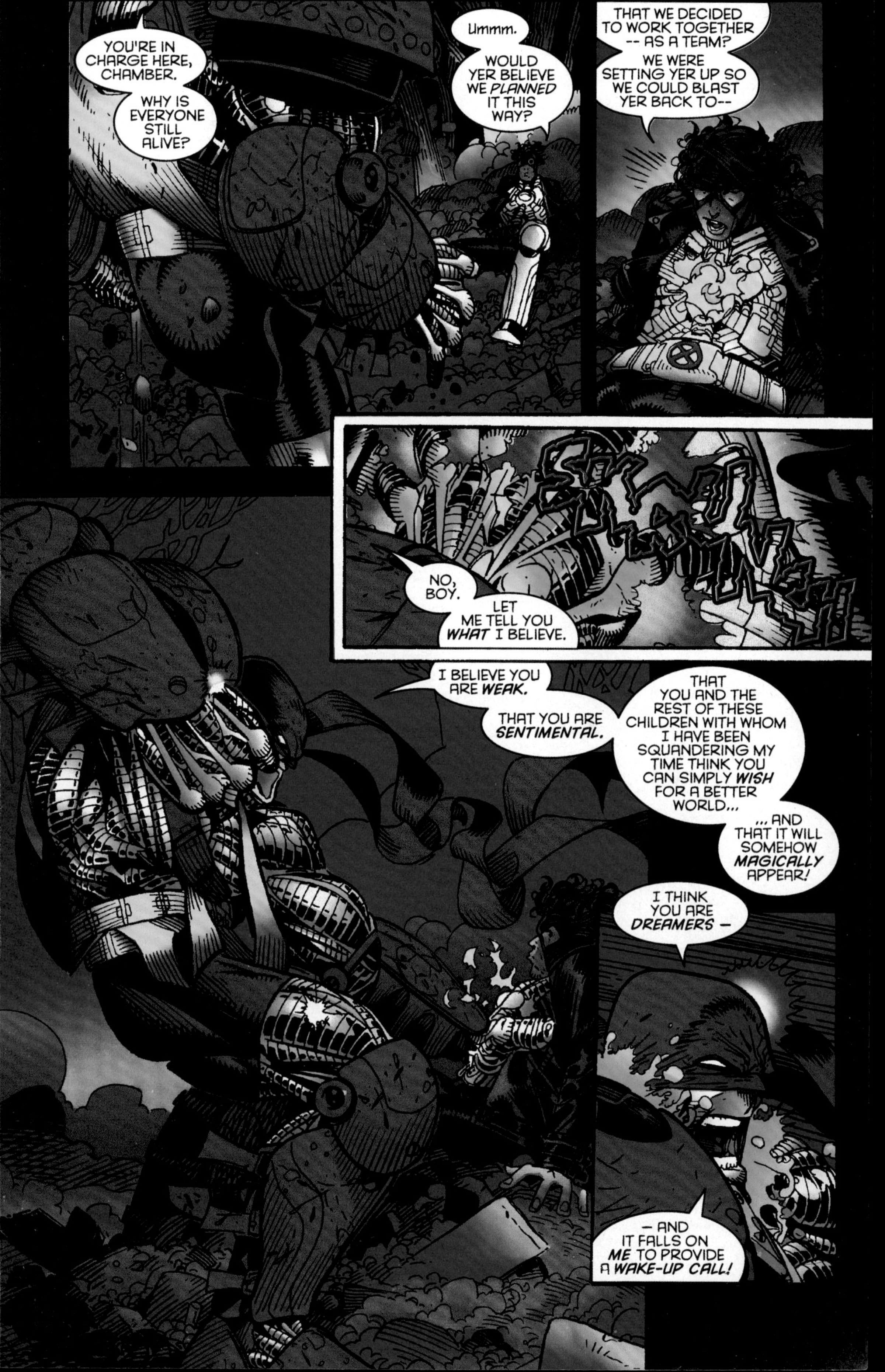
YOU'RE IN CHARGE HERE, CHAMBER.
WHY IS EVERYONE STILL ALIVE?
Ummm.
WOULD YER BELIEVE WE PLANNED IT THIS WAY?
THAT WE DECIDED TO WORK TOGETHER -- AS A TEAM?
WE WERE SETTING YER UP SO WE COULD BLAST YER BACK TO--
NO, BOY.
LET ME TELL YOU WHAT I BELIEVE.
I BELIEVE YOU ARE WEAK.
THAT YOU ARE SENTIMENTAL.
THAT YOU AND THE REST OF THESE CHILDREN WITH WHOM I HAVE BEEN SQUANDERING MY TIME THINK YOU CAN SIMPLY WISH FOR A BETTER WORLD...
... AND THAT IT WILL SOMEHOW MAGICALLY APPEAR!
I THINK YOU ARE DREAMERS –
– AND IT FALLS ON ME TO PROVIDE A WAKE-UP CALL!

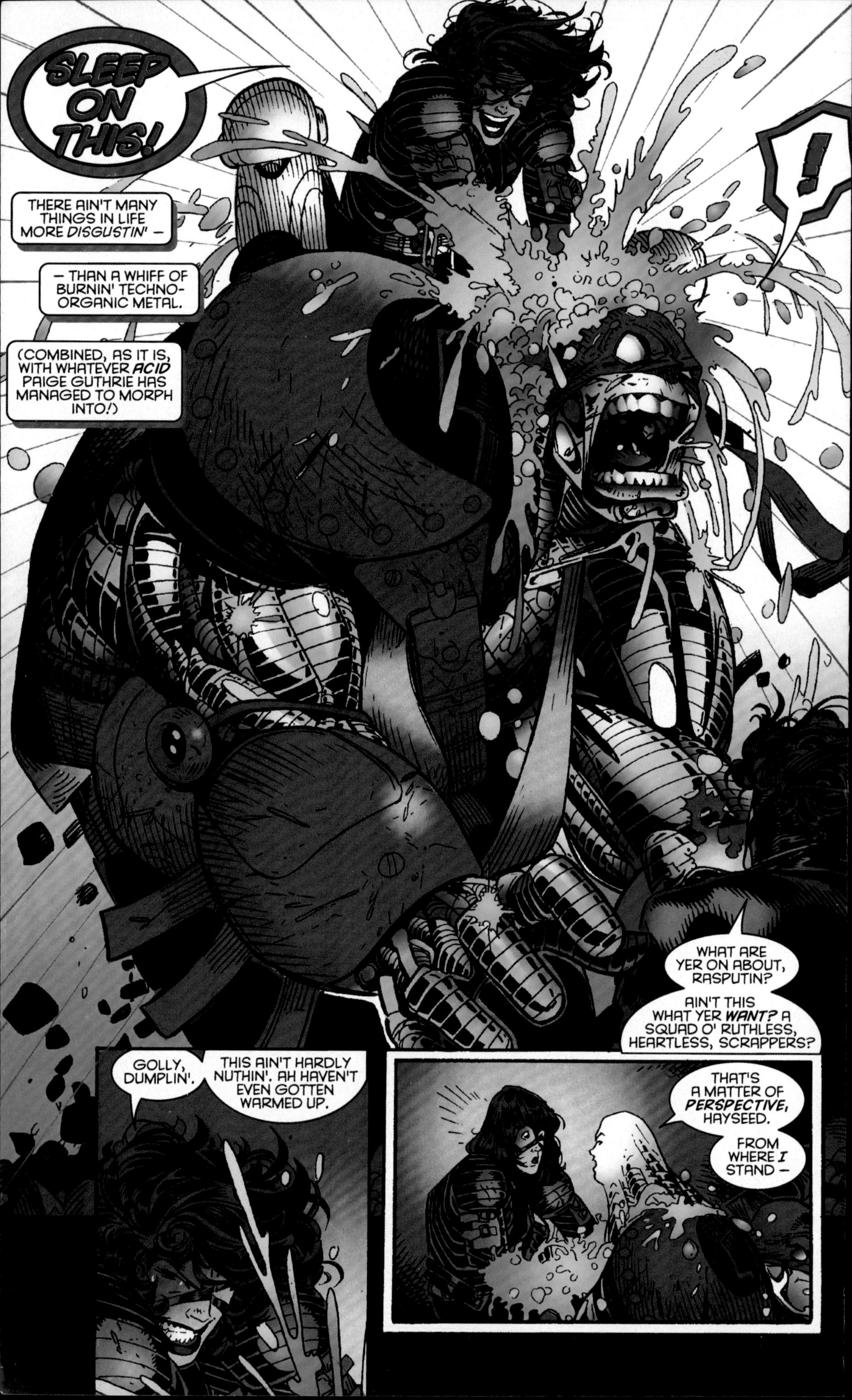
SLEEP ON THIS!
THERE AIN'T MANY THINGS IN LIFE MORE *DISGUSTIN'* —
— THAN A WHIFF OF BURNIN' TECHNO-ORGANIC METAL.
(COMBINED, AS IT IS, WITH WHATEVER *ACID* PAIGE GUTHRIE HAS MANAGED TO MORPH INTO!)
!
WHAT ARE YER ON ABOUT, RASPUTIN?
AIN'T THIS WHAT YER *WANT?* A SQUAD O' RUTHLESS, HEARTLESS, SCRAPPERS?
GOLLY, DUMPLIN'.
THIS AIN'T HARDLY NUTHIN'. AH HAVEN'T EVEN GOTTEN WARMED UP.
THAT'S A MATTER OF *PERSPECTIVE,* HAYSEED.
FROM WHERE *I* STAND —

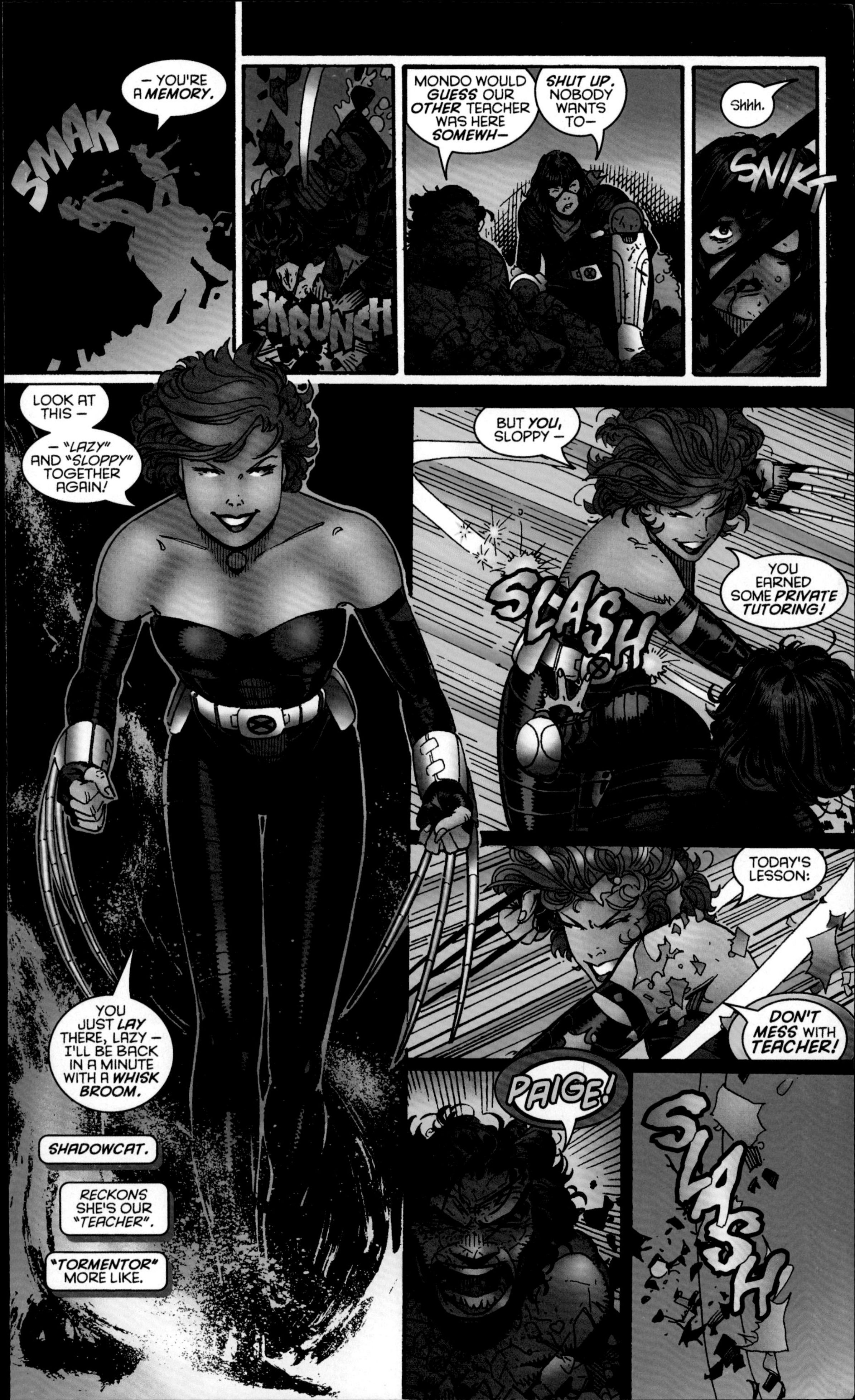

– YOU'RE A MEMORY.
SMAK
SKRUNCH
MONDO WOULD GUESS OUR OTHER TEACHER WAS HERE SOMEWH–
SHUT UP. NOBODY WANTS TO–
Shhh.
SNIKT
LOOK AT THIS –
– "LAZY" AND "SLOPPY" TOGETHER AGAIN!
YOU JUST LAY THERE, LAZY – I'LL BE BACK IN A MINUTE WITH A WHISK BROOM.
SHADOWCAT.
RECKONS SHE'S OUR "TEACHER".
"TORMENTOR" MORE LIKE.
BUT YOU, SLOPPY –
SLASH
YOU EARNED SOME PRIVATE TUTORING!
TODAY'S LESSON:
DON'T MESS WITH TEACHER!
PAIGE!
SLASH

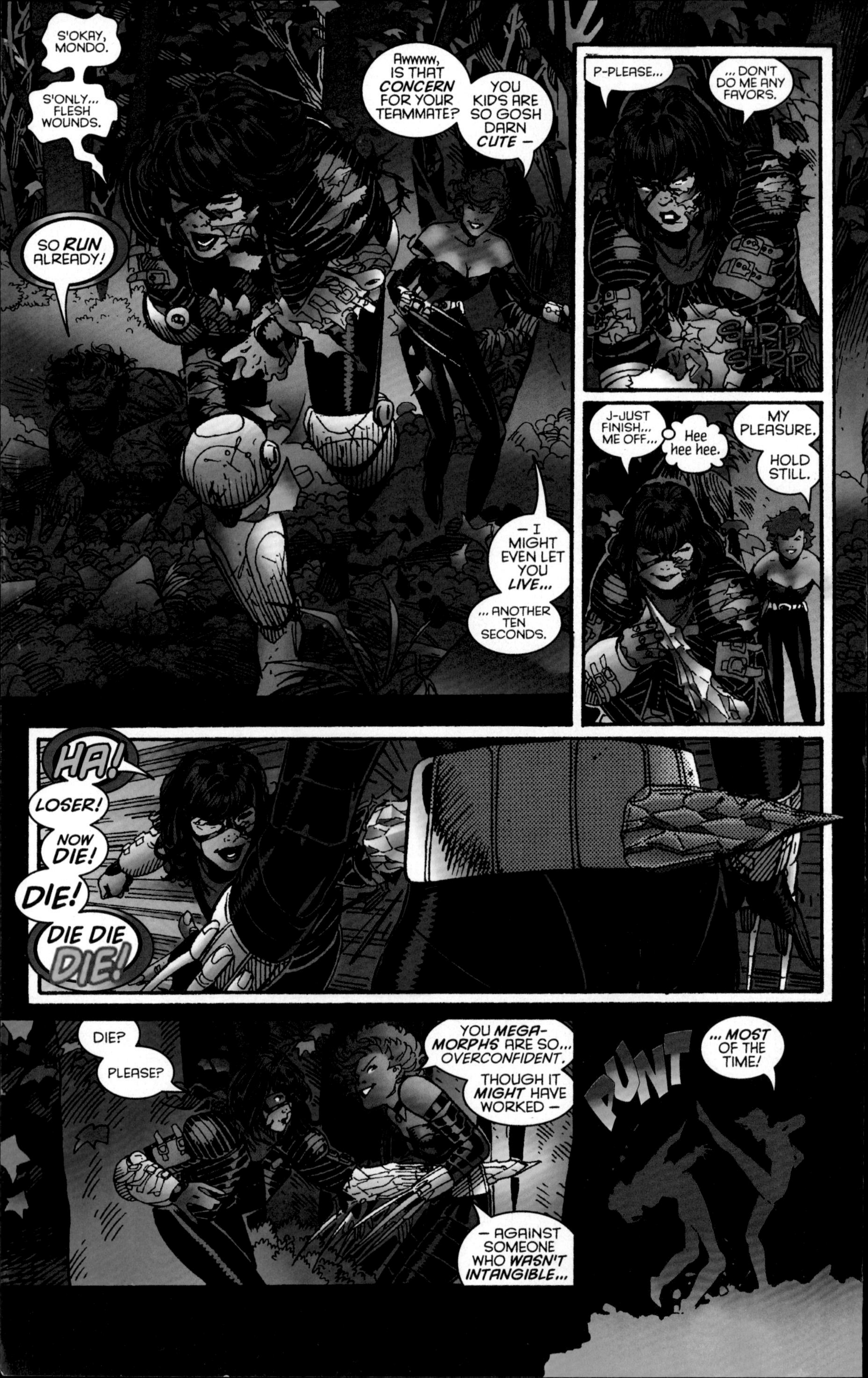
S'OKAY, MONDO.
S'ONLY... FLESH WOUNDS.
SO RUN ALREADY!
Awwwww, IS THAT CONCERN FOR YOUR TEAMMATE?
YOU KIDS ARE SO GOSH DARN CUTE —
— I MIGHT EVEN LET YOU LIVE...
... ANOTHER TEN SECONDS.
P-PLEASE...
... DON'T DO ME ANY FAVORS.
SHRIP SHRIP
J-JUST FINISH... ME OFF...
Hee hee hee.
MY PLEASURE.
HOLD STILL.
HA!
LOSER!
NOW DIE!
DIE!
DIE DIE DIE!
DIE?
PLEASE?
YOU MEGA-MORPHS ARE SO... OVERCONFIDENT.
THOUGH IT MIGHT HAVE WORKED —
— AGAINST SOMEONE WHO WASN'T INTANGIBLE...
PUNT
... MOST OF THE TIME!

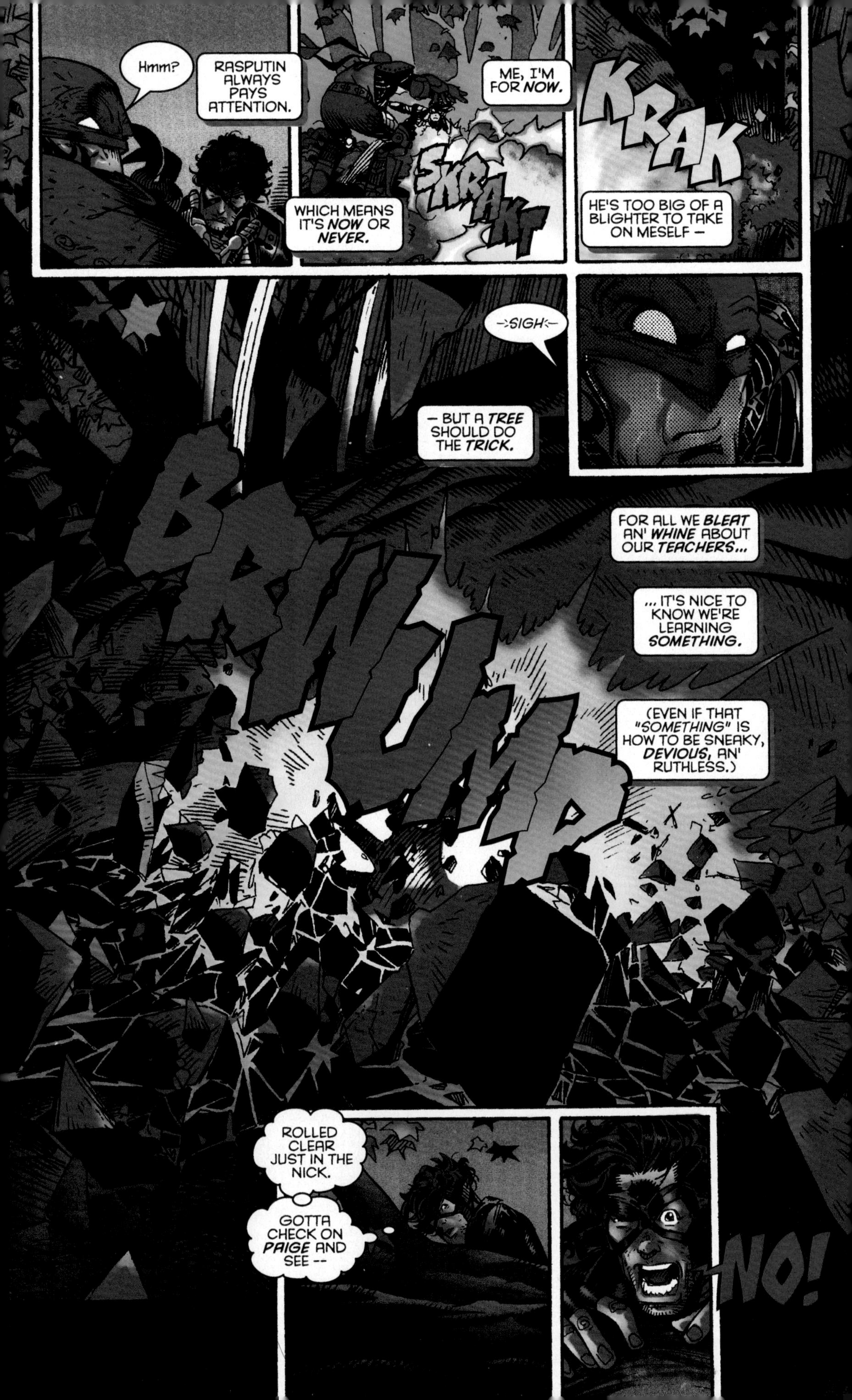
Hmm?
RASPUTIN ALWAYS PAYS ATTENTION.
WHICH MEANS IT'S NOW OR NEVER.
SKRAKT
ME, I'M FOR NOW.
KRAK
HE'S TOO BIG OF A BLIGHTER TO TAKE ON MESELF —
-SIGH-
— BUT A TREE SHOULD DO THE TRICK.
BRUMP
FOR ALL WE BLEAT AN' WHINE ABOUT OUR TEACHERS...
... IT'S NICE TO KNOW WE'RE LEARNING SOMETHING.
(EVEN IF THAT "SOMETHING" IS HOW TO BE SNEAKY, DEVIOUS, AN' RUTHLESS.)
ROLLED CLEAR JUST IN THE NICK.
GOTTA CHECK ON PAIGE AND SEE --
NO!

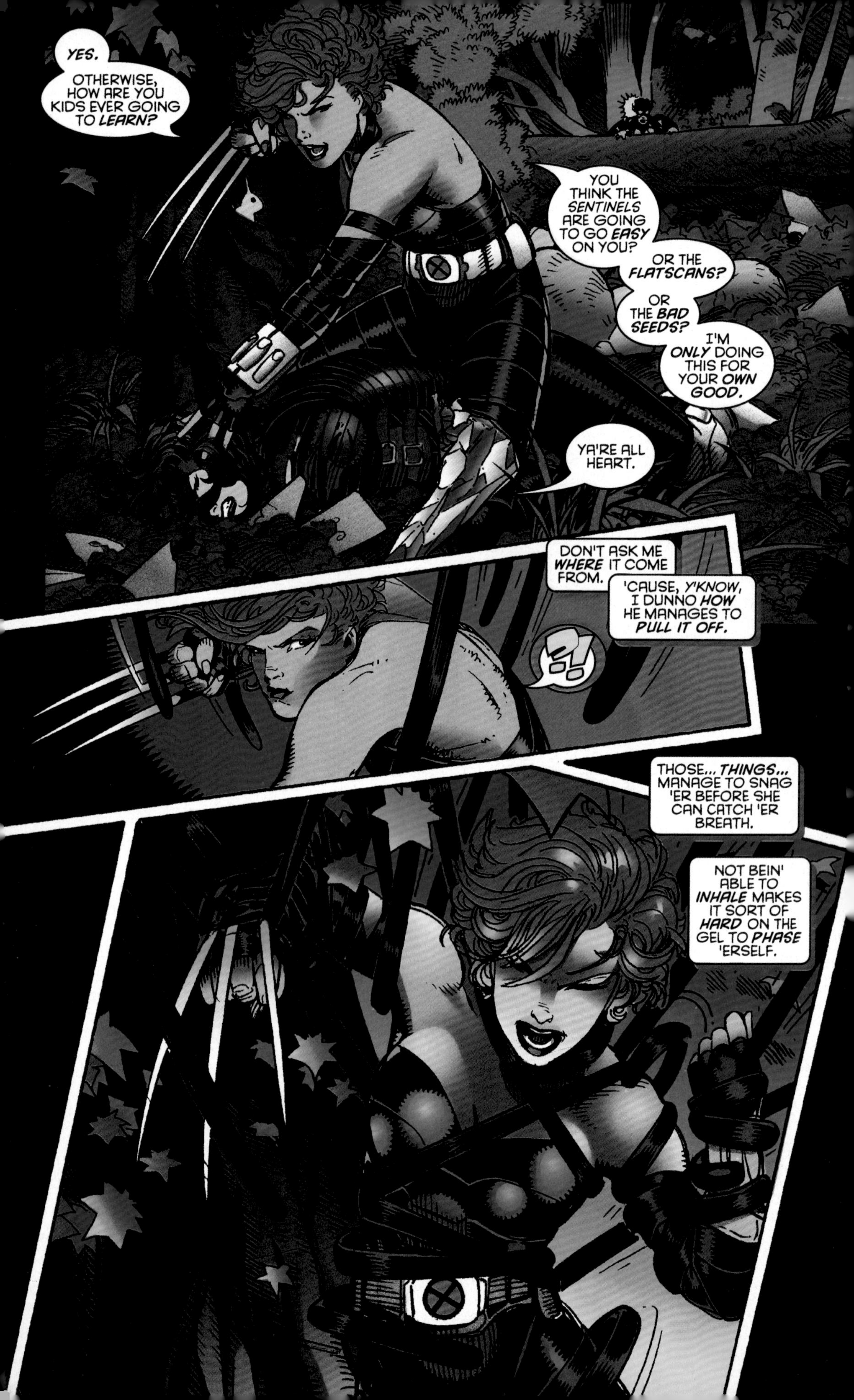
YES.
OTHERWISE, HOW ARE YOU KIDS EVER GOING TO LEARN?
YOU THINK THE SENTINELS ARE GOING TO GO EASY ON YOU?
OR THE FLATSCANS?
OR THE BAD SEEDS?
I'M ONLY DOING THIS FOR YOUR OWN GOOD.
YA'RE ALL HEART.
DON'T ASK ME WHERE IT COME FROM.
'CAUSE, Y'KNOW, I DUNNO HOW HE MANAGES TO PULL IT OFF.
THOSE... THINGS... MANAGE TO SNAG 'ER BEFORE SHE CAN CATCH 'ER BREATH.
NOT BEIN' ABLE TO INHALE MAKES IT SORT OF HARD ON THE GEL TO PHASE 'ERSELF.

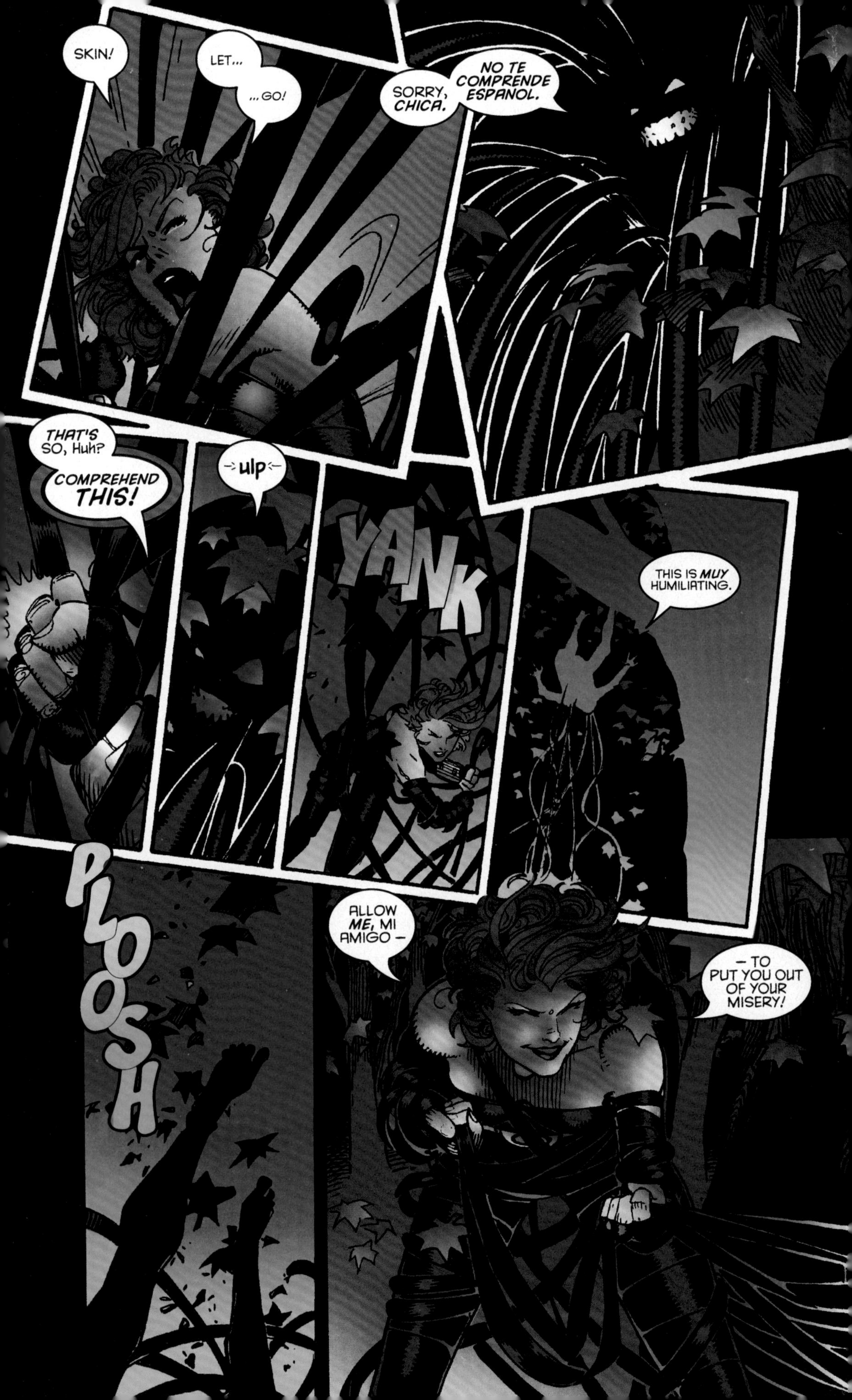

SKIN!
LET...
...GO!
SORRY, CHICA.
NO TE COMPRENDE ESPANOL.
THAT'S SO, Huh?
COMPREHEND THIS!
ulp
YANK
THIS IS MUY HUMILIATING.
PLOOSH
ALLOW ME, MI AMIGO —
— TO PUT YOU OUT OF YOUR MISERY!

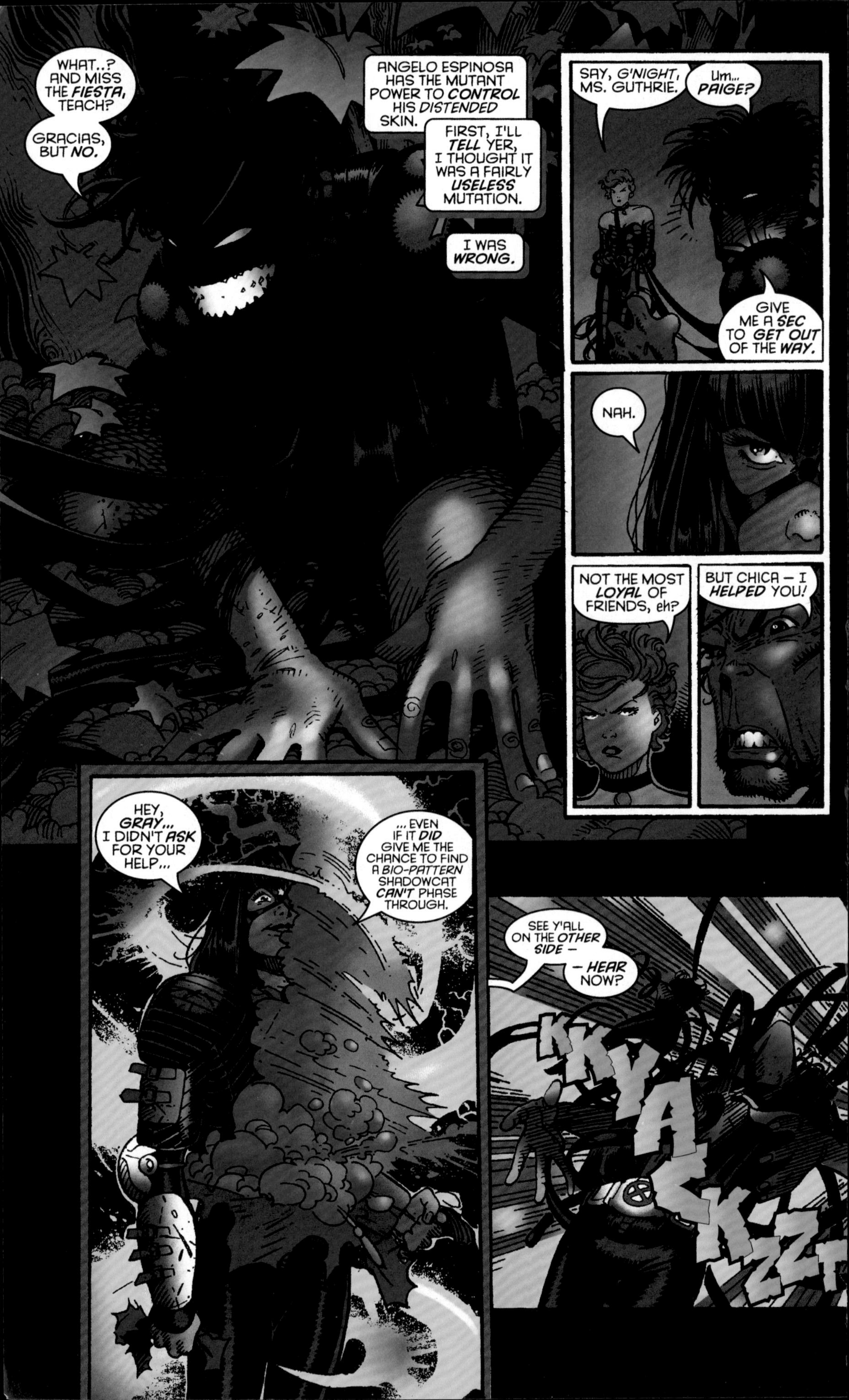
WHAT..? AND MISS THE FIESTA, TEACH?
GRACIAS, BUT NO.
ANGELO ESPINOSA HAS THE MUTANT POWER TO CONTROL HIS DISTENDED SKIN.
FIRST, I'LL TELL YER, I THOUGHT IT WAS A FAIRLY USELESS MUTATION.
I WAS WRONG.
SAY, G'NIGHT, MS. GUTHRIE.
Um... PAIGE?
GIVE ME A SEC TO GET OUT OF THE WAY.
NAH.
NOT THE MOST LOYAL OF FRIENDS, eh?
BUT CHICA — I HELPED YOU!
HEY, GRAY... I DIDN'T ASK FOR YOUR HELP...
...EVEN IF IT DID GIVE ME THE CHANCE TO FIND A BIO-PATTERN SHADOWCAT CAN'T PHASE THROUGH.
SEE Y'ALL ON THE OTHER SIDE —
— HEAR NOW?
KKYAKKZZT

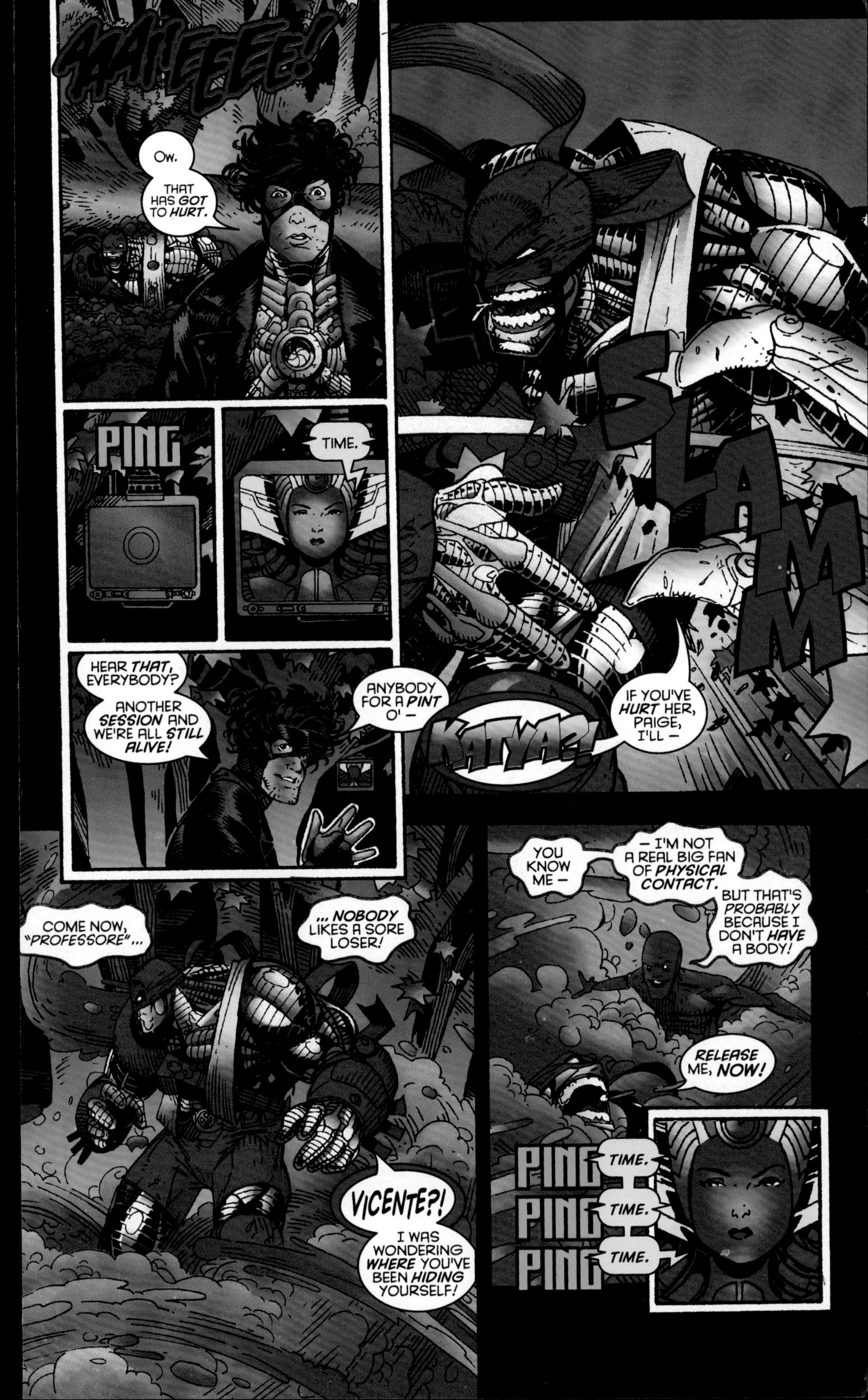
AAAIEEEEE!
OW.
THAT HAS GOT TO HURT.
PING
TIME.
HEAR THAT, EVERYBODY?
ANOTHER SESSION AND WE'RE ALL STILL ALIVE!
ANYBODY FOR A PINT O' —
KATYA?!
IF YOU'VE HURT HER, PAIGE, I'LL —
SLAMM
COME NOW, "PROFESSORE"...
... NOBODY LIKES A SORE LOSER!
VICENTE?!
I WAS WONDERING WHERE YOU'VE BEEN HIDING YOURSELF!
YOU KNOW ME —
— I'M NOT A REAL BIG FAN OF PHYSICAL CONTACT.
BUT THAT'S PROBABLY BECAUSE I DON'T HAVE A BODY!
RELEASE ME, NOW!
PING
TIME.
PING
TIME.
PING
TIME.

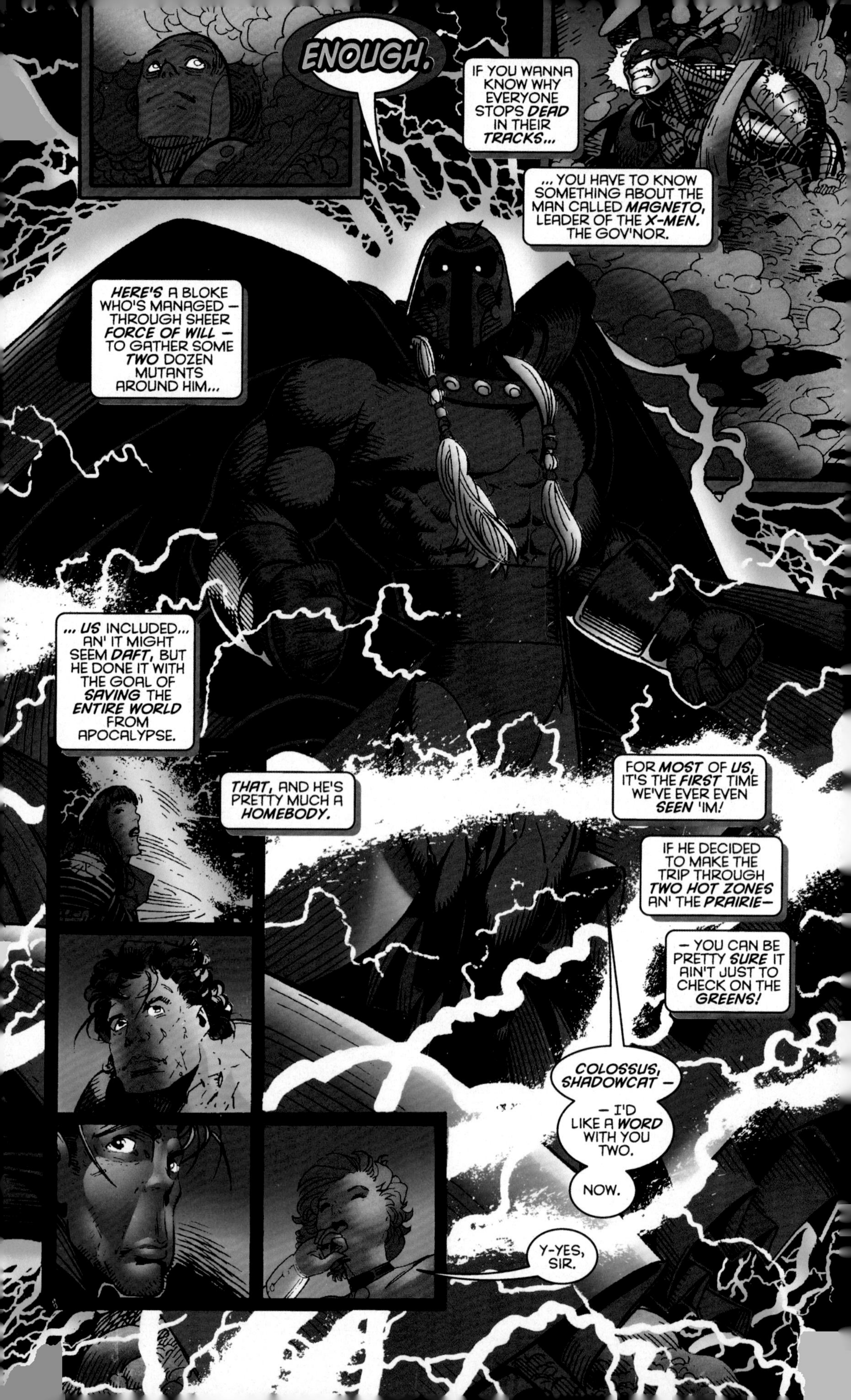
ENOUGH.
IF YOU WANNA KNOW WHY EVERYONE STOPS DEAD IN THEIR TRACKS...
...YOU HAVE TO KNOW SOMETHING ABOUT THE MAN CALLED MAGNETO, LEADER OF THE X-MEN. THE GOV'NOR.
HERE'S A BLOKE WHO'S MANAGED — THROUGH SHEER FORCE OF WILL — TO GATHER SOME TWO DOZEN MUTANTS AROUND HIM...
...US INCLUDED... AN' IT MIGHT SEEM DAFT, BUT HE DONE IT WITH THE GOAL OF SAVING THE ENTIRE WORLD FROM APOCALYPSE.
THAT, AND HE'S PRETTY MUCH A HOMEBODY.
FOR MOST OF US, IT'S THE FIRST TIME WE'VE EVER EVEN SEEN 'IM!
IF HE DECIDED TO MAKE THE TRIP THROUGH TWO HOT ZONES AN' THE PRAIRIE—
— YOU CAN BE PRETTY SURE IT AIN'T JUST TO CHECK ON THE GREENS!
COLOSSUS, SHADOWCAT —
— I'D LIKE A WORD WITH YOU TWO.
NOW.
Y-YES, SIR.

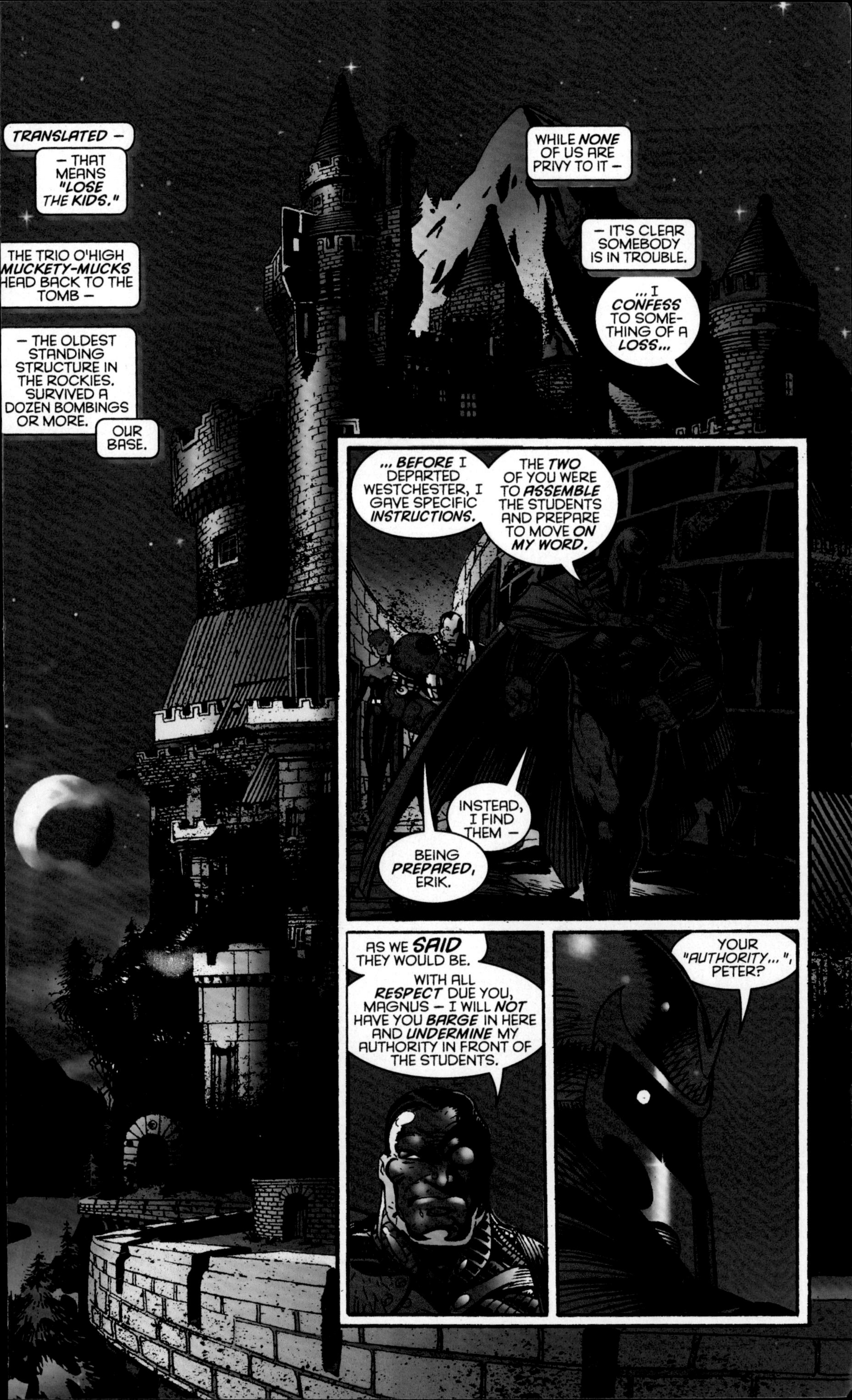
TRANSLATED —
— THAT MEANS "LOSE THE KIDS."
THE TRIO O'HIGH MUCKETY-MUCKS HEAD BACK TO THE TOMB —
— THE OLDEST STANDING STRUCTURE IN THE ROCKIES. SURVIVED A DOZEN BOMBINGS OR MORE.
OUR BASE.
WHILE NONE OF US ARE PRIVY TO IT —
— IT'S CLEAR SOMEBODY IS IN TROUBLE.
... I CONFESS TO SOMETHING OF A LOSS...
... BEFORE I DEPARTED WESTCHESTER, I GAVE SPECIFIC INSTRUCTIONS.
THE TWO OF YOU WERE TO ASSEMBLE THE STUDENTS AND PREPARE TO MOVE ON MY WORD.
INSTEAD, I FIND THEM —
BEING PREPARED, ERIK.
AS WE SAID THEY WOULD BE.
WITH ALL RESPECT DUE YOU, MAGNUS — I WILL NOT HAVE YOU BARGE IN HERE AND UNDERMINE MY AUTHORITY IN FRONT OF THE STUDENTS.
YOUR "AUTHORITY...", PETER?

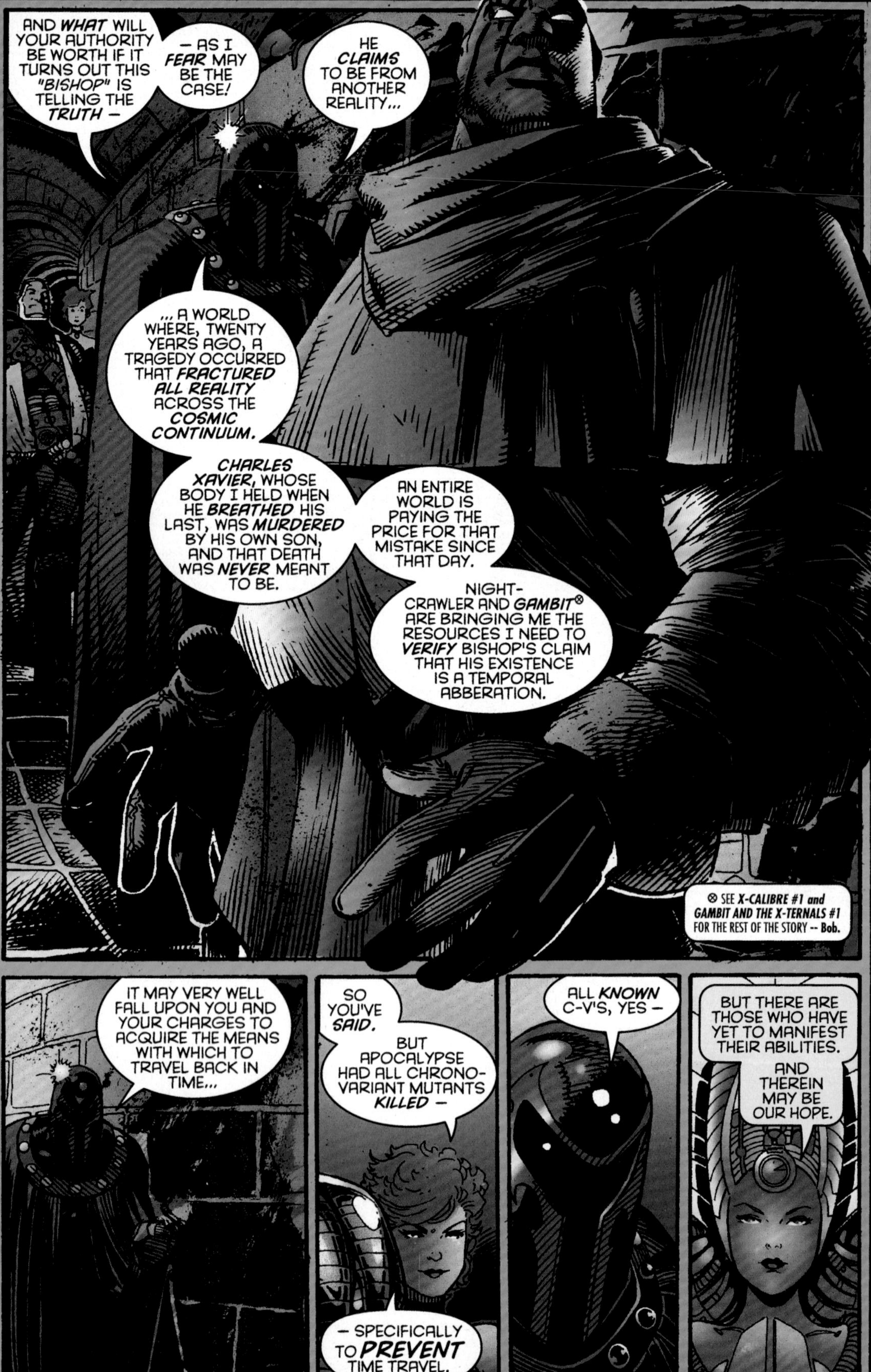
AND WHAT WILL YOUR AUTHORITY BE WORTH IF IT TURNS OUT THIS "BISHOP" IS TELLING THE TRUTH —
— AS I FEAR MAY BE THE CASE!
HE CLAIMS TO BE FROM ANOTHER REALITY...
... A WORLD WHERE, TWENTY YEARS AGO, A TRAGEDY OCCURRED THAT FRACTURED ALL REALITY ACROSS THE COSMIC CONTINUUM.
CHARLES XAVIER, WHOSE BODY I HELD WHEN HE BREATHED HIS LAST, WAS MURDERED BY HIS OWN SON, AND THAT DEATH WAS NEVER MEANT TO BE.
AN ENTIRE WORLD IS PAYING THE PRICE FOR THAT MISTAKE SINCE THAT DAY.
NIGHT-CRAWLER AND GAMBIT⊗ ARE BRINGING ME THE RESOURCES I NEED TO VERIFY BISHOP'S CLAIM THAT HIS EXISTENCE IS A TEMPORAL ABBERATION.
⊗ SEE X-CALIBRE #1 and GAMBIT AND THE X-TERNALS #1 FOR THE REST OF THE STORY -- Bob.
IT MAY VERY WELL FALL UPON YOU AND YOUR CHARGES TO ACQUIRE THE MEANS WITH WHICH TO TRAVEL BACK IN TIME...
SO YOU'VE SAID.
BUT APOCALYPSE HAD ALL CHRONO-VARIANT MUTANTS KILLED —
— SPECIFICALLY TO PREVENT TIME TRAVEL.
ALL KNOWN C-V'S, YES —
BUT THERE ARE THOSE WHO HAVE YET TO MANIFEST THEIR ABILITIES.
AND THEREIN MAY BE OUR HOPE.

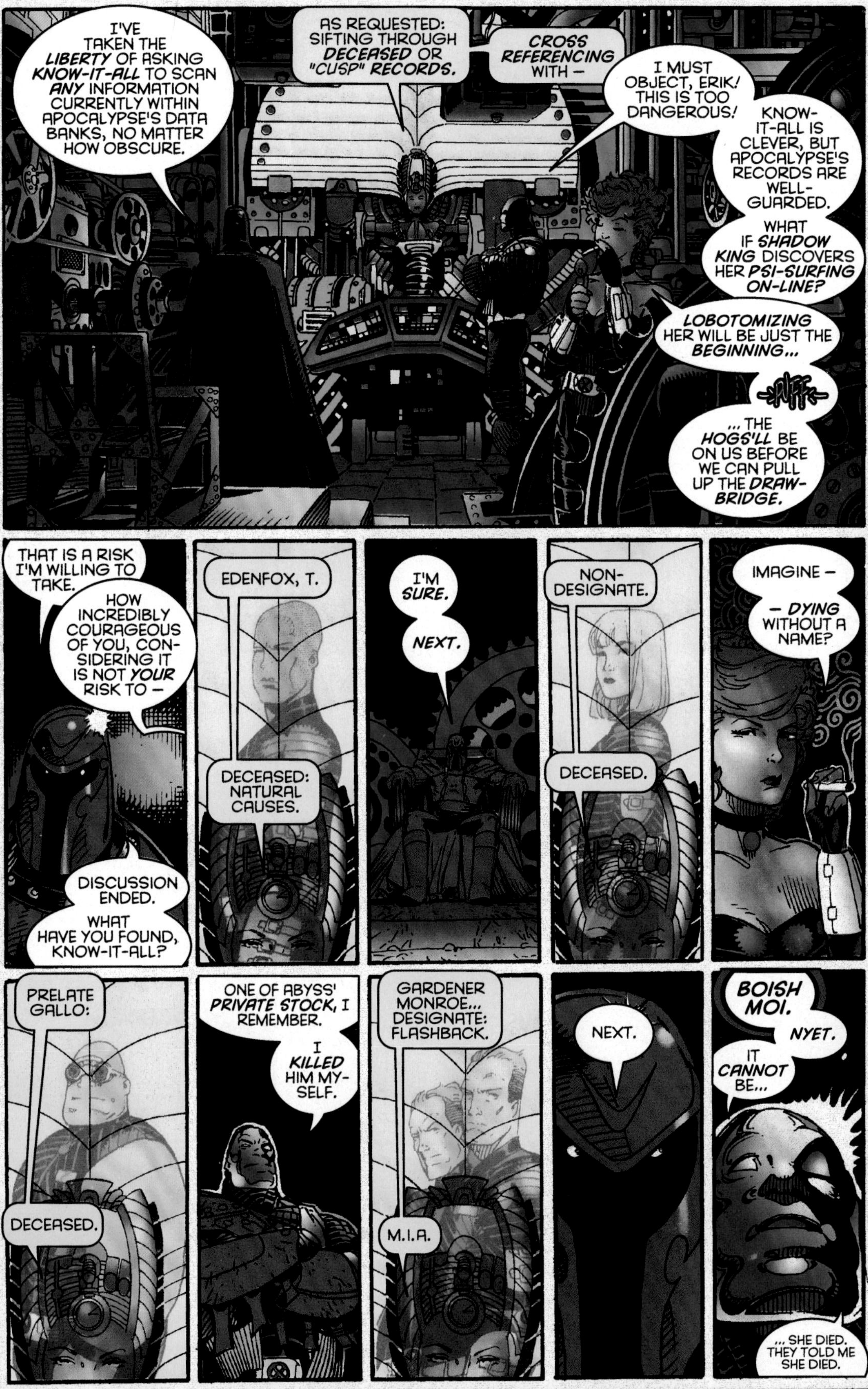

I'VE TAKEN THE LIBERTY OF ASKING KNOW-IT-ALL TO SCAN ANY INFORMATION CURRENTLY WITHIN APOCALYPSE'S DATA BANKS, NO MATTER HOW OBSCURE.
AS REQUESTED: SIFTING THROUGH DECEASED OR "CUSP" RECORDS.
CROSS REFERENCING WITH —
I MUST OBJECT, ERIK! THIS IS TOO DANGEROUS!
KNOW-IT-ALL IS CLEVER, BUT APOCALYPSE'S RECORDS ARE WELL-GUARDED.
WHAT IF SHADOW KING DISCOVERS HER PSI-SURFING ON-LINE?
LOBOTOMIZING HER WILL BE JUST THE BEGINNING...
PUFF
... THE HOGS'LL BE ON US BEFORE WE CAN PULL UP THE DRAW-BRIDGE.
THAT IS A RISK I'M WILLING TO TAKE.
HOW INCREDIBLY COURAGEOUS OF YOU, CON-SIDERING IT IS NOT YOUR RISK TO —
DISCUSSION ENDED.
WHAT HAVE YOU FOUND, KNOW-IT-ALL?
EDENFOX, T.
DECEASED: NATURAL CAUSES.
I'M SURE.
NEXT.
NON-DESIGNATE.
DECEASED.
IMAGINE —
— DYING WITHOUT A NAME?
PRELATE GALLO:
DECEASED.
ONE OF ABYSS' PRIVATE STOCK, I REMEMBER.
I KILLED HIM MY-SELF.
GARDENER MONROE... DESIGNATE: FLASHBACK.
M.I.A.
NEXT.
BOISH MOI.
NYET.
IT CANNOT BE...
... SHE DIED. THEY TOLD ME SHE DIED.

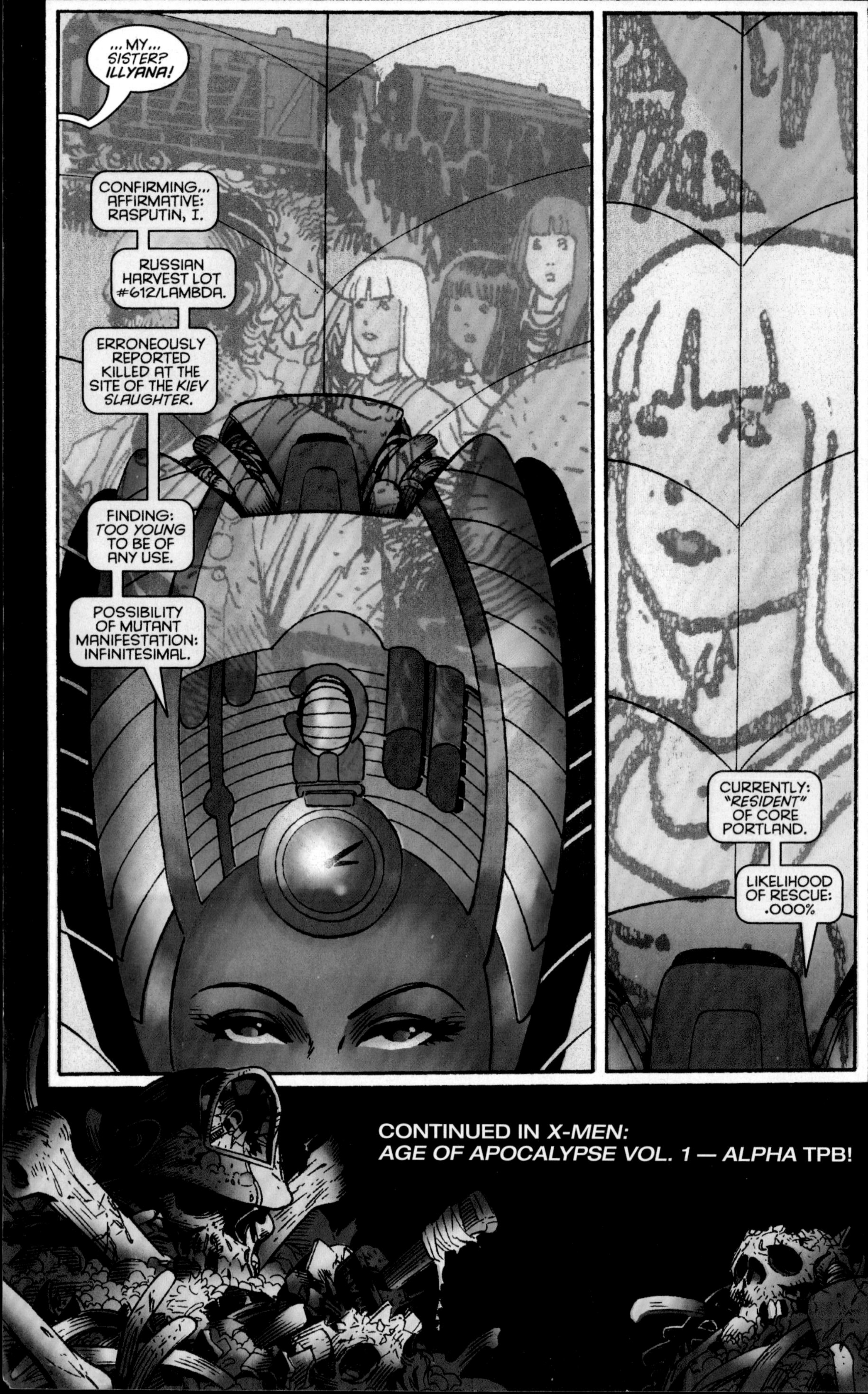

...MY... SISTER? ILLYANA!
CONFIRMING... AFFIRMATIVE: RASPUTIN, I.
RUSSIAN HARVEST LOT #612/LAMBDA.
ERRONEOUSLY REPORTED KILLED AT THE SITE OF THE KIEV SLAUGHTER.
FINDING: TOO YOUNG TO BE OF ANY USE.
POSSIBILITY OF MUTANT MANIFESTATION: INFINITESIMAL.
CURRENTLY: "RESIDENT" OF CORE PORTLAND.
LIKELIHOOD OF RESCUE: .000%

CONTINUED IN *X-MEN: AGE OF APOCALYPSE VOL. 1 — ALPHA* TPB!

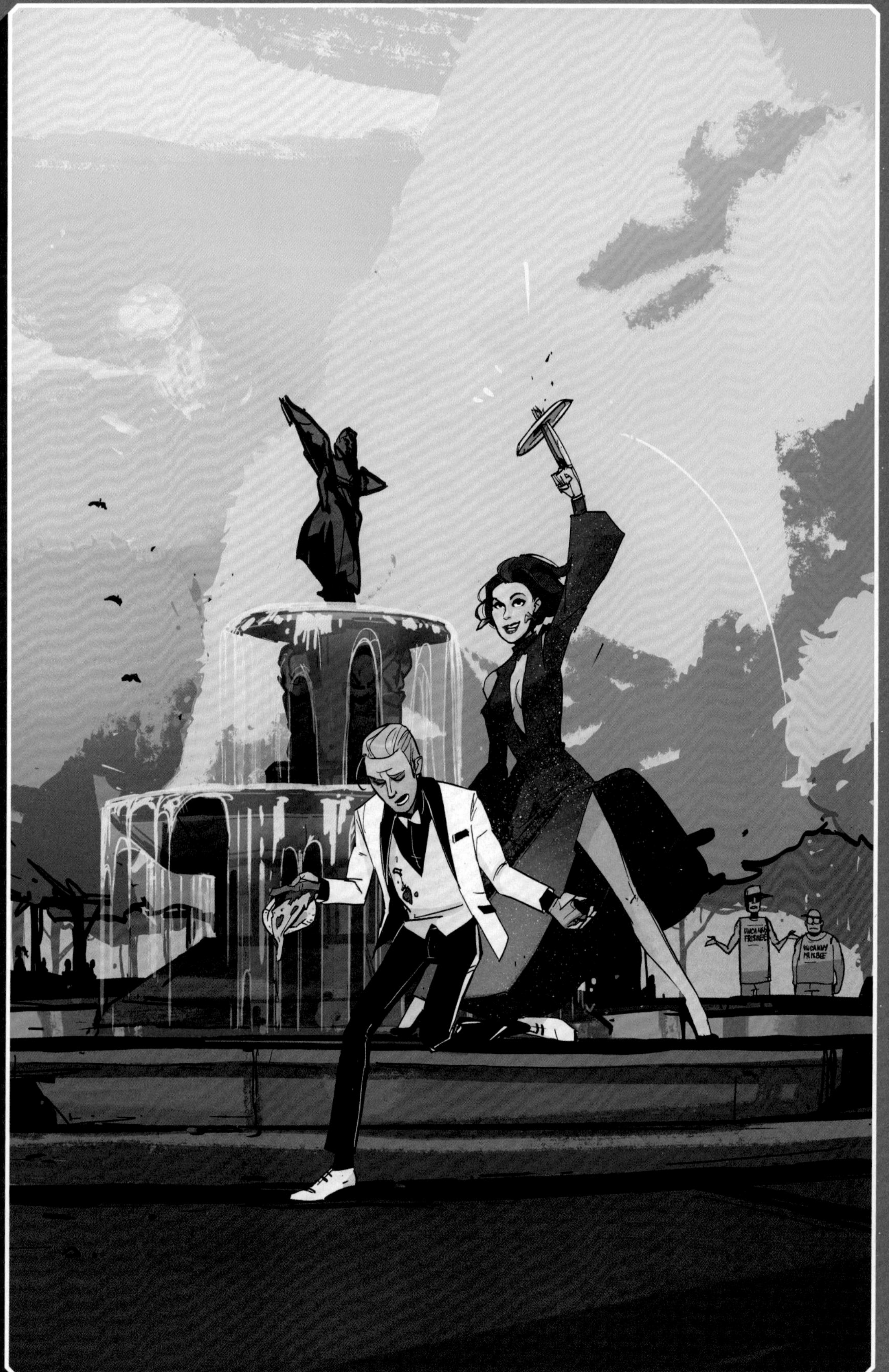

STAR LORD & KITTY PRYDE #2 variant cover
by ANNIE WU

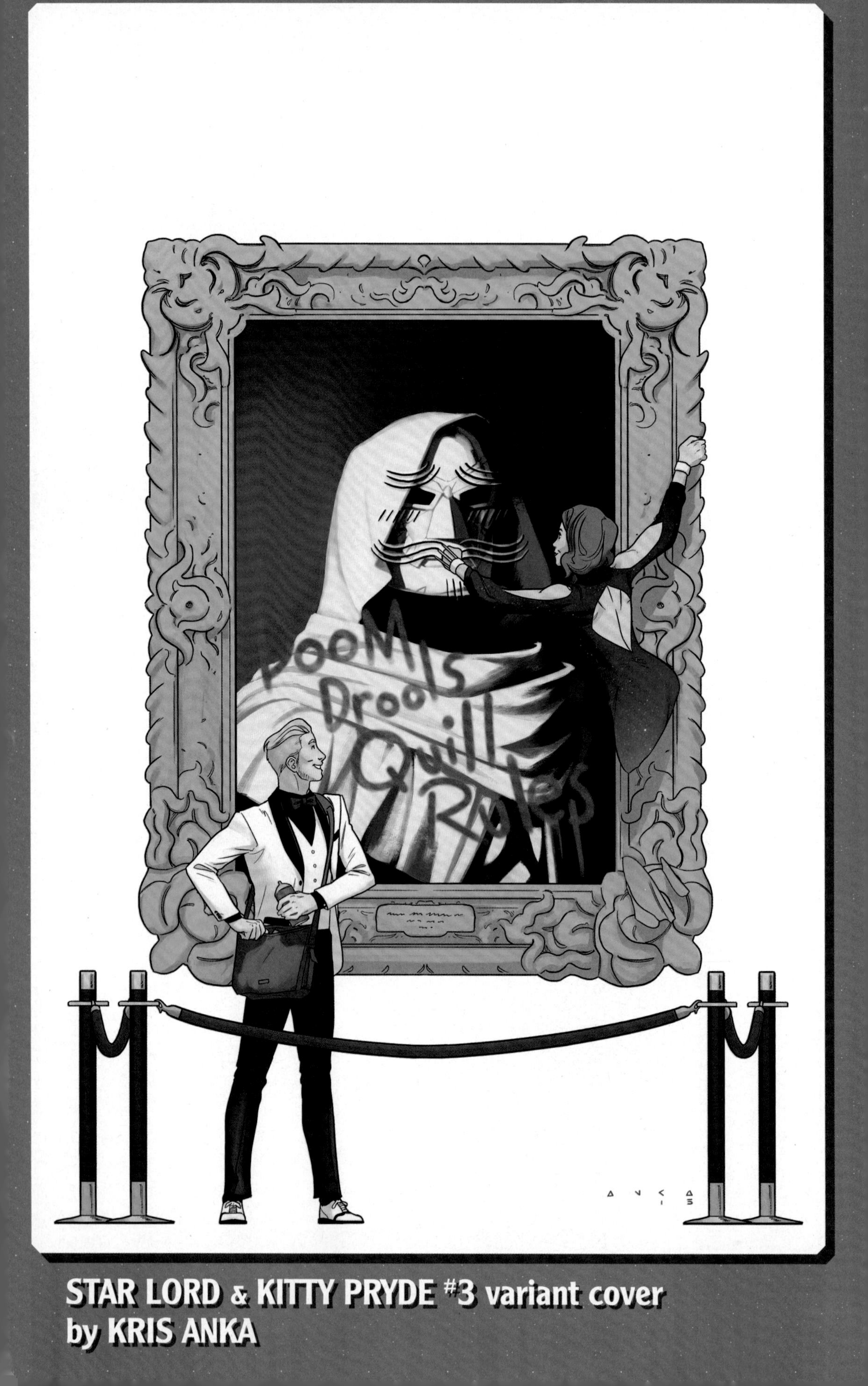
DooM Is
Drools
Quill
Rules

STAR LORD & KITTY PRYDE #3 variant cover
by KRIS ANKA

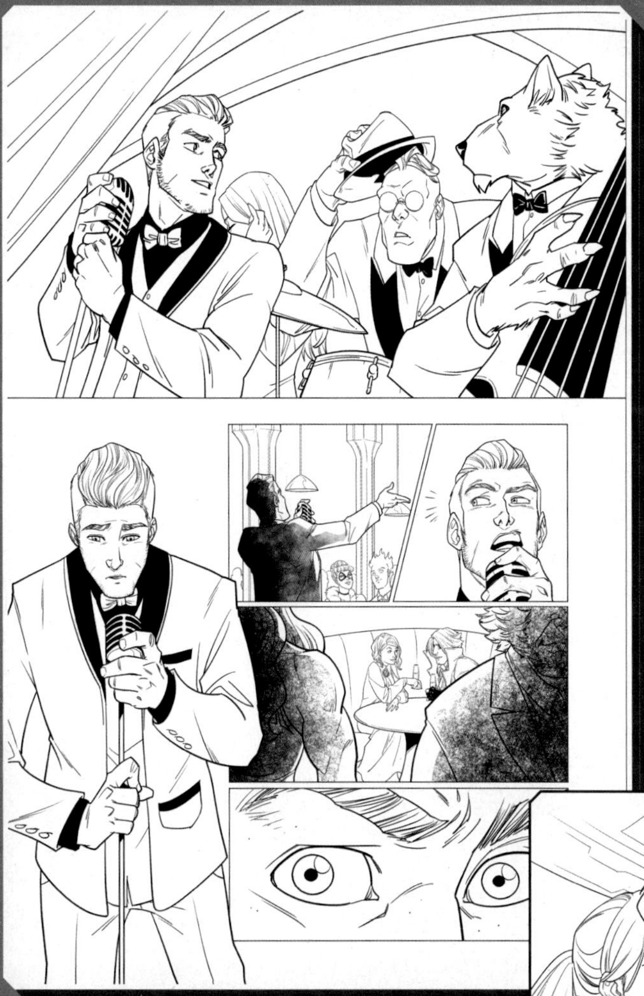

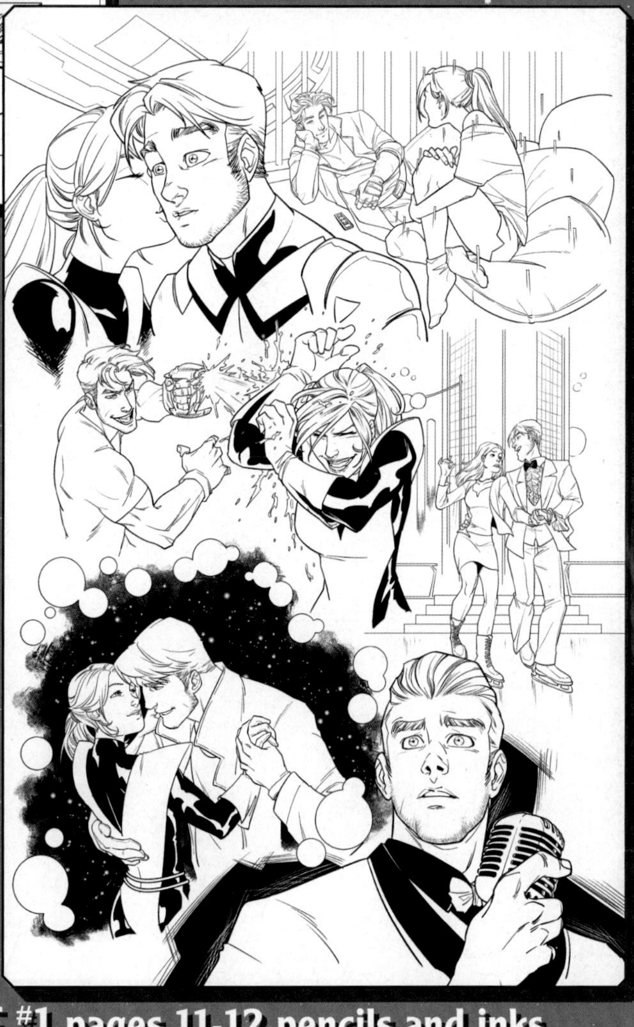

STAR LORD & KITTY PRYDE #1 pages 11-12 pencils and inks by ALTI FIRMANSYAH

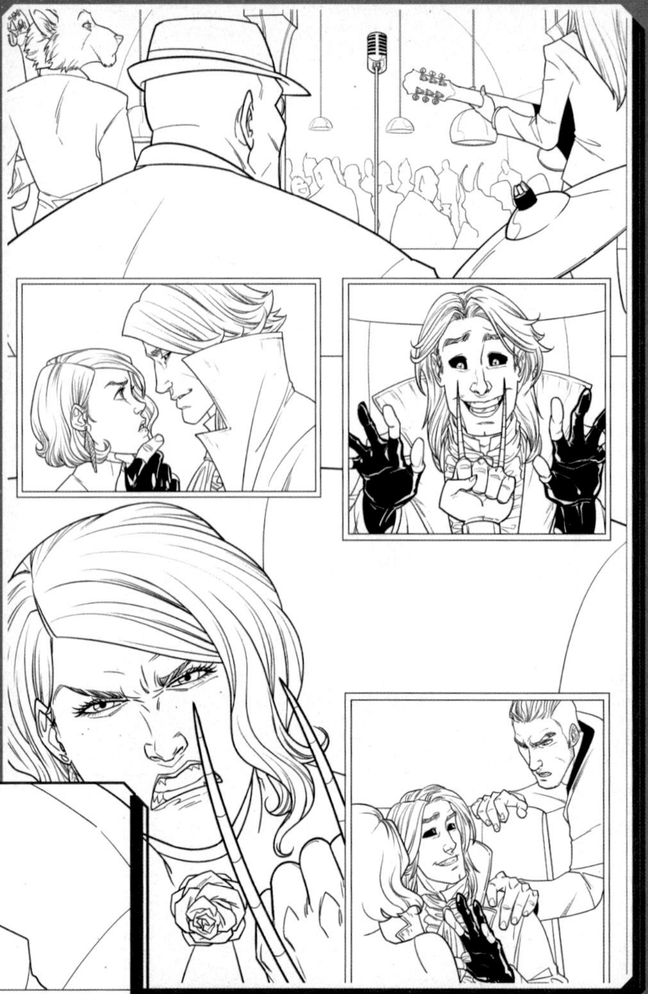

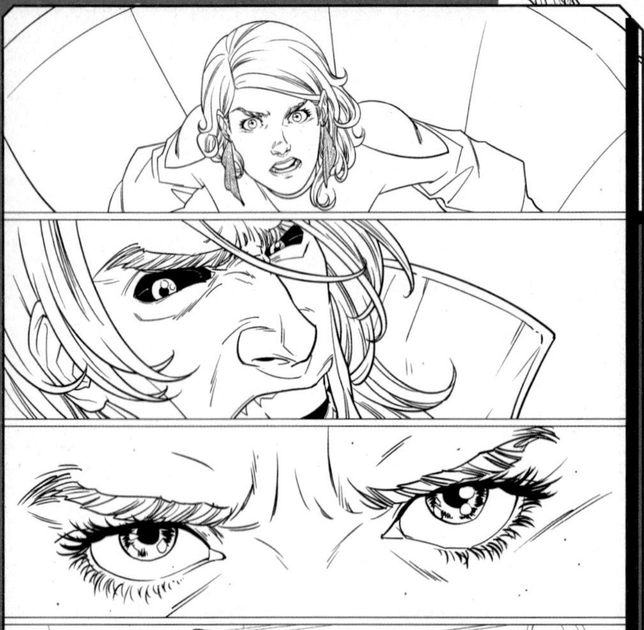

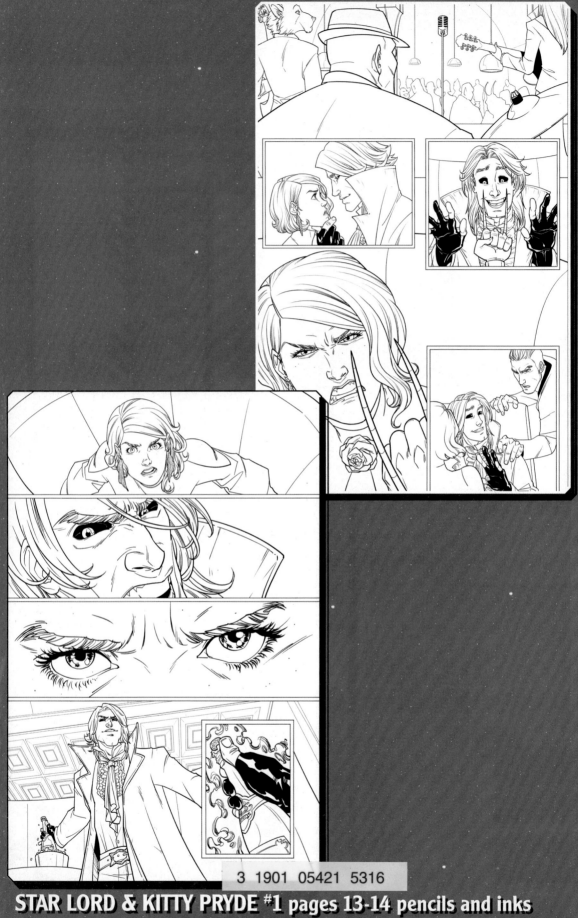

STAR LORD & KITTY PRYDE #1 pages 13-14 pencils and inks by ALTI FIRMANSYAH